HARRAP

SALES MARKETING DICTIONARY

English-French
French-English

HARRAP

First published in Great Britain in 1999
by Chambers Harrap Publishers Ltd
7 Hopetoun Crescent
Edinburgh EH7 4AY

ISBN 0245 60666 1 (UK)
ISBN 0245 50388 9 (France)

Graphics produced using Corel Draw clip art

Dépôt légal : juillet 1999

Designed and typeset by Chambers Harrap Publishers Ltd, Edinburgh
Printed and bound in France by IFC

Editor/Rédactrice
Anna Stevenson

with/avec
Alban Demode
Georges Pilard

Publishing manager/Direction éditoriale
Patrick White

Specialist consultants/Consultants spécialistes

Bob Norton
Head of Information Services
Institute of Management, Corby, UK

Cathy Smith
Systems Controller
Institute of Management, Corby, UK

Jean-François Trinquecoste
Maître de Conférences
Université Montesquieu-Bordeaux IV

Trademarks

Words considered to be trademarks have been designated in this dictionary by the symbol ®. However, no judgement is implied concerning the legal status of any trademark by virtue of the presence or absence of such a symbol.

Marques déposées

Les termes considérés comme des marques déposées sont signalés dans ce dictionnaire par le symbole ®. Cependant, la présence ou l'absence de ce symbole ne constitue nullement une indication quant à la valeur juridique de ces termes.

Contents
Table des Matières

Preface

Developed and expanded from the databases used for the **Harrap French Business Dictionary**, this completely new book brings together terms from all areas of sales and marketing, including advertising, distribution, import/ export, market research and retailing. Its breadth of coverage means that it will be an invaluable tool both for students of business French and for all businesspeople working with companies in the French-speaking world.

The growth of the consumer society, with an ever-increasing number of commodities to choose from, means that the customer's decision-making process has become more and more difficult. Good marketing is the only way to persuade the customer to choose one product over another and has thus become an indispensable tool of any business with a product to sell. As the field of marketing develops, particularly with the growth of the Internet, so too does its vocabulary. Terms such as **on-line retailer**, **e-commerce**, **electronic shopping** and **magasin électronique**, **site marchand**, **ventes en ligne** can all be found in this book.

As in all the dictionaries in Harrap's Business range, the emphasis is on providing **practical help** and putting business language in **context**.

Practical help is provided in the form of panels integrated into the dictionary text which illustrate important marketing concepts, such as the product lifecycle curve and the Four P's. There is also a useful guide to corresponding in French by letter, fax and e-mail.

Context is provided by the inclusion of many quotations from French and English books, newspapers and magazines. These quotations are presented in boxes after the relevant entry and show the application of the word or expression in the real business world.

Préface

Cet ouvrage entièrement nouveau a été conçu à partir des bases de données utilisées lors de l'élaboration du **Harrap's Business**. Il rassemble des termes et expressions issus de toutes les disciplines liées à la vente et au marketing, dont la publicité, la distribution, l'import-export et les études de marché. L'étendue des domaines couverts en fera l'outil irremplaçable des étudiants de l'anglais des affaires ainsi que de tous les hommes d'affaires.

Le nombre toujours croissant des produits disponibles sur le marché fait que le consommateur éprouve de plus en plus de difficultés à s'orienter. Seule une solide stratégie de marketing peut convaincre un consommateur d'acheter un produit plutôt qu'un autre. Les entreprises doivent donc planifier la commercialisation de leurs produits de façon efficace. L'une des conséquences de l'expansion du marketing (avec notamment le développement de l'Internet), est l'augmentation considérable du vocabulaire lié à ce domaine. Des termes tels que **on-line retailer**, **e-commerce**, **electronic shopping** et **magasin électronique**, **site marchand**, **vente en ligne** figurent dans ce livre.

Cet ouvrage, comme tous ceux de la collection **La vie des affaires** de Harrap, met l'accent sur **l'aide pratique** à l'utilisateur ainsi que sur **la mise en contexte** de la langue des affaires.

L'aide pratique à l'utilisateur est présentée sous forme d'encadrés intégrés au texte illustrant des notions de marketing essentielles telles que la courbe de cycle de vie du produit et les quatre P. Ce dictionnaire contient également un guide de correspondance commerciale en anglais.

La mise en contexte est assurée par la présence de nombreuses citations extraites de livres, de journaux et de magazines. Ces citations sont présentées dans des encadrés et montrent comment les termes en question sont réellement utilisés dans le monde des affaires.

Labels
Indications d'Usage

gloss	=	glose
[introduces an explanation]		[introduit une explication]
cultural equivalent	≃	équivalent culturel
[introduces a translation which has a roughly equivalent status in the target language]		[introduit une traduction dont les connotations dans la langue cible sont comparables]
abbreviation	*abbr, abrév*	abréviation
adjective	*adj*	adjectif
adverb	*adv*	adverbe
North American English	*Am*	anglais américain
British English	*Br*	anglais britannique
Canadian French	*Can*	canadianisme
computing	*Comptr*	informatique
customs	*Customs*	douanes
customs	*Douanes*	douanes
economics	*Econ, Écon*	économie
feminine	*f*	féminin
familiar	*Fam*	familier
masculine	*m*	masculin
masculine and feminine noun	*mf*	nom masculin ou féminin
[same form for both genders, eg **wholesaler** grossiste *mf*]		[formes identiques]
masculine and feminine noun	*m,f*	nom masculin ou féminin
[different form in the feminine, eg **consumer** utilisateur(trice) *m,f*]		[formes différentes]
noun	*n*	nom
feminine noun	*nf*	nom féminin
feminine plural noun	*nfpl*	nom féminin pluriel
masculine noun	*nm*	nom masculin

masculine and feminine noun [same form for both genders, eg **panéliste** *nmf*]	*nmf*	nom masculin ou féminin [formes identiques]
masculine and feminine noun [different form in the feminine, eg **client, -e** *nm,f*]	*nm,f*	nom masculin ou féminin [formes différentes]
masculine plural noun	*nmpl*	nom masculin pluriel
computing	*Ordinat*	informatique
plural	*pl*	pluriel
Swiss French	*Suisse*	helvétisme
intransitive verb	*vi*	verbe intransitif
reflexive verb	*vpr*	verbe pronominal
transitive verb	*vt*	verbe transitif
transitive verb used with a preposition [eg **répondre à** (to answer); il a **répondu à** la question (he answered the question)]	*vt ind*	verbe transitif indirect [par exemple : **répondre à** il a **répondu à** la question]
inseparable transitive verb [phrasal verb where the verb **and the adverb or preposition** cannot be separated, eg **call on**; he **called on** his client]	*vt insep*	verbe transitif à particule inséparable [par exemple : **call on** (rendre visite à); he **called on** his client (il a rendu visite à son client)]
separable transitive verb [phrasal verb where the verb and the adverb or preposition cannot be separated, eg **send back**; they **sent** the goods **back** or they **sent back** the goods]	*vt sep*	verbe transitif à particule séparable [par exemple : **send back** (renvoyer); they **sent** the goods **back** ou they **sent back** the goods (ils ont renvoyé les marchandises)]

AA *n* (*abbr* **Advertising Association**) = organisme britannique dont le rôle est de veiller à la qualité des publicités et de défendre les intérêts des annonceurs et des agences de publicité

ABC1 *n* = catégorie sociale allant du cadre supérieur au cadre moyen, au pouvoir d'achat élevé (*dans le cadre du système de classification sociale britannique ABC1*)

> *Stuff* had a cover price of £2.50 and was targeted at **ABC1** men aged 25-44 with an average income of around £20,000.

above-the-line **1** *n* publicité *f* média

2 *adj* média

◇ **above-the-line advertising** publicité *f* média

◇ **above-the-line costs** coûts *mpl* média

◇ **above-the-line expenditure** dépenses *fpl* média

> Sales promotion is sometimes called below-the-line adver-tising in contrast with **above-the-line expenditure** which is handled by an external advertising agency.

absolute frequency *adj* fréquence *f* absolue

acceptance test *n* test *m* d'acceptabilité

account *n* (**a**) (*in advertising, marketing*) budget *m*, compte-client *m*, client *m* ; **we lost the Guinness account** nous avons perdu la clientèle de Guinness *ou* le budget Guinness
(**b**) (*with shop, company*) compte *m* ; **to have an account with sb** avoir un compte chez qn, être en compte avec qn ; **to buy sth on account** acheter qch à crédit ; **to settle an account** régler un compte ; **put it on** *or* **charge it to my account** inscrivez-le *ou* mettez-le à mon compte ; **cash or account?** vous payez *ou* réglez comptant ou est-ce que vous avez un compte chez nous ?

◇ **account director** directeur (trice) *m,f* des comptes-clients

◇ **account executive** responsable *mf* de budget, chargé *m* de budget

ABC1 system of social classification
Système de classification sociale ABC1

Social Grade / Catégorie socio-professionnelle	Social Status / Position sociale	Chief income earner's occupation / Profession du chef de famille
A	*Upper middle class* Classe supérieure	*Higher managerial, administrative or professional* Cadres supérieurs et professions libérales
B	*Middle class* Classe moyenne	*Intermediate managerial, administrative or professional* Cadres moyens
C1	*Lower middle class* Classe moyenne inférieure	*Supervisory or clerical and junior managerial, administrative or professional* Employés
C2	*Skilled working class* Classe ouvrière supérieure	*Skilled manual workers* Ouvriers qualifiés et artisans
D	*Working class* Classe ouvrière	*Semi-skilled and unskilled manual workers* Ouvriers semi-qualifiés et non qualifiés
E	*Lower class* Classes inférieures	*State pensioners, casual workers* Retraités touchant uniquement le minimum vieillesse, travailleurs intermittents

◇ *account handler* responsable *mf* de budget, chargé *m* de budget

◇ *account manager* responsable *mf* de budget, chargé *m* de budget

▸ **account for** *vt insep (make up)* représenter; **this product accounts for 15% of all sales** ce produit représente 15% des ventes totales

accredit *vt (representative)* accréditer

accredited *adj (representative)* accrédité(e)

accumulate *vt (stock)* accumuler

accumulation *n (of stock)* accumulation *f*

ACORN *n (abbr* A Classification of Residential Neighbourhoods*)* = classement des différents types de quartiers résidentiels existant en Grande-Bretagne en 39 catégories, utilisé par les entreprises pour mieux cibler leurs clients potentiels lors de campagnes commerciales

action plan, action programme *n* plan *m* d'action

active *adj (market)* animé(e), actif(ive)

activity *n (in market, of company)* activité *f*

◇ *activity chart* graphique *m* des activités

ad *n Fam* pub *f*; *(classified)* annonce *f*

◇ *ad agency* agence *f* publicitaire, agence *f* de publicité

added value *n* valeur *f* ajoutée

address **1** *n* adresse *f*

2 *vt* **(a)** *(letter, parcel)* adresser **(b)** *(direct)* adresser (**to** à); **please address all enquiries to the after-sales department** faire parvenir toute demande de renseignements au service après-vente

addressable *adj* utile

◇ *addressable audience* audience *f* utile

◇ *addressable market* marché *m* utile

ad hoc *adj*

◇ *ad hoc panel* panel *m* ad hoc

◇ *ad hoc research* recherche *f* ad hoc

◇ *ad hoc survey* étude *f* ad hoc

adman *n Fam* publicitaire *m*

administration *n (management)* administration *f*

adopt *vt (product)* adopter

adoption *n (of product)* adoption *f*

adspend *n Fam* dépenses *fpl* de publicité

> 66
>
> Like most of its competitors, Legal & General's expansion into direct marketing has seen it increase its **adspend**.
>
> 99

advance publicity *n* publicité *f* d'amorçage

advert *n Fam (for product, service)* publicité *f*, réclame *f*

advertise **1** *vt (product,*

service) faire de la réclame *ou* de la publicité pour; **as advertised on TV** vu(e) à la télé

2 *vi (to sell product, service)* faire de la réclame *ou* de la publicité

advertisement *n (for product, service)* publicité *f*, réclame *f*

◊ **advertisement canvasser** démarcheur(euse) *m,f* en publicité

advertiser *n* annonceur *m*

advertising *n* publicité *f*

◊ **advertising account** budget *m* de publicité

◊ **advertising agency** agence *f* publicitaire, agence *f* de publicité

◊ **advertising agent** agent *m* publicitaire, agent *m* de publicité

◊ **advertising approach** optique *f* publicitaire

◊ **Advertising Association** = organisme britannique dont le rôle est de veiller à la qualité des publicités et de défendre les intérêts des annonceurs et des agences de publicité

◊ **advertising awareness** notoriété *f* publicitaire

◊ **advertising budget** budget *m* de publicité

◊ **advertising campaign** campagne *f* de publicité

◊ **advertising concept** concept *m* publicitaire

◊ **advertising consultant** conseil *m* en publicité

◊ **advertising copy** texte *m* publicitaire

◊ **advertising department** service *m* de publicité

◊ **advertising director** directeur(trice) *m,f* de la publicité

◊ **advertising effectiveness** efficacité *f* publicitaire

◊ **advertising executive** publicitaire *mf*

◊ **advertising expenses** dépenses *fpl* de la publicité

◊ **advertising gimmick** gadget *m* publicitaire

◊ **advertising goal** objectif *m* publicitaire

◊ **advertising insert** encart *m* publicitaire

◊ **advertising leaflet** dépliant *m* publicitaire

◊ **advertising material** matériel *m* publicitaire

◊ **advertising medium** organe *m* de publicité, support *m* de publicité

◊ **advertising potential** potentiel *m* publicitaire

◊ **advertising psychology** psychologie *f* de la publicité

◊ **advertising rates** tarif *m* des insertions

◊ **advertising schedule** programme *m* des annonces

◊ **advertising slogan** slogan *m* publicitaire

◊ **advertising space** espace *m* publicitaire, emplacement *m* publicitaire

◊ **advertising standards** normes *fpl* publicitaires

◊ *Br* **Advertising Standards Authority** ≃ Bureau *m* de vérification de la publicité

◊ **advertising strategy** stratégie *f* publicitaire

advertorial n publireportage m, publicité f rédactionnelle

> **"**
>
> "The indirect endorsement they offer," says Emap Elan head of research Aida Muirhead, "appears to be a strong factor in generating purchasing interest. And the more an **advertorial** style resembles the writing style and look of the publication carrying it, the better. This prevents interrupting the flow of the reader."
>
> **"**

affluent adj riche

◇ *the affluent society* la société d'abondance

affordable adj abordable

after-sales adj après-vente

◇ *after-sales department* service m après-vente

◇ *after-sales marketing* marketing m après-vente

◇ *after-sales service* service m après-vente

age group n *(in market research)* tranche f d'âge; **this product is targeted at the 18-24 age group** ce produit vise les 18-24 ans

agency n agence f

◇ *agency account* compte m agence

◇ *agency agreement* contrat m de mandat, accord m de représentation

◇ *agency contract* contrat m d'agence

◇ *agency fee* commission f de

gestion, frais mpl d'agence

agent n agent m, représentant(e) m,f; **an agent for Mercury Ltd** un représentant de Mercury Ltd; **he is our agent in the Far East** c'est notre agent pour l'Extrême-Orient

agree 1 vt *(price, conditions)* s'accorder ou se mettre d'accord sur; **to be agreed** *(price)* à débattre

2 vi **to agree and counter** approuver et contre-argumenter

agreement n *(arrangement, contract)* accord m (**on** or **about** sur); **to enter into** or **conclude an agreement with sb** passer un accord avec qn; **to come to an agreement** parvenir à un accord; **to sign an agreement** signer un accord

AIDA n *(abbr* **attention-interest-desire-action)** AIDA m

aided recall n notoriété f assistée

AIO n *(abbr* **activities, interests and opinions)** AIO

◇ *AIO research* étude f AIO

airfreight 1 n transport m par avion; *(price)* fret m, frais mpl (de transport par avion); *(cargo)* fret m aérien

2 vt *(goods)* transporter par avion

airport advertising n publicité f dans les aéroports

aisle n *(in shop)* allée f

◇ *aisle end display* tête f de gondole

all-inclusive price n prix m

forfaitaire, prix *m* à forfait

AMA *n* (*abbr* **American Market-ing Association**) = institut américain de marketing

analysis *n* analyse *f*

analyst *n* analyste *mf*

annual *adj* annuel(elle)

◇ ***annual budget*** budget *m* annuel

◇ ***annual earnings*** (*of company*) recette(s) *f(pl)* annuelle(s)

◇ ***annual sales figures*** chiffre *m* d'affaires annuel

◇ ***annual turnover*** chiffre *m* d'affaires annuel

anonymous *adj*

◇ ***anonymous buyer*** acheteur(euse) *m,f* anonyme

◇ ***anonymous research*** recherche *f* anonyme

anticipate *vt* (*expect*) prévoir; **we anticipate a good response to our advertisement** nous attendons de bons résultats de notre annonce publicitaire

◇ ***anticipated sales*** (taux *m* de) ventes *fpl* prévues

appeal **1** *n* (*of brand, product*) attrait *m*, attraction *f*
2 *vi* **to appeal to sb** attirer qn

appointed agent *n* agent *m* attitré

appro *n Br Fam* (*abbr* **approval**) **on appro** à l'essai; **to buy sth on appro** acheter qch à l'essai; **to send sth on appro** envoyer qch à titre d'essai

approval *n* (a) (*of consumer, customer*) agrément *m* (b) **on** approval à l'essai; **to buy sth on approval** acheter qch à l'essai; **to send sth on approval** envoyer qch à titre d'essai; *Am* **approvals** (*goods*) marchandises *fpl* envoyées à l'essai

◇ ***approval rating*** score *m* d'agrément

approved *adj* (*person, sample*) agréé(e)

◇ ***approved dealer*** concessionnaire *mf* agréé(e)

area *n*

◇ ***area sample*** échantillon *m* par zone

◇ ***area sampling*** échantillonnage *m* par zone

arranged interview *n* entretien *m* organisé

article *n* (*item*) article *m*

artwork *n* (*for advertisement*) illustrations *fpl*

ASA *n* (a) *Br* (*abbr* **Advertising Standards Authority**) ≃ BVP *m* (b) *Am* (*abbr* **American Standards Association**) ≃ AFNOR *f*

asking price *n* prix *m* demandé

aspirational *adj* (*product*) qui fait chic; (*consumer*) qui achète des produits de prestige; (*advertising*) qui joue sur le prestige d'un produit

◇ ***aspirational group*** groupe *m* de référence

❝

The Fosters Trading Company name is to be dropped and the clothing chain rebranded as a unisex store. … The new stores, called d2, will stock male and female clothing and accessories and will be designed to appeal to the **aspirational** consumer.

"

assortment n (of goods) assortiment m

atmosphere n (of shop, outlet) atmosphère f

attack 1 n (on market) attaque f (**on** sur); **they have just launched an attack on the mobile phone market** ils viennent de lancer une offensive sur le marché des téléphones portables

2 vt (market) attaquer

attitude n (of consumer to product) attitude f

◊ **attitude research** enquête f d'attitudes

◊ **attitude scale** échelle f d'attitudes

◊ **attitude survey** enquête f d'attitudes

attribute n (of product) attribut m

◊ **attribute list** liste f d'attributs

audience n (for product, advertisement) audience f

◊ **audience duplication** duplication f d'audience

◊ **audience exposure** exposition f au public

◊ **audience measurement** mesure f d'audience

◊ **audience research** étude f d'audience

◊ **audience study** étude f d'audience

audit 1 n audit m

2 vt (accounts) vérifier, apurer, examiner

auditor n audit m, auditeur (trice) m,f

augmented product n produit m augmenté

authorized adj

◊ **authorized agent** mandataire mf, agent m mandataire

◊ **authorized dealer** concessionnaire mf agréé(e), distributeur m agréé(e)

◊ **authorized distributor** distributeur(trice) m,f agréé(e)

◊ **authorized representative** mandataire mf, agent m mandataire

availability n disponibilité f; **this offer is subject to availability** l'offre est sujette à disponibilité

available adj disponible; **available at all branches** en vente dans toutes nos succursales; **we regret that this offer is no longer available** nous avons le regret de vous annoncer que cette offre n'est plus valable; **these items are available from stock** nous avons ces articles en magasin

◊ **available market** marché m effectif

"

And they indicate that there are excellent opportunities opening up in the United Kingdom bottled water market. ... The total **available market** consists of thirty percent of the total population of the United Kingdom. But this market is expanding at a rate of at least five percent and predictions and calculations show that this is far in excess of this base rate.

"

average 1 *n* moyenne *f*; **our monthly sales average is increasing steadily** la moyenne mensuelle de nos ventes est en constante augmentation **2** *adj* moyen(enne)

◇ **average cost per unit** coût *m* unitaire moyen

◇ **average price** prix *m* moyen

◇ **average sample** échantillon *m* normal

awareness *n* (of product) notoriété *f*

◇ **awareness rating** taux *m* de notoriété

◇ **awareness study** étude *f* de notoriété

baby boomer *n* enfant *mf* du baby boom

backward integration *n* *Econ* intégration *f* en amont

banded pack *n* lot *m*

◇ **banded pack selling** vente *f* par lot

banner *n* *Comptr* (*for advertising on Internet*) bandeau *m* publicitaire, bannière *f* publicitaire

◇ **banner campaign** campagne *f* publicitaire sur Internet utilisant des bandeaux publicitaires

bar *n*

◇ **bar chart** diagramme *m* à bâtons, graphique *m* à *ou* en barres, graphique *m* en colonnes

◇ **bar code** code-barre *m*

bargain 1 *n* (**a**) (*agreement*) marché *m*, affaire *f*; **to strike** *or* **make a bargain with sb** conclure *ou* faire un marché avec qn (**b**) (*good buy*) affaire *f*, occasion *f*

2 *vi* (**a**) (*negotiate*) entrer en négociations, négocier, traiter (**with** avec) (**b**) (*haggle*) **to bargain with sb** marchander avec qn; **to bargain over sth** marchander qch

◇ **bargain counter** rayon *m* des soldes

◇ **bargain offer** offre *f* exceptionnelle

◇ **bargain price** prix *m* exceptionnel

barrier *n* (*to goods, trade*) barrière *f*

baseline sales *npl* ventes *fpl* de base

basic *adj*

◇ **basic commodity** article *m* de première nécessité

◇ **basic consumer goods** denrées *fpl* de consommation courante

◇ **basic offer** offre *f* de base

◇ **basic population** population *f* mère

batch *n* (*of goods*) lot *m*

behaviour *n* (*of buyer, consumer*) comportement *m*

◇ **behaviour segmentation** segmentation *f* comportementale

behavioural study *n* étude *f* du comportement

below-the-line 1 *n* publicité *f* hors-média
2 *adj* hors-média

◇ **below-the-line advertising** publicité *f* hors-média

◇ **below-the-line costs** coûts *mpl* hors-média

◇ **below-the-line promotion** promotion *f* hors-média

> "
> Ayres will handle new product development for and manage advertising and relationship marketing campaigns. There is likely to be an increased emphasis on **below-the-line** activity because of the high proportion of custom that comes from repeat visitors.
> "

benchmark *n* (*product*) point *m* de repère, référence *f*

◇ **benchmark market** marché *m* de référence

benchmarking *n* benchmarking *m*

benefit segmentation *n* segmentation *f* par avantages recherchés

best-before date *n* date *f* limite de consommation

best-in-class *n* chef *m* de file

best-of-breed *n* nec *m* plus ultra

best-perceived *adj* mieux perçu(e); **the best-perceived product** le produit le mieux perçu

> "
> But most important for Adidas is that it has toppled Reebok as the UK's **best-perceived** sports goods brand, knocking Nike into third place. This is a crucial victory for Adidas, which is engaged in a mammoth battle with Nike.
> "

best-selling *adj* à grand succès, de grosse vente

better *vt* (*improve*) améliorer; (*surpass*) faire mieux que; **we must try to better last year's figures** nous devons essayer d'obtenir de meilleurs résultats que l'an dernier; **the company has bettered the competition for the second year running** c'est la deuxième année consécutive que l'entreprise a fait mieux que la concurrence

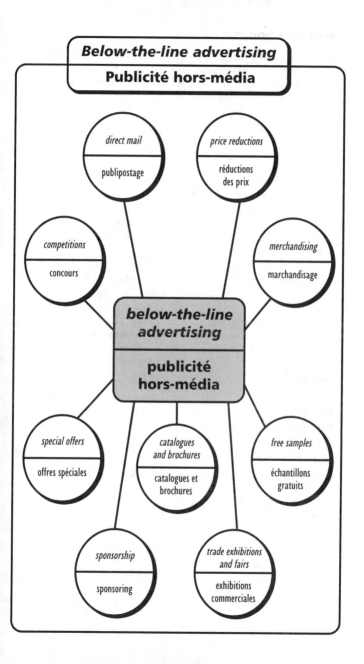

Big Idea, big idea n Fam idée-force f; **new product development is all about coming up with a Big Idea** le développement de nouveaux produits démarre toujours avec une idée-force

bill 1 n (notice of payment due) facture f; **to pay a bill** payer ou régler une facture

   2 vt facturer; **they billed us twice for the order** ils nous ont facturé la commande deux fois

◊ **bill of sale** acte m de vente, contrat m de vente

billboard n panneau m d'affichage, panneau m publicitaire

◊ **billboard advertising** publicité f sur panneau

◊ **billboard site** emplacement m d'affichage

bill-poster n afficheur m publicitaire

bill-posting n affichage m

bill-sticker n afficheur m publicitaire

bill-sticking n affichage m

binding adj obligatoire; (contrat, agreement) qui engage ou lie; **it is binding on the buyer to make immediate payment** l'acheteur est tenu de payer immédiatement

black 1 n **to be in the black** (of person, company) être solvable; (of account) être créditeur(trice)

   2 adj

◊ **black economy** économie f souterraine, économie f parallèle

◊ **black market** marché m noir; **to buy on the black market** acheter au noir

◊ **black marketeer** = personne qui fait du marché noir

blanket adj général(e), global(e)

◊ **blanket family name** nom m de famille global

blind adj

◊ **blind test** test m aveugle

◊ **blind testing** tests mpl aveugles

blister pack n blister m, emballage-bulle m

blitz n campagne f de marketing intensive; **we are already preparing for the pre-Christmas advertising blitz** nous préparons déjà la campagne de marketing de Noël

❝
Yes we want sales in Edinburgh but we're not going to launch a billboard **blitz**. It will be gradually, year by year.
❞

blurb n baratin m publicitaire; (on book jacket) texte m publicitaire

bonanza adj prospère, favorable; **1999 was a bonanza year for us** nous avons connu une année exceptionnelle en 1999

bonded adj Customs (goods) entreposé(e), en entrepôt

◊ **bonded warehouse** entrepôt m de ou en douane, entrepôt m réel

bonus n prime f

◇ **bonus pack** prime f produit en plus

boom 1 n boom m, essor m économique

2 vi **business is booming** les affaires marchent bien ou sont en plein essor; **car sales are booming** les ventes de voitures connaissent une forte progression

boost 1 n to give sth a boost (sales, exports) faire augmenter qch, doper qch

2 vt (sales) faire augmenter, doper; **the new marketing campaign should boost sales** la nouvelle campagne commerciale devrait faire augmenter ou doper les ventes

Boston matrix n matrice f BCG

▸ **bottom out** vi (of price) atteindre son minimum; **sales bottomed out at £40,000** à leur niveau le plus bas, les ventes sont tombées à 40 000 livres

bottom-of-the-range adj bas de gamme

brainstorming n remue-méninges m, brainstorming m

◇ **brainstorming session** réunion f de remue-méninges, brainstorming m

branch n (of shop, company) succursale f; **this product has sold well in all the London branches** ce produit s'est bien vendu dans toutes les succursales de Londres

brand 1 n (of product) marque f

2 vt (product) marquer

◇ **brand acceptability, brand acceptance** acceptabilité f de la marque

◇ **brand advertising** publicité f de marque, publicité f sur la marque

◇ **brand awareness** notoriété f de la marque

◇ **brand bonding** attachement m à la marque

◇ **brand building** création f de marque

◇ **brand competition** concurrence f entre marques

◇ **brand concept** concept m de marque

◇ **brand equity** capital-marque m

◇ **brand exclusivity** exclusivité f à la marque

◇ **brand extension** extension f de la marque

◇ **brand familiarity** connaissance f de la marque

◇ **brand identifier** identificateur m de marque

◇ **brand identity** identité f de marque

◇ **brand image** image f de marque

◇ **brand leader** marque f de tête

◇ **brand lifecycle** cycle m de vie de la marque

◇ **brand loyalty** fidélité f à la marque

◇ **brand management** gestion f de marque

◇ **brand manager** chef m de marque, directeur(trice) m,f de marque

◇ **brand mark** emblème m de marque

⋄ *brand name* marque *f*

⋄ *brand name product* produit *m* de marque

⋄ *brand name recall* mémo-marque *f*, mémorisation *f* de la marque

⋄ *brand perception* perception *f* de marque

⋄ *brand policy* politique *f* de marque

⋄ *brand portfolio* portefeuille *m* de marques

⋄ *brand positioning* positionnement *m* de la marque

⋄ *brand preference* préférence *f* pour une marque

⋄ *brand recognition* identification *f* de la marque

⋄ *brand sensitivity* sensibilité *f* aux marques

⋄ *brand strategy* stratégie *f* de la marque

⋄ *brand switching* changement *m* de marque

44

It follows the much vaunted launch that month of *The Independent's* first **brand building** campaign for nearly two years, using cinema and posters. The agency change is the latest in a series of measures by the paper's new management to build a stronger **brand** and halt the circulation slide.

77

branded *adj*

⋄ *branded goods* produits *mpl* de marque

⋄ *branded product* produit *m* de marque

branding *n* marquage *m*

⋄ *branding campaign* campagne *f* d'image de marque

brand-led *adj* conditionné(e) par la marque, piloté(e) par la marque

44

Merloni is hoping to adopt a more **brand-led** approach to its advertising in the white goods market, which is growing by about six per cent year on year.

77

brand-loyal *adj* fidèle à la marque

brand-sensitive *adj* sensible aux marques

▸ **break even** *vi (of person, company)* rentrer dans ses frais

▸ **break into** *vt insep (market)* percer sur; **many companies are trying to break into the Japanese market** de nombreuses entreprises essaient de percer sur le marché japonais

break-even **1** *n* seuil *m* de rentabilité; **to reach break-even** atteindre le seuil de rentabilité

2 *adj*

⋄ *break-even deal* affaire *f* blanche

⋄ *break-even point* seuil *m* de rentabilité

⋄ *break-even price* prix *m* minimum rentable

breakthrough *n (of market)* percée *f*

brief 1 n (instructions) brief m, mission f; **my brief was to develop sales** la tâche ou la mission qui m'a été confiée était de développer les ventes
2 vt (inform) mettre au courant (**on** de); (instruct) donner des instructions ou des directives à; **have you been briefed?** (brought up to date) est-ce que vous avez été mis au courant?; (given instructions) est-ce qu'on vous a donné vos instructions?

briefing n briefing m

▸ **bring out** vt sep (product) lancer, sortir

broadcast 1 n (programme) émission f
2 vt (advertisement, programme) diffuser

◇ **broadcast sponsorship** parrainage m audiovisuel

44

The deal, worth £1.5m, is the first time Volvo has signed up for **broadcast sponsorship**. This is also the first time the US hospital drama, which delivers an audience of 3.2 million a week, has been sponsored on Channel 4.

77

broadcasting n (of advertisement, programme) diffusion f

brochure n brochure f, prospectus m

broker n (for goods) courtier m (de commerce)

◇ **broker's commission** (frais mpl de) courtage m

◇ **broker's contract** courtage m

brokerage n (a) (profession of broker) courtage m (b) (fee) (frais mpl de) courtage m

◇ **brokerage house** maison f de courtage

brown goods npl produits mpl électroménagers (tel que télévisions, magnétoscopes)

BS n (abbr **British Standard**) = indique que le chiffre qui suit renvoie au numéro de la norme fixée par l'Institut britannique de normalisation

b/s n (abbr **bill of sale**) acte m de vente, contrat m de vente

BSI n (abbr **British Standards Institution**) = association britannique de normalisation, ≃ AFNOR f

bubble pack, bubble wrap n emballage-bulle m

budget 1 n (financial plan) budget m; (allocated ceiling) enveloppe f budgétaire; **to be within budget** être dans les limites du budget; **we are already well over budget** on a déjà largement dépassé le budget qui était alloué pour le projet
2 vt budgétiser; **our main competitor is budgeting a loss this year** notre concurrent principal s'attend à enregistrer une perte pour l'année qui s'achève et prépare son nouveau budget en conséquence
3 vi **to budget for sth** budgétiser qch

◇ **budget account** (with shop) compte m crédit

◇ *budget estimates* prévisions *fpl* budgétaires

◇ *budget forecasts* prévisions *fpl* budgétaires

◇ *budget planning* planification *f* budgétaire

build *vt* to build a brand créer une marque

▸ **build up** *vt sep* (**a**) *(advertise)* faire de la publicité pour (**b**) *(stock)* accumuler

build-up *n* (**a**) *(advertising)* publicité *f*; **to give sth a big build-up** faire beaucoup de publicité pour qch (**b**) *(of stock)* accumulation *f*

built-in obsolescence *n* obsolescence *f* programmée

bulk **1** *n* in bulk en gros; **to buy in bulk** acheter en gros, acheter en grande quantité; **to ship sth in bulk** transporter qch en vrac

2 *vt (packages)* grouper

◇ *bulk buying* achat *m* en gros

◇ *bulk carrier* vraquier *m*

◇ *bulk discount* remise *f* quantitative *ou* pour quantité *ou* sur la quantité

◇ *bulk goods* marchandises *fpl* en vrac

◇ *bulk order* grosse commande *f*, commande *f* par quantité

bulking *n (of packages)* groupage *m*

bumper *adj (profits, year)* exceptionnel(elle)

bundle *vt* to bundle sth with sth offrir qch en plus de qch; **to come bundled with sth** être vendu(e) avec qch

> Recently, this computer has been selling **bundled** with £400-£500 worth of software for £1000. At this price it has come under increasing pressure from its main competitor, which starts at the same price and attracts similar discounts.

bundling *n (of products)* groupage *m*

business *n (trade)* affaires *fpl*; *(commerce)* commerce *m*; **to lose business** perdre de la clientèle; **to do business with sb** faire affaire *ou* des affaires avec qn; **supermarkets have put many small shops out of business** les supermarchés ont obligé beaucoup de petits magasins à fermer; **we have lost business to foreign competitors** nous avons perdu une partie de notre clientèle au profit de concurrents étrangers

◇ *business buyer* acheteur (euse) *m,f* industriel(elle)

◇ *business call* visite *f* d'affaires

◇ *business manager* responsable *mf* commercial(e)

◇ *business mission* mission *f* d'activité, mission *f* de l'entreprise

◇ *business portfolio* portefeuille *m* d'activités

buy **1** *n (purchase)* **a good/bad buy** une bonne/mauvaise affaire; **to make a good/bad**

buy faire une bonne/mauvaise affaire

2 vt acheter; **to buy sth from sb** acheter qch à qn; **to buy sth in bulk** acheter qch en grande quantité; **to buy sth wholesale/retail** acheter qch en gros/en détail; **to buy sth on credit** acheter qch à crédit, acheter qch à terme

3 vi acheter

▸ **buy in** vt sep (goods, commodities) s'approvisionner de

▸ **buy out** vt sep (partner) racheter la part de, désintéresser; **he was bought out for £50,000** on lui a racheté sa part dans l'affaire pour 50 000 livres

▸ **buy up** vt sep (goods, supplies) acheter en masse

buyback n reprise f

◇ **buyback agreement** accord m de reprise

buyer n (**a**) (consumer) acheteur(euse) m,f, acquéreur m (**b**) (for company, shop) acheteur(euse) m,f; **head buyer** acheteur(euse) m,f principal(e)

◇ **buyer behaviour** comportement m de l'acheteur

◇ **buyer credit** crédit-acheteur m

◇ **buyer's market** marché m d'acheteurs

◇ **buyer readiness** prédisposition f à l'achat

buying n achat m; **buying and selling** l'achat et la vente

◇ **buying behaviour** comportement m d'achat

◇ **buying behaviour model** modèle m de comportement d'achat

◇ **buying decision** décision f d'achat

◇ **buying department** service m des achats

◇ **buying incentive** incitation f à l'achat

◇ **buying inducement** mobile m d'achat

◇ **buying motive** motif m d'achat, motivation f d'achat

◇ Econ **buying power** pouvoir m d'achat

◇ **buying situation** situation f d'achat, scénario m d'achat

by-product n sous-produit m, (produit m) dérivé m

cachet *n* label *m*

CACI *n* (*abbr* **California Analysis Centers Inc**) = institut international de sondages

call *n* (*of representative*) visite *f*; **to pay** *or* **make a call on sb** rendre visite à qn

▸ **call on** *vt insep* (*visit*) rendre visite à; **the sales reps call on us monthly** les représentants de commerce nous rendent visite une fois par mois

campaign *n* campagne *f*

C&F, C and F (*abbr* **cost and freight**) coût *m* et fret *m*

C&I, C and I (*abbr* **cost and insurance**) C&A *m*

cannibalization *n* cannibalisme *m*

cannibalize *vt* cannibaliser

canvass 1 *vt* (*person*) démarcher, solliciter des commandes de; (*area*) prospecter

　2 *vi* faire du démarchage; **to canvass for customers** prospecter la clientèle

canvasser *n* placier *m*, démarcheur(euse) *m,f*

canvassing *n* (*for orders*) sollicitation *f*; (*for custom*) prospection *f*, démarchage *m*

caption *n* légende *f*

captive *adj* captif(ive)

◇ *captive audience* audience captive

◇ *captive market* clientèle captive, marché *m* captif

◇ *captive product* produit *m* lié

captive-product pricing fixation *f* du prix des produits liés

capture *vt* (*market*) accaparer; **in one year they have captured a large part of the mail-order market** en un an il se sont emparés d'une part importante du marché de la vente par correspondance

carriage *n* (*transportation*) transport *m*; (*cost*) (frais *mp* de) port *m*; **to pay the carriage** payer le transport; **carriage forward** port dû, port avancé; **carriage free** franc de port, franco; **carriage insurance paid** port payé, assurance comprise; **carriage paid** port payé

◇ *carriage expenses* frais *mp* de port

carrier *n* entrepreneur *m* de transports, transporteur *m*

carry *vt* (a) (*keep in stock*)

vendre, avoir; **do you carry computer accessories?** est-ce que vous vendez des accessoires pour ordinateurs? (**b**) *(transport)* transporter

▸**carry out** *vt sep (market research)* effectuer

carrying *n (transport)* transport *m*

◇ *carrying charges, carrying cost* frais *mpl* de transport

case study *n* étude *f* de cas

cash *n (coins, banknotes)* liquide *m*, espèces *fpl*; **to pay (in) cash** *(not credit)* payer comptant; *(not by cheque)* payer en liquide, payer en espèces; **to buy/sell sth for cash** acheter/vendre qch comptant; **cash against documents** comptant contre documents; *Br* **cash on delivery** paiement à la livraison, livraison contre remboursement; **cash with order** paiement *m* à la commande, envoi *m* contre paiement

◇ *cash budget* budget *m* de trésorerie

◇ *cash and carry* cash and carry *m*

◇ *cash cow (product)* vache *f* à lait

◇ *cash desk* caisse *f*

◇ *cash discount* remise *f* sur paiement (au) comptant

◇ *cash payment* paiement *m* (au) comptant, paiement *m* en espèces

◇ *cash price* prix *m* au comptant

◇ *cash purchase* achat *m* au comptant

◇ *cash register* caisse *f* (enregistreuse)

◇ *cash sale* vente *f* au comptant

◇ *cash settlement* liquidation *f* en espèces

CASM *n Comptr (abbr* **computer-aided sales and marketing**) vente-marketing *f* assistée par ordinateur

catalogue, *Am* **catalog** **1** *n* catalogue *m*; **to buy sth by catalogue** acheter qch sur catalogue

2 *vt* cataloguer

◇ *catalogue price* prix *m* catalogue

category *n* catégorie *f*

◇ *category leader* chef *m* de file dans sa catégorie

> **″**
>
> Sky Networks … has signed up St Lukes to handle an £18m creative advertising account. … St Lukes will now work across Sky Networks' entire portfolio of eight wholly-owned brands - which include Sky News, Sky Sports and Sky Box Office - in a bid to create strong **category leaders**.
>
> **″**

CCI *n (abbr* **Chamber of Commerce and Industry**) CCI *f*

central *adj*

◇ *central purchasing department (in company)* centrale *f* d'achat(s)

◇ *Central Office of Information* = organisme chargé

d'organiser les campagnes d'information du gouvernement britannique

◇ **central purchasing group, central purchasing office** centrale *f* d'achat(s)

centralized purchasing *n* achats *mpl* centralisés

certificate *n* certificat *m*

◇ **certificate of origin** certificat *m* d'origine, label *m* d'origine

◇ **certificate of quality** certificat *m* de qualité

certification mark *n* marque *f* de garantie

chain *n* (shops) chaîne *f*

◇ **chain of distribution** circuit *m* de distribution, réseau *m* de distribution

◇ **chain store** magasin *m* à succursales (multiples); (individual store) succursale *f*

challenger *n* challengeur *m*, prétendant(e) *m,f*

> **❝**
>
> Rank has ploughed £139m into a two-year redevelopment programme, the fruits of which will be apparent in spring. ... To modernise itself and respond to **challengers**, such as CenterParcs, Butlins has ditched 'cheesy' comedians, beauty contests and seaside entertainment in favour of a more 1990s mix.
>
> **❞**

Chamber *n*

◇ **Chamber of Commerce** Chambre *f* de commerce

◇ **Chamber of Commerce and Industry** Chambre *f* de commerce et d'industrie

channel *n* (means) canal *m*; **to open up new channels for trade** créer de nouveaux débouchés pour le commerce

◇ **channel of distribution** circuit *m* de distribution, canal *m* de distribution

charge 1 *n* (cost) frais *mpl*, prix *m*; (to an account) imputation *f*; *Am* **will that be cash or charge?** vous payez comptant ou vous le portez à votre compte?

2 *vt* (a) (defer payment of) **charge it** mettez-le sur mon compte; **charge it to the company's account** mettez-le sur le compte de l'entreprise (b) (person) faire payer; (sum) faire payer, prendre; (commission) prélever; **they charged us $50 for delivery** ils nous ont fait payer 50 dollars pour la livraison; **how much will you charge for the lot?** combien demandez-vous pour le tout?; **you will be charged for postage** les frais postaux seront à votre charge

3 *vi* (demand payment) faire payer; **they don't charge for postage and packing** ils ne font pas payer le port et l'emballage

◇ *Am* **charge account** compte *m* crédit d'achats

◇ **charge card** carte *f* de paiement

▶ **charge up** *vt sep* **to charge sth up to sb's account** mettre qch sur le compte de qn; **could**

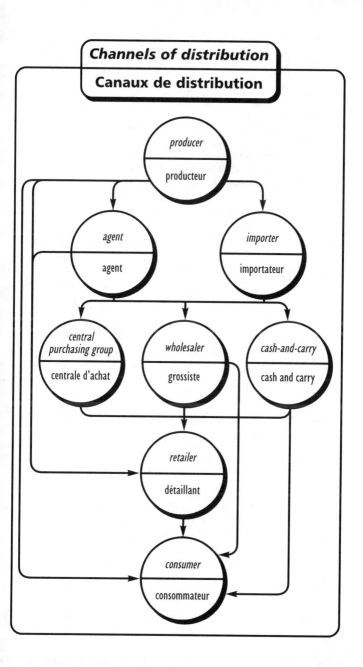

Channels of distribution

Canaux de distribution

producer
producteur

agent
agent

importer
importateur

central purchasing group
centrale d'achat

wholesaler
grossiste

cash-and-carry
cash and carry

retailer
détaillant

consumer
consommateur

you charge it up? pourriez-vous le mettre sur mon compte?

chargeable *adj (to an account)* imputable; **to be chargeable to sb** *(payable by)* être à la charge de qn; **who is it chargeable to?** c'est à la charge de qui?; **could you make that chargeable to Crown Ltd?** est-ce que vous pourriez facturer Crown Ltd?

◊ **chargeable expenses** frais *mpl* facturables

chart 1 *n (diagram)* graphique *m* 2 *vt (on diagram)* faire le graphique de; **this graph charts sales over the last ten years** ce graphique montre l'évolution des ventes au cours des dix dernières années

cheap *adj* bon marché, pas cher (chère); **to buy sth cheap** acheter qch (à) bon marché; **it works out cheaper to buy 10 kilos** cela revient moins cher d'acheter 10 kilos à la fois

cheaply *adv* (à) bon marché; **they can manufacture more cheaply than we can** ils sont à même de fabriquer à meilleur marché que nous

check *n (test)* contrôle *m*
◊ **check question** question *f* de contrôle, question *f* témoin
◊ **check sample** échantillon *m* témoin
check-out *n (in supermarket)* caisse *f*
◊ **check-out display** devant *m* de caisse
◊ **check-out operator** caissier (ère) *m,f*

choice 1 *n (selection)* choix *m*; **the product of choice** le premier choix
2 *adj (product)* de choix, de première qualité
◊ **choice set** ensemble *m* de considérations, éventail *m* de choix

CIF, cif *n (abbr* **cost, insurance and freight)** CAF *m*

CIM *n (abbr* **Chartered Institute of Marketing)** = institut britannique de marketing

cinema advertising *n* publicité *f* au cinéma

claim 1 *n* promesse *f*; **they have been making all sorts of claims about their new product** ils ont paré leur nouveau produit de toutes sortes de qualités
2 *vt* affirmer; **they claim that their product is the best on the market** ils affirment que leur produit est le meilleur sur le marché

classified advertisements *npl* annonces *fpl* classées, petites annonces *fpl*

client *n* client(e) *m,f*
◊ **client confidence** confiance *f* de la clientèle, confiance *f* du client
◊ **client file** dossier *m* client, fichier *m* client
◊ **client list** liste *f* de clients
clientele *n* clientèle *f*

close *vt (deal)* conclure, clore

closed-ended *adj (question)* fermé(e)

close substitute *n* substitut *m* rapproché

closing-down n (of shop, business) fermeture f

◊ **closing-down sale** solde m de fermeture

closing-out n Am fermeture f

◊ **closing-out sale** solde m de fermeture

closure n (of shop, business) fermeture f

cluster n

◊ **cluster analysis** analyse f par segments

◊ **cluster sample** échantillon m aréolaire, échantillon m par grappes

◊ **cluster sampling** échantillonnage m aréolaire, échantillonnage m par grappes

> "
> A further way of reducing the spread of sampling is to use what is called **cluster sampling**, a device by which subunits are grouped together and work concentrated on them. A simple example in the case of the university student population would be to take the faculties of the university … and take a sample of two of them.
> "

co-branding n alliance f de marque, co-branding m

COD, cod adv (abbr Br **cash** or Am **collect on delivery**) paiement à la livraison, livraison contre remboursement; **all goods are sent COD** toutes les marchandises doivent être payées à la livraison

cognitive dissonance n (of buyer) dissonance f cognitive

COI n (abbr **Central Office of Information**) = organisme chargé d'organiser les campagnes d'information du gouvernement britannique

cold adj

◊ **cold call** visite f à froid; (on phone) appel m à froid

◊ **cold calling** approche f directe

◊ **cold call sales** ventes fpl par approche directe

collect on delivery adv Am paiement à la livraison, livraison contre remboursement

comment card n fiche f d'observations

commerce n commerce m

commercial 1 n (advertisement) publicité f
2 adj commercial(e)

◊ **commercial break** écran m publicitaire

◊ **commercial channel** circuit m commercial

◊ **commercial directory** annuaire m du commerce

commercialization n commercialisation f

commercialize vt (make commercial) commercialiser

commercialized adj (commercial) commercialisé(e)

commercially adv commercialement; **commercially available** disponible dans le commerce

commission 1 n (payment)

commission *f*; **to get 3% commission** toucher 3% de commission; **to work on a commission basis** travailler à la commission

2 *vt (order)* commander; **to commission sb to do sth** charger qn de faire qch

◇ *commission agent* commissionnaire *mf*

◇ *commission sale* vente *f* à (la) commission

commodity *n (product)* marchandise *f*, produit *m*; *(foodstuff)* denrée *f*

communications channel *n* canal *m* de communication

company *n* société *f*, entreprise *f*

comparative *adj*

◇ *comparative advantage* avantage *m* comparatif

◇ *comparative advertising* publicité *f* comparative

◇ *comparative test* essai *m* comparatif

◇ *comparative testing* essais *mpl* comparatifs

comparison *n*

◇ *comparison advertising* publicité *f* comparative

◇ *comparison shopping* achats *mpl* comparatifs

compete *vi (of one company)* faire (de la) concurrence (**with** à); *(of two companies)* se faire concurrence; **they compete with foreign companies for contracts** ils sont en concurrence avec des entreprises étrangères pour obtenir des contrats; **we have to compete on an international level** nous devons être à la hauteur de la concurrence sur le plan international

competition *n (between companies, candidates)* concurrence *f*; **the competition** *(rivals)* la concurrence; **the company has to stay ahead of the competition** la société doit rester plus compétitive que les autres

competitive *adj (product)* concurrentiel(elle); *(company, price)* compétitif(ive); **the advertising industry has become very competitive** l'industrie de la publicité est devenue très concurrentielle

◇ *competitive advantage* avantage *m* concurrentiel

◇ *competitive advertising* publicité *f* concurrentielle

◇ *competitive analysis* analyse *f* des concurrents

◇ *competitive awareness* sensibilité *f* compétitive

◇ *competitive marketplace* marché *m* de concurrence

◇ *competitive position* position *f* concurrentielle

◇ *competitive positioning* positionnement *m* concurrentiel

◇ *competitive pricing* fixation *f* des prix compétitifs

◇ *competitive scope* domaine *m* concurrentiel, champ *m* concurrentiel

> Some factors in the **competitive analysis** will relate to market attractiveness. If the competition offered no alternative to the proposed new product it would score highly. Since the competition is the market leader it attracts a low score.

competitively adv **to be competitively priced** être vendu(e) à un prix compétitif

competitiveness n (of product) concurrence f; (of company, price) compétitivité f

competitor n concurrent(e) m,f

completion date n (of sale) date f d'exécution

computer-assisted interview n entretien m assisté par ordinateur

concentrated marketing n marketing m concentré

concept n concept m

◇ **concept development** élaboration f de concept

◇ **concept test** test m de concept

◇ **concept testing** tests mpl de concept

concession n (a) (within larger store) concession f (b) (discount) réduction f; **we offer a 10% concession to retailers** nous accordons une remise de 10% aux détaillants

condition n (a) (stipulation) condition f; **conditions of sale**

conditions fpl de vente (b) (state) état m; **in good/bad condition** (goods) en bon/mauvais état

conjoint analysis n analyse f conjointe

conquer vt (market, market share) conquérir

conquest n (of market, market share) conquête f

consideration set n ensemble m de considérations

consign vt (goods) envoyer, expédier

consignee n consignataire mf

consigner n consignateur (trice) m,f, expéditeur(trice) m,f

consignment n (a) (goods) arrivage m, livraison f; **a consignment of machinery** un envoi de machines (b) (dispatch) envoi m, expédition f; **on consignment** en consignation, en dépôt (permanent); **for consignment abroad** à destination de l'étranger

◇ **consignment invoice** facture f de consignation

◇ **consignment note** bordereau m d'expédition

consignor n consignateur (trice) m,f, expéditeur(trice) m,f

consolidate vt (orders, consignments) grouper

consolidated adj (orders, consignments) groupé(e)

consolidation n (of orders, consignments) groupage m

consumable 1 n **consumables**

produits *mpl* de consommation
2 *adj* consomptible

◇ **consumable goods** produits *mpl* de consommation

consumer *n* consommateur(trice) *m,f*

◇ **consumer acceptance** réceptivité *f* des consommateurs

◇ **Consumers' Assocation** = association britannique de consommateurs

◇ **consumer attitude** attitude *f* du consommateur

◇ **consumer behaviour** comportement *m* du consommateur

◇ **consumer behaviour study** étude *f* du comportement du consommateur

◇ **consumer benefit** bénéfice *m* consommateur

◇ **consumer brand** marque *f* grand public

◇ **consumer credit** crédit *m* à la consommation

◇ **consumer demand** demande *f* des consommateurs

◇ **consumer durables** biens *mpl* de consommation

◇ **consumer expenditure** dépenses *fpl* de consommation

◇ **consumer goods** biens *mpl* de (grande) consommation

◇ **consumer goods industry** industrie *f* de consommation

◇ **consumer group** groupe *m* de consommateurs

◇ **consumer industry** industrie *f* de consommation

◇ **consumer market** marché *m* de la consommation

◇ **consumer organization** or-

ganisme *m* de défense des consommateurs

◇ **consumer panel** groupe-témoin *m*, panel *m* de consommateurs

◇ **consumer preference** préférence *f* du consommateur

◇ **consumer price index** indice *m* des prix à la consommation

◇ **consumer product** bien *m* de consommation

◇ **consumer profile** profil *m* du consommateur

◇ **consumer protection** défense *f* du consommateur

◇ **consumer protection movement** mouvement *m* de défense du consommateur

◇ **consumer psychology** psychologie *f* des consommateurs

◇ **consumer research** recherche *f* sur les besoins des consommateurs

◇ **consumer resistance** résistance *f* des consommateurs

◇ **consumer society** société *f* de consommation

◇ **consumer spending** dépenses *fpl* de consommation

◇ **consumer survey** enquête *f* auprès des consommateurs

◇ **consumer test** test *m* auprès des consommateurs

◇ **consumer test group** groupe *m* test de consommateurs

◇ **consumer testing** tests *mp* auprès des consommateurs

◇ **consumer trends** tendances *fpl* de la consommation

◇ **consumer welfare** intérêt *m* du consommateur

> 66
>
> It is important to recognise that whilst the UK business economy may soon see a recovery, the adverse effects of the current recession on the **consumer market** will continue to be felt long after the economy has begun to recover.
>
> 99

consumerism n (consumer protection) consumérisme m; (consumption) consommation f à outrance

consumption n consommation f

container n récipient m; (for transport) conteneur m

◇ **container premium** prime f contenant

continuous adj

◇ **continuous innovation** innovation f continue

◇ **continuous research** recherche f longitudinale

control n

◇ **control group** groupe-témoin m

◇ **control market** marché m témoin

◇ **control question** question f de contrôle

controlled price n taxe f; to sell sth at the controlled price vendre qch à la taxe

convenience n

◇ **convenience goods** produits mpl de consommation courante

◇ **convenience sample** échantillon m de convenance

cooling-off period n période f de réflexion, délai m de réflexion

> 66
>
> Companies are not regarded as individuals under the Act and are therefore unable to break contracts once signed. Crucially, they cannot take advantage of the two week **cooling-off period** available to individuals.
>
> 99

co-operative n co-opérative f

copy n (text of advertisement) texte m (publicitaire)

◇ **copy strategy** copy f stratégie

◇ **copy test** pré-test m publicitaire

◇ **copy testing** pré-tests mpl publicitaires

copywriter n rédacteur (trice) m,f publicitaire, concepteur m rédacteur

core adj principal(e)

◇ **core brand** marque f phare

◇ **core business** activité f centrale

◇ **core market** marché m principal, marché m de référence

◇ **core message** (of advertisement) message m principal

> 66
>
> While the short-term outlook for Russian TV companies and media agencies is gloomy, Sears is confident the industry will pull throught the crisis. While his clients … are spending less money and

> focusing only on **core brands**, he believes none will pull out completely.
> **"**

corner 1 *n* monopole *m*; **to make** *or* **have a corner in sth** accaparer qch

2 *vt (market)* accaparer; **in two years they've cornered the market in software packages** en deux ans, ils ont accaparé le marché du progiciel

cornering *n (of market)* accaparement *m*

corporate *adj* corporatif(ive), d'entreprise

◊ *corporate advertising* publicité *f* institutionnelle, publicité *f* d'entreprise

◊ *corporate hospitality* = fait, pour une entreprise, d'organiser des divertissements pour ses clients établis ou potentiels

◊ *corporate identity* image *f* de marque

◊ *corporate image* image *f* de marque; **the company cares about its corporate image** la société se préoccupe de son image

◊ *corporate licensing* cession *f* de licence de marque

◊ *corporate literature* = brochures décrivant une société

◊ *corporate sponsorship* sponsoring *m*, parrainage *m* d'entreprises

cost 1 *n (price)* coût *m*, frais *mpl*; **cost, insurance and freight** coût, assurance, fret; **cost per thousand** coût *m* par mille, CPM *m*

2 *vt* **(a)** *(be priced at)* coûter; **how much does it cost?** combien cela coûte-t-il?; **it costs $25** ça coûte 25 dollars

(b) *(estimate cost of) (article)* établir le prix de revient de; *(job)* évaluer le coût de; **how much was it costed at?** *(of work)* à combien est-ce que le coût a été évalué?

3 *vi Fam (be expensive)* coûter cher, ne pas être donné; **we can do it but it will cost** on peut le faire mais ça ne sera pas donné

◊ *cost analysis* analyse *f* des coûts, analyse *f* du prix de revient

◊ *cost curve* courbe *f* des coûts

◊ *cost factor* facteur *m* coût

◊ *cost of living* coût *m* de la vie

◊ *cost management* gestion *f* des coûts

◊ *cost price* prix *m* coûtant, prix *m* de revient

◊ *cost unit* unité *f* de coût

> **"**
> Media costs are usually assessed in terms of **cost per thousand**: the number of pence (or pounds) it takes to reach an audience of 1000 (adults, housewives, men under 45 or whatever) with a given ad or campaign.
> **"**

cost-benefit analysis *n* analyse *f* coût-profit, analyse *f* des coûts et rendements

cost-conscious *adj* qui fait attention aux dépenses

cost-effective *adj* rentable

cost-effectiveness *n* rentabilité *f*

costing *n (of article)* établissement *m* du prix de revient; *(of job)* évaluation *f* du coût

country *n* pays *m*

◇ *country of origin* pays *m* d'origine

coupon *n (exchangeable voucher)* bon *m*, coupon *m*

◇ *coupon offer* offre *f* de bon de réduction

couponing *n* couponing *m*, couponnage *m*

coverage *n* couverture *f*

crack *vt (market)* percer sur

▸ **crack open** *vt sep (market)* percer sur

cream *vt Am* to cream the market écrémer le marché

creative **1** *n (department, work)* création *f; (person)* créatif(ive) *m,f;* **we prefer creative to be handled out of house** nous préférons que tout ce qui est création artistique soit réalisé à l'extérieur
2 *adj* créatif(ive)

◇ *creative copy strategy* copy *f* stratégie créative

◇ *creative department* service *m* de création

◇ *creative director* directeur (trice) *m,f* de la création

◇ *creative marketing* créativité *f* commerciale

◇ *creative team* équipe *f* de création

> It is funding the press work from its own budgets. **Creative** will be handled in-house and media buying by BMP interactive.

creativity *n* créativité *f*

credit *n (for future payment)* crédit *m;* **to give sb credit** faire crédit à qn; **to buy/sell sth on credit** acheter/vendre qch à crédit

◇ *credit account* compte *m* crédit d'achats

◇ *credit agency, Am* **credit bureau** agence *f* de notation

◇ *credit card* carte *f* de crédit

◇ *credit ceiling* plafond *m* de crédit

◇ *credit control* encadrement *m* des crédits

◇ *credit facilities* facilités *fpl* de crédit

◇ *credit freeze* blocage *m* du crédit

◇ *credit limit* limite *f* de crédit, plafond *m* de crédit

◇ *credit note (in shop)* avoir *m*

◇ *credit options* formules *fpl* de crédit

◇ *credit organization* organisme *m* de crédit

◇ *credit period* délai *m* de crédit

◇ *credit purchase* achat *m* à crédit

◇ *credit rating* degré *m* de solvabilité

◇ *credit rating agency* agence *f* de notation

◇ *credit sale* vente *f* à crédit

creditor *n* créancier(ère) *m,f*

critical *adj*
◇ *critical path* chemin *m* critique
◇ *critical path method* méthode *f* du chemin critique
◇ *critical path model* modèle *m* du chemin critique

cumulative audience *n* audience *f* cumulée

curve *n* courbe *f*; **the graph shows an upward/downward curve** la courbe accuse une hausse/une baisse

custom *n (act of buying)* clientèle *f*

customer *n* client(e) *m,f*
◇ *customer appeal* séduction *f* du client
◇ *customer base* base *f* de clientèle, base *f* de consommateurs
◇ *customer care* = qualité du service fourni à la clientèle
◇ *customer confidence* confiance *f* de la clientèle, confiance *f* du client
◇ *Comptr customer database* base *f* de données de consommateurs
◇ *customer list* liste *f* de clients
◇ *customer loyalty* fidélité *f* de la clientèle
◇ *customer loyalty discount* remise *f* de fidélité
◇ *customer orientation* orientation *f* clientèle
◇ *customer profile* profil *m* de la clientèle
◇ *customer record* fiche *f* client
◇ *customer relations* relations *fpl* clientèle
◇ *customer satisfaction* satisfaction *f* de la clientèle

◇ *customer satisfaction survey* étude *f* de satisfaction de la clientèle
◇ *customer service* service *m* clientèle, service *m* clients
◇ *customer service department* service *m* clientèle, service *m* clients

❝
It will also give the Pru a chance to develop a new **customer base**, by attracting young professionals with its internet-based service.
❞

customer-focused *adj* tributaire du consommateur

❝
M&S used to be held up as a brand with strong values and connections to its customers. But it has failed to keep pace with the market, and other major retailers have slowly stripped away its claims to be the most **customer-focused** of major retailers.
❞

customize *vt* faire sur mesure(s); **we provide a customized service for all our clients** nous fournissons à tous nos clients un service adapté à leurs besoins
◇ *customized marketing* marketing *m* sur mesure

cwo (*abbr* **cash with order**) envoi *m* contre paiement

cycle *n (in distribution)* cycle *m*

data *n* données *fpl*; **an item of data** une donnée; **to collect data on sb/sth** recueillir des données sur qn/qch

◇ *data acquisition* collecte *f* de données, saisie *f* de données

◇ *data bank* banque *f* de données

◇ *data collection* recueil *m* de données, collecte *f* de données

◇ *data processing* traitement *m* de données

database *n Comptr* base *f* de données

day-after recall *n* mémorisation *f* un jour après

◇ *day-after recall test* test *m* du lendemain

deadline *n* délai *m* (d'exécution); **I'm working to a deadline** j'ai un délai à respecter

dealer *n* (*trader*) négociant(e) *m,f*, marchand(e) *m,f* (**in** en); (*in cars*) concessionnaire *mf*

dealership *n* concession *f*

debit card *n* carte *f* de débit, carte *f* de paiement

debriefing *n* debriefing *m*

debt *n* dette *f*; (*to be recovered*)

créance *f*; **to be in debt** être endetté(e), avoir des dettes; **to pay off a debt** rembourser *ou* payer une dette

debtor *n* débiteur(trice) *m,f*

decision *n* décision *f*

◇ *decision model* modèle *m* décisionnel, modèle *m* de décision

◇ *decision theory* théorie *f* de la décision

◇ *decision tree* arbre *m* décisionnel, arbre *m* de décision

decision-making *n* prise *f* de décision(s)

◇ *decision-making model* modèle *m* de prise de décision(s)

◇ *decision-making process* processus *m* de prise de décision(s)

decline **1** *n* déclin *m*; **to be on the decline** être en déclin
2 *vi* (*of prices, sales*) être en baisse

◇ *decline stage* (*of product*) phase *f* de déclin

declining *adj* en baisse

deep discount *n* forte remise *f*

delist *vt* (*product*) déréférencer

delisting *n (of product)* déréférencement *m*

deliver 1 *vt (goods)* livrer (**to à**); **to have sth delivered** faire livrer qch
2 *vi (of supplier)* livrer

delivery *n (of goods)* livraison *f*; **to accept or take delivery of sth** prendre livraison de qch, réceptionner qch; **awaiting delivery** en souffrance; **for immediate delivery** à livrer de suite; **to pay on delivery** payer à *ou* sur livraison; **free delivery** (envoi) livraison franco; **next day delivery** livraison lendemain

◇ *delivery address* adresse *f* de livraison

◇ *delivery charges* frais *mpl* de livraison

◇ *delivery date* date *f* de livraison

◇ *delivery note* bon *m* de livraison, bordereau *m* de livraison

◇ *delivery order* bon *m* de livraison

◇ *delivery point* lieu *m* de livraison

◇ *delivery schedule* planning *m* de livraison

◇ *delivery time* délai *m* de livraison

demand *n Econ* demande *f*; **supply and demand** l'offre et la demande; **to be in (great) demand** être (très) demandé(e) *ou* recherché(e); **there isn't much demand for this product** ce produit n'est pas très demandé

◇ *demand curve* courbe *f*

(d'évolution) de la demande

◇ *demand factor* facteur *m* de demande

◇ *demand function* fonction *f* de demande

demarketing *n* démarketing *m*

demographic 1 *n Fam (segment)* segment *m* démographique
2 *adj* démographique

◇ *demographic analysis* analyse *f* démographique

◇ *demographic data* données *fpl* démographiques

◇ *demographic profile* profil *m* démographique

◇ *demographic segment* segment *m* démographique

◇ *demographic segmentation* segmentation *f* démographique

"

Demographic segmentation involves the sub-division of markets on the basis of variables such as age, sex, occupation and class, for example. Magazines and journals are examples of products which are directed towards carefully segmented markets (readership). In addition to the basic reading material, the advertising contained in each edition reflects the segmentation.

"

demographics *n* statistiques *fpl* démographiques

demography *n* démographie *f*

demonstration *n (of product)* démonstration *f*

department *n (in company)* service *m*; *(in shop)* rayon *m*

◊ *department manager (in company)* chef *m* de service; *(in shop)* chef *m* de rayon

◊ *department store* grand magasin *m*

deplete *vt (stock)* épuiser

depletion *n (of stock)* épuisement *m*

deposition *vt (product)* dépositionner

depressed *adj (market, trade)* déprimé(e)

depth *n (of product)* profondeur *f*

◊ *depth interview* entretien *m* en profondeur

> Not a great deal in the way of interpretation or conclusion should be hung on answers to a single question about liking a product. Only a **depth interview** of several hours can be expected to provide a complete picture of overall positive and negative feelings experienced by the consumer in relation to that product.

design **1** *n (planning)* conception *f*, design *m*; *(style)* modèle *m*; **our latest design** notre dernier modèle

2 *vt (plan)* concevoir; **they have designed a product to appeal to younger customers** ils ont conçu un produit ciblé sur le marché de la jeunesse

◊ *design agency* agence *f* de design

◊ *design department* bureau *m* de design

◊ *design team* équipe *f* des concepteurs

designer *n (in advertising)* créatif(ive) *m,f*

desire *n (of consumer for product)* désir *m*

desk research *n* recherche *f* documentaire

destination purchase *n* achat *m* prévu

develop *vt (idea, market, product)* développer

development *n (of idea, market, product)* développement *m*

◊ *development stage (of product)* phase *f* de développement

diagram *n* diagramme *m*

dichotomous question *n (in survey)* question *f* dichotomique

differential *n* différentiel *m*

differentiated marketing *n* marketing *m* de différenciation, marketing *m* différencié

differentiation *n* différenciation *f*

◊ *differentiation strategy* stratégie *f* de différenciation

dinosaur *n (product)* poids *m* mort, produit *m* dodo

direct *adj* direct(e)

◇ *direct advertising* publicité *f* directe

◇ *direct competition* concurrence *f* directe

◇ *direct mail* publipostage *m*, publicité *f* directe

◇ *direct mail advertising* publicité *f* directe, publicité *f* par publipostage

◇ *direct mail campaign* campagne *f* de publicité directe

◇ *direct marketing* marketing *m* direct

◇ *direct marketing agency* agence *f* de marketing direct

◇ *direct purchasing* achats *mpl* directs

◇ *direct response advertisement* publicité *f* à réponse directe

◇ *direct response advertising* publicité *f* à réponse directe

◇ *direct sale* vente *f* directe

◇ *direct selling* vente *f* directe

❝

To comply with European legislation, Oftel plans to ban the use of telephone directories as a source of data for telemarketing and **direct mail**. Residential phone customers would be given the opportunity to flag their directory entries to ensure that their details are not used for **direct marketing** purposes.

❞

director *n (of company)* directeur(trice) *m,f*

directory *n (list of addresses)* annuaire *m*

discontinue *vt (product)* interrompre; **that item has been discontinued** cet article n'est plus suivi

◇ *discontinued line* fin *f* de série

discount **1** *n (reduction in price)* remise *f*, rabais *m*; **to give sb a discount** faire une remise à qn; **to buy/sell sth at a discount** acheter/vendre qch au rabais; **to allow a discount of 10% (on sth)** consentir un rabais de 10% (sur qch)

2 *vt (price)* baisser; *(goods)* solder

◇ *discount card* carte *f* de réduction

◇ *discount price* prix *m* réduit, prix *m* faible

◇ *discount rate* taux *m* d'escompte

◇ *discount store* magasin *m* de discount

discounter *n* discounter *m*

dispatch **1** *n (of goods)* expédition *f*, envoi *m*

2 *vt (goods)* expédier, envoyer

◇ *dispatch department* service *m* des expéditions

◇ *dispatch note* bulletin *m* d'expédition, bordereau *m* d'expédition

dispatcher *n* expéditeur (trice) *m,f*

display **1** *n (goods, activity)* étalage *m*, exposition *f*

2 *vt (goods)* étaler, exposer, présenter

◇ *display advertisement* placard *m* publicitaire

◇ *display advertising* étalage

m publicitaire

◇ *display area* espace *m* d'exposition

◇ *display material* matériel *m* de présentation

◇ *display pack* emballage *m* de présentation, emballage *m* présentoir

◇ *display space* surface *f* d'exposition

◇ *display stand, display unit* présentoir *m*

◇ *display window* vitrine *f*, étalage *m*

displayed price *n* prix *m* affiché, prix *m* à la vente

disposable 1 *n* disposables biens *mpl* de consommation non durables

2 *adj (packaging, product)* jetable

◇ *disposable goods* biens *mpl* de consommation non durables

◇ *disposable income* surplus *m*, revenu *m* disponible

distinctive value *n* valeur *f* distinctive

distribute *vt (goods)* distribuer; **Hammond Ltd is the only company allowed to distribute our products** l'entreprise Hammond Ltd est notre distributeur exclusif

distribution *n* distribution *f*, diffusion *f*; **wholesale and retail distribution** commerce *m* de gros et de détail

◇ *distribution agency* agence *f* de distribution

◇ *distribution agent* agent *m* de distribution

◇ *distribution centre* centre *m* de distribution

◇ *distribution chain* chaîne *f* de distribution

◇ *distribution channel* canal *m* de distribution

◇ *distribution costs* frais *mpl* de distribution, coût *m* de la distribution

◇ *distribution depot* dépôt *m* de distribution

◇ *distribution network* réseau *m* de distribution, circuit *m* de distribution

◇ *distribution outlet* point *m* de distribution

◇ *distribution policy* politique *f* de distribution

◇ *distribution process* processus *m* de distribution

◇ *distribution rights* droits *mpl* de distribution, droits *mpl* de diffusion

◇ *distribution system* système *m* de distribution

distributor *n* distributeur (trice) *m,f*

◇ *distributor's brand* marque *f* de distributeur

◇ *distributor's margin* marge *f* de distributeur

◇ *distributor panel* panel *m* de distributeurs

diversification *n* diversification *f*; **the company's recent diversification into cosmetics** la diversification qu'a récemment entreprise la société en pénétrant le marché des cosmétiques

◇ *diversification strategy* stratégie *f* de diversification

diversify 1 *vt (production)* diversifier; **we must aim to diversify our product portfolio** il nous faut essayer de diversifier notre portefeuille de produits

2 *vi (of company)* se diversifier; **to diversify into a new market** se diversifier en pénétrant un nouveau marché; **to diversify into a new product** se diversifier en fabriquant un nouveau produit

documentation *n* documentation *f*

dog *n (product, company)* poids *m* mort, gouffre *m* financier

"

For the marketing executive guessing the future is more than a routine parlour game to be indulged in at the beginning of each new year. Getting it right or getting it wrong is the difference between being regarded as a star or a **dog**.

"

domestic *adj*

◇ **domestic market** marché *m* intérieur

◇ **domestic products** denrées *fpl* du pays, produits *mpl* d'origine nationale

◇ **domestic trade** commerce *m* intérieur

dominant brand *n* marque *f* dominante

door drop *n* distribution *f* à domicile

"

The promotion also includes

a complementary TV advertising campaign, which hit the screens just after Christmas, and a nationwide **door drop** of free samples of the product and redemption coupons.

"

door-to-door *adj*

◇ **door-to-door salesman** démarcheur *m*

◇ **door-to-door selling** (vente de) porte-à-porte *m*

downmarket **1** *adj* bas de gamme

2 *adv* **to move downmarket** se repositionner à la baisse

drip advertising *n* publicité continue, publicité *f* goutte à goutte

drive *n (campaign)* campagne *f*; **the company is having a sales drive** la société fait une campagne de vente

drop **1** *n (in prices)* chute *f*, baisse *f* (**in** de); **sales show a drop of 10%** les ventes accusent une baisse de 10%

2 *vi (of prices, inflation)* baisser; **sales have dropped by 10%** les ventes ont baissé de 10%

dual-branded *adj* sous marque double

"

Last Wednesday's launch saw BAT unveil **dual-branded** cars to begin racing in March, in open defiance of the F1 establishment. Former world champion Jacques

Villeneuve's car and suit were decorated in the colours of BAT's Lucky Strike brand while his deputy Ricardo Zonta flew the flag of State Express 555.

"

dummy 1 *n (product)* objet *m* factice
  2 *adj* factice
◇ *dummy pack* emballage *m* factice
dump bin *n* panier *m* de présentation en vrac, panier *m* présentoir
duopoly *n* duopole *m*
durable 1 *n* durables biens *mpl* (de consommation) durables
  2 *adj*
◇ *durable goods* biens *mpl* (de

consommation) durables
duty *n Customs* droit *m*; **to pay duty on sth** payer une taxe sur qch
duty-free *Customs* 1 *n Fam* (**a**) *(goods)* marchandises *fpl* hors taxe, marchandises *fpl* en franchise
  (**b**) *(shop)* magasin *m* hors taxe
  2 *adj (goods)* hors taxe, en franchise
◇ *duty-free allowance* = quantité de produits hors taxe autorisée
◇ *duty-free import* importation *f* en franchise
◇ *duty-free shop* magasin *m* hors taxe
duty-paid *adj Customs (goods)* acquitté(e), dédouané(e)

early *adj*

◇ *early adopter* réceptif *m* précoce, adopteur *m* précoce

◇ *early majority* majorité *f* innovatrice

e-cash *n Comptr* argent *m* électronique, argent *m* virtuel, e-cash *m*

e-commerce *n Comptr* commerce *m* électronique

economic *adj* (a) *(relating to the economy)* économique (b) *Br (profitable)* rentable; **to make sth economic** rentabiliser qch

◇ *economic analysis* analyse *f* économique

◇ *economic appraisal* évaluation *f* économique

◇ *economic climate* climat *m* économique

◇ *economic forecast* prévisions *fpl* économiques

◇ *economic growth* croissance *f* économique

◇ *economic indicators* indicateurs *mpl* économiques

◇ *economic life* *(of product)* vie *f* économique

◇ *economic recovery* reprise *f* économique

◇ *economic situation* conjoncture *f* économique

economical *adj* *(person)* économe; *(method, approach)* économique

economically *adv* (a) *(relating to the economy)* économiquement (b) *(with economy)* de manière économe; **economically viable** *(campaign, product)* économiquement viable

economics *npl* *(profitability)* rentabilité *f*; *(financial aspects)* aspects *mpl* financiers; **we must consider the economics of the project before making any decisions** nous devons considérer l'aspect financier du projet avant de prendre une décision

economy *n* économie *f*

◇ *economy brand* marque *f* économique

◇ *economy pack* paquet *m* économique

◇ *economies of scale* économies *fpl* d'échelle

effective *adj* *(method, campaign)* efficace

effectiveness *n* *(of method, campaign)* efficacité *f*

EFT *n Comptr* *(abbr electronic funds transfer)* transfert *m* de fonds électronique

EFTPOS *n Comptr (abbr elec-tronic* **electronic funds transfer at point of sale**) transfert *m* de fonds électronique au point de vente

elastic *adj (price, demand)* élastique

elasticity *n (of price, demand)* élasticité *f*

electronic *adj Comptr* électronique

◇ *electronic catalogue* catalogue *m* en ligne

◇ *electronic commerce* commerce *m* électronique

◇ *electronic funds transfer* transfert *m* de fonds électronique

◇ *electronic funds transfer at point of sale* transfert *m* de fonds électronique au point de vente

◇ *electronic payment* paiement *m* électronique

◇ *electronic payment terminal* terminal *m* électronique de paiement

◇ *electronic point of sale* point *m* de vente électronique

◇ *electronic shopping* achats *mpl* en ligne, téléachat *m*

emotional *adj (reaction, response)* émotionnel(elle)

◇ *emotional purchase* achat *m* d'émotion

> 〝
> The importance of image in fashion retailing cannot be underestimated: "It is 90% an **emotional purchase**," says Kindleysides. His view is supported by academic re-search: "Store design in this market … is crucial in the first place for attracting customers to the store and then for creating the right atmosphere for purchase."
> 〞

encirclement *n*

◇ *encirclement attack* attaque *f* par encerclement

◇ *encirclement strategy* stratégie *f* d'encerclement

end-consumer *n* utilisateur (trice) *m,f* final(e)

endgame *n* objectif *m*

end product *n* produit *m* fini

end-user *n* utilisateur(trice) *m,f* final(e)

enter *vt (market)* entrer dans; **all goods entering the country are subject to duty** toutes les marchandises importées sont passibles de droits

EPOS *n Comptr (abbr* **electronic point of sale**) point *m* de vente électronique

Euro *n* euro *m*

European Standards Commission *n* comité *m* européen de normalisation

event *n*

◇ *event advertising* publicité *f* par l'événement

◇ *event promotion* communication *f* événementielle

evoked set *n* ensemble *m* évoqué

exchange rate *n* cours *m* du change, taux *m* de change; **at the current exchange rate** au cours du jour

exclusive *adj* exclusif(ive)

◊ *exclusive distribution* distribution *f* exclusive

◊ *exclusive distribution agreement* accord *m* de distribution exclusive

◊ *exclusive licence* licence *f* exclusive

◊ *exclusive rights* droits *mpl* exclusifs, exclusivité *f*

◊ *exclusive selling rights* droits *mpl* de vente exclusifs

◊ *exclusive shipment* expédition *f* exclusive

◊ *exclusive territory* territoire *m* exclusif

exclusivity *n* exclusivité *f*

◊ *exclusivity agreement* accord *m* d'exclusivité

◊ *exclusivity clause* clause *f* d'exclusivité

exempt *adj* Customs *(from duty)* exempté(e), en franchise

exemption *n* Customs *(from duty)* exemption *f*, franchise *f*

exhibit 1 *n* objet *m* exposé
2 *vt (object, goods)* exhiber, montrer

exhibition *n* (a) *(of goods)* étalage *m* (b) *(show)* exposition *f*

◊ *exhibition hall* salle *f* d'exposition

◊ *exhibition stand* stand *m* (d'exposition)

exhibitor *n (at exhibition)* exposant(e) *m,f*

existing *adj*

◊ *existing customer* client(e) *m,f* actuel(elle)

◊ *existing market* marché *m* existant, marché *m* actuel .

expand 1 *vt (company, market)* agrandir
2 *vi (of market)* s'agrandir; **the computer games market is expanding** le marché des jeux vidéo est en expansion

"

These light buyers, he suggested, were a market to concentrate on and convert to medium (4 to 9 books) and heavy (10 plus) book buyers. In seeking to **expand** the market, publishers and booksellers would have to take into account a number of factors.

"

expenditure *n* (a) *(spending)* dépense *f* (b) *(amount spent)* dépenses *fpl*; **it entails heavy expenditure** cela entraîne de fortes dépenses

expense *n (cost)* dépense *f*, frais *mpl*; **at great expense** à grands frais

experience *n* expérience *f*

◊ *experience curve* courbe *f* d'expérience

◊ *experience effect* effet *m* d'expérience

explore *vt (market)* prospecter

export 1 *n* (a) *(product)* article *m* d'exportation; **exports** *(of country)* exportations *fpl* (b) *(activity)* exportation *f*; **for export only, reserved for export** réservé à l'exportation

2 *vt (goods)* exporter

3 *vi* exporter; **the firm exports all over the world** l'entreprise exporte dans le monde entier

◇ *export agent* commissionnaire *mf* exportateur(trice), agent *m* exportateur

◇ *export ban* interdiction *f* d'exporter; **to impose an export ban on sth** interdire qch d'exportation

◇ *export company* entreprise *f* exportatrice

◇ *export credit* crédit *m* à l'exportation

◇ *export department* service *m* des exportations

◇ *export duty* droit *m* de sortie, droit *m* d'exportation

◇ *export firm* maison *f* d'exportation

◇ *export goods* marchandises *fpl* à l'export

◇ *export label* label *m* d'exportation

◇ *export management* direction *f* export

◇ *export manager* directeur (trice) *m,f* des exportations

◇ *export market* marché *m* à l'exportation

◇ *export order* commande *f* export, commande *f* pour l'exportation

◇ *export price* prix *m* à l'exportation, prix *m* (à l')export

◇ *export sales* ventes *fpl* export, ventes *fpl* à l'exportation

◇ *export tax* taxe *f* à l'exportation

◇ *export trade* commerce *m* d'exportation

exportation *n (of goods)* exportation *f*

exporter *n (person)* exportateur(trice) *m,f; (country)* pays *m* exportateur; **France is one of the world's biggest exporters of wine** la France est l'un des plus grands pays exportateurs de vin; **this country is a net exporter of manufactured goods** ce pays est un exportateur net de produits manufacturés

exporting *adj* exportateur (trice)

◇ *exporting country* pays *m* exportateur

exposure *n (publicity)* couverture *f;* **to get a lot of exposure** *(of company, product)* faire l'objet d'une couverture médiatique importante; **exposure to the media is important for a new product** il est important de bénéficier d'une couverture médiatique pour un nouveau produit

express delivery *n* envoi *m* exprès

external *adj (audit, auditor)* externe

extrapolate **1** *vt* extrapoler; **we can extrapolate sales figures of the last ten years to predict future trends** on peut extrapoler les tendances à venir à partir des chiffres de vente de ces dix dernières années

2 *vi* extrapoler; **to extrapolate from sth** extrapoler à partir de qch

extrapolation *n* extrapolation *f*

facility n (possibility) facilité f; **facilities for payment** facilités fpl de paiement; **we offer credit facilities** nous offrons des facilités de crédit

factor n (a) (in multiplication) indice m, coefficient m; **the sales increased by a factor of ten** les ventes sont dix fois plus élevées, l'indice des ventes est dix fois plus haut (b) (element) facteur m

◇ Econ **factor of production** facteur m de production

factory n usine f

◇ **factory price** prix m usine, prix m sortie usine

◇ **factory shop** magasin m d'usine

▸ **fall off** vi (of profits, takings, sales) diminuer

falling off n diminution f, baisse f; **there has been a recent falling-off in sales** les ventes ont accusé une baisse ces derniers temps

false claim n promesse f mensongère

family n (of products) famille f

◇ **family brand** marque f générale

◇ **family lifecycle** cycle m de vie familiale

◇ **family model** modèle m familial

family-sized adj (packet, box) familial(e)

fast mover n (product) article m à forte rotation

fast-moving adj à forte rotation

◇ **fast-moving consumer goods** biens mpl de (grande) consommation à forte rotation

feasibility n (of plan) faisabilité f

◇ **feasibility report** rapport m de faisabilité

◇ **feasibility stage** phase f de faisabilité

◇ **feasibility study** étude f de faisabilité

◇ **feasibility test** essai m probatoire

feature n (of product) caractéristique f

feedback n réactions fpl, échos mpl; **we welcome feedback from our customers** nous sommes toujours heureux d'avoir les impressions ou les réactions de nos clients; **we**

need more feedback nous avons besoin de plus d'informations en retour; **this will provide us with much-needed feedback on public opinion** ceci nous fournira des informations dont nous avons grand besoin sur l'opinion publique

field n (a) (for product) marché m (b) (practice as opposed to theory) terrain m; **in the field** sur le terrain

◇ **field marketing** marketing m sur le terrain

◇ **field research** études fpl sur le terrain, recherches fpl sur le terrain

◇ **field study** enquête f sur le terrain, étude f sur le terrain

◇ **field work** travail m sur le terrain

FIFO (abbr first in, first out) (stock control system) PEPS

firm 1 n (company) société f, entreprise f, firme f
   2 adj (order) ferme

first-time user n nouvel(elle) utilisateur(trice) m,f

fixed adj (price, rate) fixe

flagship n

◇ **flagship branch** succursale f vedette

◇ **flagship brand** marque f étendard, marque f fer de lance

◇ **flagship product** produit m fer de lance, produit m vedette

◇ **flagship store** magasin m vitrine

flank attack n (on market) attaque f latérale

flat price n prix m unique

flood vt (market) inonder, encombrer; **the market is flooded with computer games** il y a une surabondance de jeux électroniques sur le marché

floor n

◇ **floor ad** publicité f au sol

◇ **floor display** présentation f au sol

◇ **floor manager** (in department store) chef m de rayon

◇ **floor space** surface f au sol

◇ **floor stand** présentatoir m au sol

floorwalker n (in department store) chef m de rayon

flow chart n graphique m d'évolution, organigramme m

flyer n (leaflet) prospectus m

FMCG npl (abbr **fast-moving consumer goods**) biens mpl de (grande) consommation à forte rotation

focus group n groupe-témoin m

◇ **focus group interview** entretien m avec les membres du groupe-témoin

▸ **follow up** 1 vt sep (letter) faire suivre d'une seconde lettre; (customer) relancer; **follow up your initial phone call with a letter** confirmez votre coup de téléphone par écrit

2 vi (in selling) faire de la relance

follower n (company, product) suiveur m

follow-me product n produit m tactique

follow-up n (of advertising, client) relance f; (of order) suivi m, suite f

◇ **follow-up letter** lettre f de relance

◇ **follow-up visit** visite f de relance

◇ **follow-up work** travail m complémentaire

food n aliments mpl

◇ **food products** produits mpl alimentaires, comestibles mpl, denrées fpl

foodstuffs npl produits mpl alimentaires, comestibles mpl, denrées fpl

footfall n fréquentation f

forecast 1 n prévisions fpl

2 vt prévoir; **he forecasts sale of £2m** il prévoit un chiffre d vente de 2 millions de livres

◇ **forecast plan** plan m pré visionnel

foreign adj étranger(ère)

◇ **foreign currency** devises f étrangères

◇ **foreign exchange** devises f étrangères

◇ **foreign goods** marchandise fpl qui viennent de l'étranger

◇ **foreign market** marché extérieur

◇ **foreign trade** commerce extérieur

format n (of advertisement format m

forward vt (goods) expédie envoyer; **to forward sth to s** faire parvenir qch à qn

◇ Econ **forward integratio** intégration f en aval, inté gration f descendante

forwarding n expédition envoi m

◇ **forwarding address** (fc goods) adresse f pour l'ex pédition

◇ **forwarding agent** (agent m transitaire m, agent m de fre

◇ *forwarding charges* frais *mpl* d'expédition

◇ *forwarding office* bureau *m* d'expédition

franchise 1 *n* franchise *f*
2 *vt* franchiser, accorder une franchise à

◇ *franchise agreement* accord *m* de franchise

◇ *franchise outlet* boutique *f* franchisée, magasin *m* franchisé

franchisee *n* franchisé(e) *m,f*

franchiser *n* franchiseur (euse) *m,f*

franchising *n* franchisage *m*

◇ *franchising operation* franchisage *m*

franchisor = **franchiser**

free 1 *adj* **(a)** *(without charge)* gratuit(e) **(b)** *(unrestricted)* libre
2 *adv* gratuitement; **they will deliver free of charge** ils livreront gratuitement

◇ *free agent* agent *m* indépendant

◇ *free competition* libre concurrence *f*

◇ *free credit* crédit *m* gratuit

◇ *free delivery* livraison *f* gratuite, livraison *f* franco

◇ *free gift* prime *f*, cadeau *m*

◇ *free import* entrée *f* en franchise

◇ *free sample* échantillon *m* gratuit

◇ *free trial* essai *m* gratuit

◇ *free trial period* période *f* d'essai gratuit

freebie *n Fam* cadeau *m* (publicitaire)

freeze 1 *n* *(on prices)* gel *m*
2 *vt* *(prices)* geler

freight 1 *n* **(a)** *(transport)* fret *m*, transport *m* de marchandises; **to send goods by freight** envoyer des marchandises par régime ordinaire
(b) *(cargo, load)* fret *m*, cargaison *f*; **to take in freight** prendre du fret
(c) *(goods)* marchandises *fpl* (transportées)
(d) *(cost)* (frais *mpl* de) port *m*; **freight by weight** fret *m* au poids; **freight charges paid** port payé; **freight forward** port avancé
2 *vt* *(goods)* transporter

◇ *freight forwarder* agent *m* de fret

◇ *freight note* note *f* de fret

◇ *freight price* prix *m* de fret, prix *m* de transport

◇ *freight release* bon *m* à délivrer

frequency *n* fréquence *f*

◇ *frequency rate* taux *m* de répétition

frequent user card *n* carte *f* de fidélité

full *adj*

◇ *full demand* demande *f* soutenue

◇ *full warranty* garantie *f* totale

full-cost pricing *n* fixation *f* du prix en fonction du coût

full-line strategy *n* stratégie *f* de gamme complète

gameplan *n* stratégie *f* (de marketing)

game theory *n* théorie *f* des jeux

gap *n* écart *m*; **a gap in the market** un créneau

◇ *gap analysis* étude *f* des créneaux

◇ *gap level* écart *m* de performance

gatekeeper *n* *(in purchasing department)* contrôleur *m*, relais *m*, filtre *m*

> " ... the supplier's marketing department must try to identify and reach technical specialists, engineers, technical buyers etc. This will depend on how accessible these people are, and on how effective are the **gatekeepers** whose role includes filtering out what they, or the influencer, deem to be undesirable or unnecessary information. "

generic **1** *n* produit *m* générique
2 *adj* générique

◇ *generic advertising* publicité *f* générique

◇ *generic brand* marque *f* générique

◇ *generic market* marché *m* générique

◇ *generic name* nom *m* générique

◇ *generic product* produit *m* générique

geodemographic *adj* géodémographique

◇ *geodemographic data* données *fpl* géodémographiques

◇ *geodemographic profile* profil *m* géodémographique

◇ *geodemographic segment* segment *m* géodémographique

◇ *geodemographic segmentation* segmentation *f* géodémographique

geographic *adj*

◇ *geographic pricing* tarification *f* géographique

◇ *geographic segment* segment *m* géographique

◇ *geographic segmentation* segmentation *f* géographique

geomarketing *n* géomarketing *m*

giant-sized *adj* *(pack, box)* géant(e)

gift token, gift voucher *n* chèque-cadeau *m*

giveaway *n Fam (free gift)* prime *f*, cadeau *m (publicitaire)*

◇ *giveaway material* cadeaux *mpl (publicitaires)*

◇ *giveaway paper* journal *m* gratuit

global *adj (worldwide)* mondial(e), global(e)

◇ *global audience* audience *f* globale

◇ *global market* marché *m* global

◇ *global marketing* marketing *m* global, marketing *m* international

◇ *global strategy* stratégie *f* globale

globalization *n* globalisation *f*, mondialisation *f*

◇ *globalization strategy* stratégie *f* de globalisation

globalize *vt* globaliser, mondialiser

glut **1** *n (on market)* encombrement *m* ; *(of commodity)* surabondance *f*

2 *vt (market, economy)* encombrer, inonder ; **the market is glutted with luxury goods** il y a une surabondance d'objets de luxe sur le marché

going-rate pricing *n* alignement *m* sur les prix du marché

gondola *n (for displaying goods)* gondole *f*

◇ *gondola end* tête *f* de gondole

goods *npl (articles)* marchandises *fpl*, articles *mpl* ; **send us the goods by rail** envoyez-nous la marchandise par chemin de fer

graph *n* graphique *m*, diagramme *m* ; **to plot a graph** tracer un graphique

grass-roots forecasting *n* prévisions *fpl* de la base

gray market *Am* = **grey market**

green *adj (concerning the environment)* vert(e), écologique

◇ *green marketing* marketing *m* vert, marketing *m* écologique

◇ *green product* produit *m* vert, produit *m* écologique

grey market, *Am* **gray market** *n* marché *m* gris

gross *adj* brut(e)

◇ *gross margin* marge *f* brute

◇ *gross profit* bénéfice *m* brut

◇ *gross profit margin* marge *f* commerciale brute

group **1** *n* groupe *m*

2 *vt (orders, deliveries, consignments)* grouper

◇ *group advertising* publicité *f* collective

⋄ *group meeting* (for marketing survey) réunion f de groupe

groupage n (of orders, deliveries, consignments) groupage m

grow 1 vt **to grow the business** augmenter le chiffre d'affaires; **to grow a company** développer une entreprise

2 vi (increase) augmenter, s'accroître; **our market share has grown by 5% in the last year** notre part de marché a augmenté de 5% au cours de l'année dernière

❝

He thinks he can **grow the business** into a significant piece of change, much of it coming perhaps from the Microsoft arena where, as much as Lachman is a self-admitted Unix bigot, he knows he has to enter.

❞

growth n (of market) croissance f, expansion f; **the experts predict a 2% growth in imports** les experts prédisent une croissance des importations de 2%; **to go for growth** favoriser la croissance

⋄ *growth area* secteur m en expansion

⋄ *growth curve* courbe f de croissance

⋄ *growth market* marché m porteur

⋄ *growth sector* secteur m en expansion

⋄ *growth strategy* stratégie de croissance

growth-share matrix matrice f croissance-part de marché

guarantee 1 n (document, promise) garantie f; **this computer has a five-year guarantee** cet ordinateur est garanti cinq ans; **under guarantee** sous garantie

2 vt (product, appliance) garantir; **this computer is guaranteed for five years** cet ordinateur est garanti cinq ans

⋄ *guarantee certificate* certificat m de garantie

guaranteed adj garanti(e)

⋄ *guaranteed delivery period* délai m garanti de livraison

guerilla attack n guérilla f

guided interview n entretien m directif

habitual buying behaviour *n* comportement *m* d'achat habituel

halo effect *n* effet *m* de halo

handle *vt (account, campaign)* s'occuper de

handout *n (brochure)* prospectus *m*; *(sample)* cadeau *m* (publicitaire)

hard-core *adj*

◇ **hard-core loyal** fidèle *mf* absolu(e)

◇ **hard-core loyalty** fidélité *f* absolue

hard sell *n* vente *f* agressive; **to give sb the hard sell** imposer une vente à qn; **to give sth the hard sell** promouvoir qch de façon agressive

◇ **hard sell techniques** méthode *f* de vente agressive

hard selling *n* vente *f* agressive

◇ **hard selling techniques** méthode *f* de vente agressive

hazard forecasting *n* prévision *f* événementielle

head-on attack *n (on market)* attaque *f* frontale

heterogeneous *adj (market, goods)* hétérogène

high *adj (price)* élevé(e)

◇ **high end** *(of market)* haut *m*

◇ **high involvement** *(of consumer)* forte participation *f*

◇ *Br* **the high street** *(street)* la grand-rue, la rue principale; *(shops)* les commerçants *mpl*, le commerce; **the high street has been badly hit by the recession** la récession a frappé durement les commerçants *ou* le commerce

high-end *adj (goods)* haut de gamme

high-income group n groupe m de contribuables à revenus élevés

high-involvement adj (purchasing) à forte participation des consommateurs

high-quality adj de qualité supérieure, de première qualité

high-street shops npl the high-street shops les commerçants mpl, le commerce

hire purchase n achat m à crédit, achat m à tempérament; **to buy sth on hire purchase** acheter qch à crédit ou à tempérament

◇ **hire purchase agreement** contrat m de location-vente

hoarding n Br (billboard) panneau m d'affichage, panneau m publicitaire

◇ **hoarding site** emplacement m d'affichage

home n
◇ Econ **home consumption** consommation f intérieure
◇ **home market** marché m intérieur
◇ **home sales** ventes fpl sur le marché intérieur
◇ **home shopping** téléachat m
◇ **home trade** commerce m intérieur

homogeneous adj (market, goods) homogène

horizontal integration Econ intégration f horizontale

household n Econ ménage m, foyer m
◇ **household consumptio** consommation f des mé nages
◇ **household expenses** déper ses fpl du ménage
◇ **household goods** biens m d'équipement ménagers
◇ **household name** nom m d marque connu

house-to-house adj (sell ing) à domicile
◇ **house-to-house canvassin** porte-à-porte m, démar chage m

HP n (abbr hire purchase) acha m à crédit, achat m à tem pérament

hype Fam 1 n (publicity) bat tage m publicitaire
2 vt (publicize) faire du bat tage publicitaire pour

▸ **hype up** vt sep Fam (publi cize) faire du battage publici taire pour

hypermarket n hypermarch m, grande surface f

hypersegmentation n hy persegmentation f

ICC *n* (*abbr* **International Chamber of Commerce**) CCI *f*

image *n* image *f*; **their brief is to update the product's image** ils ont pour mission de moderniser l'image du produit; **the company is suffering from an image problem** l'entreprise a un problème d'image

◇ *image pricing* fixation *f* de prix en fonction de l'image

imitative product *n* produit *m* d'imitation

impact *n* (*of campaign, advertisement*) impact *m*

◇ *impact study* étude *f* d'impact

implement *vt* (*product, campaign*) mettre en œuvre

implementation *n* (*of product, campaign*) mise *f* en œuvre

import 1 *n* (**a**) (*product*) article *m* d'importation; **imports** (*of country*) importations *fpl*
(**b**) (*activity*) importation *f*; **import and export** l'importation *f* et l'exportation *f*
2 *vt* (*goods*) importer (**from** de)

◇ *import agent* commissionnaire *mf* importateur(trice), agent *m* importateur

◇ *import ban* interdiction *f* d'importation; **to impose an import ban on sth** interdire qch d'importation

◇ *import controls* contrôles *mpl* à l'importation

◇ *import duty* droit *m* de douane à l'importation

◇ *import firm* maison *f* d'importation

◇ *import goods* marchandises *fpl* à l'import

◇ *import list* liste *f* des importations; (*of prices*) tarif *m* d'entrée

◇ *import price* prix *m* à l'importation, prix *m* (à l')import

◇ *import tax* taxe *f* à l'importation

◇ *import trade* commerce *m* d'importation

importation *n* (**a**) (*of goods*) importation *f*; **for temporary importation** en franchise temporaire (**b**) *Am* (*imported article*) article *m* d'importation, importation *f*

importer *n* (*person*) importateur(trice) *m,f*; (*country*) pays *m* importateur; **this country is a big importer of luxury goods** ce pays est un gros importateur de produits de luxe; **Japan is still a net importer of technology** le Japon est toujours un importateur net de technologie

◇ *importer's margin* marge *f* de l'importateur

import-export *n* import-export *m*

impulse *n*

◇ *impulse buy* achat *m* spontané, achat *m* d'impulsion, achat *m* impulsif

◇ *impulse buyer* acheteur (euse) *m,f* impulsif(ive)

◇ *impulse buying* achats *mpl* spontanés, achats *mpl* d'impulsion, achats *mpl* impulsif

◇ *impulse purchase* achat *m* spontané, achat *m* d'impulsion, achat *m* impulsif

◇ *impulse purchaser* acheteur (euse) *m,f* impulsif(ive)

◇ *impulse purchasing* achats *mpl* spontanés, achats *mpl* d'impulsion, achats *mpl* impulsifs

incentive *n* stimulation *f*; *(reduction, free gift)* stimulant *m*

◇ *incentive marketing* marketing *m* de stimulation

◇ *incentive scheme* programme *m* de stimulation

increase 1 *n* *(in price, sales)* augmentation *f*, hausse *f* (**in** de) **2** *vt* augmenter; **we must increase sales by 10%** il faut augmenter les ventes de 10%

3 *vi* augmenter; **to increase in price** devenir plus cher (chère), augmenter de prix; **the growth rate is likely to increase** le taux de croissance va probablement augmenter

independent retailer *n* détaillant(e) *m,f* indépendant(e)

indirect *adj* indirect(e)

◇ *indirect costs* coûts *mpl* indirects

◇ *indirect promotional costs* coûts *mpl* de promotion indirects

◇ *indirect selling* vente *f* indirecte

individual *adj (packet, format)* individuel(elle)

industrial *adj* industriel(elle)

◇ *industrial market* marché *m* industriel

◇ *industrial marketer* mercaticien(enne) *m,f* industriel (elle)

◇ *industrial marketing* marketing *m* industriel

inertia selling *n* vente *f* forcée

inferior *adj (goods, quality)* inférieur(e)

inflation *n Econ* inflation *f*; **inflation is down/up on last year** l'inflation est en baisse/ en hausse par rapport à l'année dernière; **inflation now stands at 5%** l'inflation est maintenant à 5%

inflationary *adj Econ* inflationniste

inflation-proof *adj Econ* protégé(e) contre les effets de l'inflation

influencer *n* préconisateur *m*, influencer *m*

infomercial *n* infomercial *m*

information *n (news, data)*

informations *fpl*, renseignements *mpl*; **a piece of information** une information, un renseignement; **I am sending you this price list for your information** je vous envoie cette liste des prix à titre d'information *ou* de renseignement

informative advertising *n* publicité *f* informative

ingoing inventory *n* inventaire *m* d'entrée

inhibitor *n* (product) inhibiteur *m*

in-house **1** *adj* interne; (staff) qui travaille sur place
2 *adv* sur place
◇ *in-house magazine* magazine *m* d'entreprise
◇ *in-house team* équipe *f* en interne

initiator *n* (of purchasing process) initiateur *m*

innovating company *n* entreprise *f* (in)novatrice

innovation *n* innovation *f*

innovative *adj* (in)novateur (trice)
◇ *innovative product* produit *m* (in)novateur

innovator *n* (in)novateur (trice) *m,f*

insert *n* (leaflet) encart *m*

instalment, *Am* **installment** *n* (part payment) acompte *m*, versement *m*; **to pay in** *or* **by instalments** payer par versements échelonnés
◇ *Am* **installment plan** vente *f* à

tempérament; **to buy sth on the installment plan** acheter qch à tempérament *ou* à crédit

instantaneous audience *n* audience *f* instantanée

institutional advertising *n* publicité *f* institutionnelle

in-store *adj*
◇ *in-store advertising* PLV *f*, publicité *f* sur le lieu de vente
◇ *in-store advertising space* espace *m* de PLV, espace *m* de publicité sur le lieu de vente
◇ *in-store demonstration* démonstration *f* sur le lieu de vente
◇ *in-store promotion* promotion *f* sur le lieu de vente

integration *n Econ* intégration *f*, concentration *f*

intensive distribution *n* distribution *f* intensive
◇ *intensive distribution strategy* stratégie *f* de distribution intensive

intention to buy *n* intention *f* d'achat

intention-to-buy-scale *n* échelle *f* des intentions d'achat

interactive marketing *n* marketing *m* interactif

intercept interview *n* entretien *m* spontané

interest *n* (on loan, investment) intérêt(s) *m(pl)* (**on** sur)
◇ *interest rate* taux *m* d'intérêt; **the interest rate is 4%** le taux d'intérêt est de 4%

interest-free *adj* (credit) gratuit(e)

internal adj (audit, auditor) interne
◇ **internal marketing** marketing m interne

international adj international(e)
◇ **International Chamber of Commerce** Chambre f de commerce internationale
◇ **International Standards Organization** Organisation f internationale de normalisation

Internet n Comptr Internet m; **to buy/sell sth on** or **over the Internet** acheter/vendre qch par l'Internet

interview 1 n entretien m
2 vt interroger

interviewee n enquêté(e) m,f, personne f interrogée

interviewer n enquêteur (trice) m,f

introduce vt (product) lancer

introduction stage n (of product) phase f d'introduction

introductory adj
◇ **introductory offer** offre f de lancement
◇ **introductory price** prix m de lancement

inventory 1 n (stock) stock(s) m(pl)
2 vt (goods) inventorier

◇ **inventory control** contrôle m des stocks
◇ **inventory turnround** rotation f des stocks

invoice 1 n facture f; **to make out an invoice** établir ou faire une facture; **to settle an invoice** régler une facture; **as per invoice** conformément à la facture; **payment should be made within 30 days of invoice** les factures doivent être réglées sous 30 jours; **payable against invoice** à payer à réception de la facture
2 vt (goods) facturer, porter sur une facture; (person, company) envoyer la facture à; **to invoice sb for sth** facturer qch à qn

◇ **invoice date** date f de facturation
◇ **invoice price** prix m facturé, prix m de facture

invoicing n (of goods) facturation f
◇ **invoicing address** adresse f de facturation

island n (for displaying goods) îlot m

ISO n (abbr International Standards Organization) ISO f

item n (article) article m; **please send us the following items** prière de nous envoyer les articles suivants

jingle *n* jingle *m*, sonal *m*

JIT *adj* (*abbr* **just in time**) juste à temps, JAT

◇ *JIT distribution* distribution *f* JAT

◇ *JIT production* production *f* JAT

◇ *JIT purchasing* achat *m* JAT

judg(e)ment *n*

◇ *judg(e)ment sample* échantillon *m* discrétionnaire

◇ *judg(e)ment sampling* échantillonnage *m* discrétionnaire

junk mail *n* courrier *m* publicitaire

just-in-time *adj* juste à temps

◇ *just-in-time distribution* distribution *f* juste à temps

◇ *just-in-time production* production *f* juste à temps

◇ *just-in-time purchasing* achat *m* juste à temps

key *n*

◇ *key account* compte-clé *m*

◇ *key brand* marque *f* clé

◇ *key position* position *f* clé

key-account *adj*

◇ *key-account management* gestion *f* de comptes-clés

◇ *key-account sales* ventes *fpl* aux comptes-clés

knockdown price *n Br Fam* **for sale at knockdown prices** en vente à des prix imbattables; **I got it for a knockdown price** je l'ai eu pour trois fois rien

knocking copy *n* publicité *f* comparative dénigrante

label 1 *n* étiquette *f*, label *m*
2 *vt* étiqueter

◇ *label of origin* label *m* d'origine

labelling, *Am* **labeling** *n* étiquetage *m*

laggard *n* innovateur(trice) *m,f* tardif(ive)

late *adj*

◇ *late adopter* utilisateur-(trice) *m,f* tardif(ive)

◇ *late entrant* concurrent(e) *m,f* tardif(ive)

◇ *late entry* lancement *m* tardif

◇ *late majority* majorité *f* conservatrice

launch 1 *n* *(of product)* lancement *m*
2 *vt (product)* lancer

layout *n* *(of advertisement)* mise *f* en page, maquette *f*; *(of store)* agencement *m*

> Analysts argue that M&S has failed to make its store **layouts** help shoppers bring clothing together to make outfits.

lead *n* *(advantage)* avance *f*;

we are managing to retain our lead over the competition nous parvenons à maintenir notre avance sur nos concurrents

◇ *lead time (for production)* délai *m* de production; *(for delivery)* délai *m* de livraison

◇ *lead user* utilisateur(trice) *m,f* pilote

leader *n* **(a)** *(leading product)* leader *m*; *Am (loss leader)* produit *m* d'appel **(b)** *(company)* chef *m* de file, leader *m* **(c)** *(of focus group)* animateur (trice) *m,f*

leaflet *n* prospectus *m*

◇ *leaflet drop* distribution *f* de prospectus

learning *n* *(by consumer)* apprentissage *m*

leisure industry *n* industrie *f* des loisirs

letter *n* *(mail)* lettre *f*

▸ **level off, level out** *vi (of prices, demand, sales)* se stabiliser, s'équilibrer

licence, *Am* **license[1]** *n (to manufacture, sell)* licence *f*; **under licence** sous licence

◇ *licence agreement* contrat *m* de concession

license² *vt* accorder une licence à; **to be licensed to manufacture/sell sth** avoir l'autorhisation de fabriquer/vendre qch

"
Toy giant Mattel is negotiating with the world's leading Formula 1 racing teams to secure the rights to **license** toy cars, games, puzzles and clothing linked to the sport's most famous brands.
"

licensed *adj* sous licence

◇ *licensed brand name* nom *m* de marque sous licence

◇ *licensed product* produit *m* sous licence

licensing *n* autorisation *f*

◇ *licensing agreement* accord *m* de licence

◇ *licensing requirements* conditions *fpl* d'autorisation

lifecycle *n (of product)* cycle *m* de vie

◇ *lifecycle curve* courbe *f* du cycle de vie

life expectancy *n (of product)* durée *f* (utile) de vie, espérance *f* de vie

lifestyle *n (of consumer, client)* style *m* de vie

◇ *lifestyle analysis* analyse *f* du style de vie

◇ *lifestyle data* données *fpl* de style de vie

◇ *lifestyle group* socio-style *m*

◇ *lifestyle segmentation* segmentation *f* par styles de vie

"
Although the **lifestyle data** culled from questionnaires has become popular, some DM practitioners say it is worth exercising caution in their use. "If you are writing to someone saying: 'You have two children so we think you would enjoy holiday X,' you'd better be very sure they do have two children," warns Murray.
"

LIFO *(abbr last in, first out)* *(stock control system)* DEPS

light user *n* faible utilisateur (trice) *m,f*

limited warranty *n* garantie *f* limitée

line *n (of goods)* ligne *f*, série *f*

◇ *line addition* ajout *m* à la ligne

◇ *line chart* graphe *m* en ligne

◇ *line differentiation* différenciation *f* de ligne

◇ *line extension* extension *f* de ligne

◇ *line filling* consolidation *f* de ligne

◇ *line stretching* extension *f* de ligne

linear *adj* linéaire

◇ *linear metre* mètre *m* linéaire

"
This form of calculation is very useful to the retailer. It helps him to work out present and expected sales, and to find out how much profit he has made. For example: a unit displaying tins of soup has a

> total **linear** measurement of 5 metres. From it the retailer sells tins of soup to the value of £200 per month so each **linear metre** of space sells £40.
>
> **"**

list price n (of product) prix m (de) catalogue

literature n (information) documentation f

location n (of company) emplacement m

◇ **location pricing** fixation f des prix selon l'endroit

logo n logo m, identité f graphique

longitudinal adj (research, study) longitudinal(e)

loose adj (goods) en vrac

lose vt (custom, market share, money) perdre; **they are losing their markets to the Koreans** ils perdent leurs marchés au profit des Coréens

loss n (of custom, market share) perte f; (financial) déficit m; **to make a loss** perdre de l'argent, être déficitaire; **to sell sth at a loss** vendre qch à perte

◇ **loss leader** produit m d'appel

◇ **loss leader price** prix m d'appel

◇ **loss leader pricing** fixation f d'un prix d'appel

low adj (price) bas (basse)

◇ **low end** (of market) bas m

low-cost adj

◇ **low-cost purchase** achat m à petit prix

◇ **low-cost purchasing** achats mpl à petits prix

low-end adj (goods) bas de gamme

low-grade adj de qualité inférieure

low-income group n groupe m de contribuables à faibles revenus

low-involvement adj (purchasing) à faible participation des consommateurs

loyal adj (customer) fidèle

loyal-customer discount n remise f de fidélité

loyalty n (of customer) fidélité f

◇ **loyalty card** carte f de fidélité

◇ **loyalty discount** remise f de fidélité

◇ **loyalty magazine** = magazine publié par une chaîne de magasins, une banque etc pour ses clients

◇ **loyalty programme, loyalty scheme** programme m de fidélisation

> **"**
>
> In a bid to capitalise on the growth of relationship marketing, AT&T is preparing to launch a managed **loyalty programme** linking the functions of a **loyalty card**, call centre, customer database analysis and campaign management.
>
> **"**

luxury adj de luxe

◇ **luxury goods** articles mpl de luxe

◇ **luxury tax** taxe f de luxe

m

macroenvironment *n* macroenvironnement *m*

macromarketing *n* macromarketing *m*

macrosegment *n* macrosegment *m*

macrosegmentation *n* macrosegmentation *f*

mail 1 *n* (a) *(letters, parcels)* courrier *m* (b) *(postal service)* poste *f*
   2 *vt (put in post)* poster
◊ *mail order* vente *f* par correspondance; **to buy sth by mail order** acheter qch par correspondance
◊ *mail survey* enquête *f* postale

mailer *n* mailing *m*, publipostage *m*

mailing *n* mailing *m*, publipostage *m*
◊ *mailing card* carte *f* de publicité
◊ *mailing list* liste *f* de publipostage
◊ *mailing shot* mailing *m*, publipostage *m*

mailmerge *n* publipostage *m*

mail-order *adj*
◊ *mail-order catalogue* catalogue *m* de vente par correspondance
◊ *mail-order company* maison *f* de vente par correspondance
◊ *mail-order organization* vépéciste *m*
◊ *mail-order retailing* vente *f* par correspondance

mailshot *n* mailing *m*, publipostage *m*; **to do** *or* **send a mailshot** faire un mailing

maker *n* fabricant(e) *m,f*
◊ *maker's price* prix *m* de fabrique
◊ *maker's trademark* cachet *m* de fabrique

mall *n* Am *(shopping centre)* galerie *f* marchande

management *n* *(action)* gestion *f*, direction *f*; *(managers)* administration *f*, direction *f*

manager n (of company, department, project) directeur (trice) m,f

manufacture 1 n fabrication f **2** vt fabriquer, manufacturer

◇ *manufactured goods* produits mpl manufacturés

manufacturer n fabricant(e) m,f

◇ *manufacturer's agent* agent m exclusif

◇ *manufacturer's brand* marque f de fabricant

◇ *manufacturer's liability* responsabilité f du fabricant

◇ *manufacturer's price* prix m de fabrique

◇ *manufacturer's recommended price* prix m conseillé par le fabricant

manufacturing n fabrication f

◇ *manufacturing costs* frais mpl de fabrication

◇ *manufacturing rights* droits mpl de fabrication

mapping n mapping m

margin n (profit) marge f; **to have a low/high margin** avoir une faible/forte marge; **the margins are very tight** les marges sont très réduites; **we make a 10% margin** nous faisons 10% de marge

▸ **mark down** vt sep (price) baisser; (goods) baisser le prix de, démarquer; **everything has been marked down to half price** tout a été réduit à moitié prix

▸ **mark up** vt sep (price) augmenter; (goods) augmenter le prix de, majorer

mark-down n (article) article m démarqué; (action) démarque f

marked price n prix m marqué

market 1 n marché m; **to be on the market** être en vente; **to come onto the market** arriver sur le marché; **to put sth on the market** mettre qch sur le marché; **to take sth off the market** retirer qch du marché; **to find a market for sth** trouver un débouché ou des acheteurs pour qch; **to price oneself out of the market** perdre sa clientèle en demandant trop cher; **the bottom has fallen out of the market** le marché s'est effondré

2 vt (goods) commercialiser; (launch) lancer

◇ *market analysis* analyse f du marché

◇ *market analyst* analyste m,f du marché

◇ *market appeal* attrait m commercial

◇ *market appraisal* évaluation f du marché

◇ *market challenger* challengeur m

◇ *market choice* choix m sur le marché; (product) choix m du marché

◇ *market conditions* conditions fpl du marché

◇ *market demand* demande f du marché

◇ *market development* développement m du marché

◇ *market entry* lancement m sur le marché

⋄ **market expansion** extension f de marché

⋄ **market exploration** prospection f du marché

⋄ **market exposure** exposition f sur le marché

⋄ **market follower** suiveur m (sur le marché)

⋄ Econ **market forces** forces fpl du marché

⋄ **market forecast** prévisions fpl du marché, pronostic m du marché

⋄ **market growth** croissance f du marché

⋄ **market intelligence** information f commerciale

⋄ **market leader** leader m sur le marché

⋄ **market mechanism** mécanisme m du marché

⋄ **market orientation** orientation f marché

⋄ **market participant** intervenant(e) m,f sur le marché, acteur m sur le marché

⋄ **market penetration** pénétration f du marché

⋄ **market penetration pricing** tarification f de pénétration du marché

⋄ **market positioning** positionnement m sur le marché

⋄ **market potential** (of product) potentiel m sur le marché; (of market) potentiel m du marché

⋄ **market profile** profil m du marché

⋄ **market prospects** perspectives fpl commerciales

⋄ **market report** rapport m commercial, bilan m commercial

⋄ **market research** étude f de marché; **market research has shown that the idea is viable** des études de marché ont montré que l'idée a des chances de réussir

⋄ **market research company** société f d'études de marché

⋄ **market researcher** chargé m d'étude de marché

⋄ Br **Market Research Society** = société d'étude de marché britannique

⋄ **market segment** segment m de marché

⋄ **market segmentation** segmentation f du marché

⋄ **market share** part f de marché

⋄ **market size** (of product) part f de marché; (of market) taille f du marché

⋄ **market study** étude f de marché

⋄ **market survey** enquête f de marché

⋄ **market test** test m de marché, test m de vente

⋄ **market thrust** percée f commerciale

"

In a letter from Tom Touzmazis, managing director of Emap's radio sales house Emap on Air, to media agencies, the changes were described as part of an ongoing strategy to become **market leader** in London in the highly competitive 15–24 demographic.

"

marketability n (of goods, product) possibilité f de commercialisation

marketable adj (goods, product) commercialisable

marketer n mercaticien(enne) m,f, spécialiste mf en marketing

marketing n (theory, field) marketing m, mercatique f; (of product) commercialisation f; **to work in marketing** travailler dans le marketing

◇ **marketing agreement** accord m de commercialisation

◇ **marketing approach** démarche f marketing

◇ **marketing audit** audit m marketing

◇ **marketing auditor** audit m marketing, auditeur(trice) m,f marketing

◇ **marketing budget** budget m marketing

◇ **marketing campaign** campagne f commerciale

◇ **marketing communications channel** canal m de communication commerciale

◇ **marketing company** entreprise f de marketing

◇ **marketing concept** concept m de marketing

◇ **marketing consultant** conseiller(ère) m,f commercial(e), mercaticien(enne) m,f

◇ **marketing costs** frais mpl de commercialisation

◇ **marketing department** service m du marketing

◇ **marketing efficiency** efficacité f du marketing

◇ **marketing efficiency study** contrôle m d'efficacité du marketing

◇ **marketing environment** environnement m commercial, environnement m marketing

◇ **marketing expert** mercaticien(enne) m,f

◇ **marketing fit** ajustement m stratégique

◇ **marketing implementation** mise f en place marketing

◇ **marketing information system** système m d'information marketing

◇ **marketing intelligence** intelligence f marketing

◇ **marketing intelligence system** système m d'intelligence marketing

◇ **marketing management** gestion f du marketing

◇ **marketing manager** directeur(trice) m,f du marketing

◇ **marketing mix** marchéage m, marketing mix m

◇ **marketing myopia** myopie f marketing

◇ **marketing orientation** optique f marketing

◇ **marketing plan** plan m marketing

◇ **marketing policy** politique f de commercialisation

◇ **marketing research** recherche f commerciale

◇ **marketing spectrum** marchéage m

◇ **marketing spend** dépenses fpl de marketing

◇ **marketing strategy** stratégie f marketing

◇ **marketing study** étude commerciale, étude f marketing

◇ *marketing target* cible *f* commerciale

◇ *marketing team* équipe *f* commerciale

◇ *marketing techniques* techniques *fpl* commerciales

◇ *marketing tool* outil *m* de marketing

> 〝
> While some of the findings of the survey may be controversial, there is one of which there is unanimous agreement by telemarketing professionals. This is that telemarketing is seen as one of the most important functions in the **marketing mix**.
> 〞

marketplace *n Econ* marché *m*; **the products in the marketplace** les produits sur le marché

mark-up *n* majoration *f*; **we operate a 20% mark-up** nous appliquons une marge de 20%

◇ *mark-up pricing* fixation *f* du prix au coût moyen majoré

mass *adj*

◇ *mass consumption* consommation *f* de masse

◇ *mass display* présentation *f* en masse

◇ *mass distribution* grande distribution *f*

◇ *mass distribution sector* secteur *m* de la grande distribution

◇ *mass mailing* envoi *m* en nombre

◇ *mass market* marché *m* de masse

◇ *mass marketing* marketing *m*

de grande consommation, marketing *m* de masse

◇ *mass media* mass médias *mpl*

masterbrand *n* marque *f* vedette

> 〝
> As well as Kellogg and Nestlé, Cadbury has made a concerted effort to increase the prominence of its name on all confectionery and spin-off products and spent £870,000 on the **masterbrand** "Tastes Like Heaven" campaign in the year to May.
> 〞

material *n (for marketing, promotion)* matériel *m*

maturity *n (of market)* maturité *f*

media *n* médias *mpl*

◇ *media advertising* publicité *f* média

◇ *media analysis* analyse *f* des médias

◇ *media analyst* analyste *mf* des médias

◇ *media buyer* acheteur(euse) *m,f* d'espaces (publicitaires)

◇ *media buying* achat *m* d'espace

◇ *media consultant* conseil *m* en communication

◇ *media coverage* couverture *f* médiatique, médiatisation *f*

◇ *media hype* battage *m* médiatique

◇ *media mix* mix média *m*

◇ *media plan* plan *m* média

◇ *media planner* médiaplaneur *m*, média planner *m*

◇ *media planning* média planning *m*

◇ *media research* médialogie *f*

◇ *media schedule* calendrier *m* de campagne

◇ *media vehicle* support *m* publicitaire

> **"**
>
> Carlton will use a wide-ranging **media mix** of radio, posters, press and television to inform the public, advertising and business communities of its programme and corporate format prior to launch.
>
> **"**

medium *n (means of communication)* médium *m*, support *m*

merchandise 1 *n* marchandises *fpl*
2 *vt* marchandiser, commercialiser

merchandiser *n (object)* présentoir *m*; *(person)* marchandiseur *m*

merchandising *n* marchandisage *m*, commercialisation *f*

◇ *merchandising techniques* techniques *fpl* marchandes

merchantable quality *n* qualité *f* marchande; **all goods must be of merchantable quality** tous les articles doivent être vendables

methodology *n* méthodologie *f*

me-too *adj*

◇ *me-too product* produit *m* tactique

◇ *me-too strategy* stratégie *f* d'imitation

micromarketing *n* micromarketing *m*

microsegment *n* microsegment *m*

microsegmentation *n* microsegmentation *f*

middle-income group *n* groupe *m* de contribuables à revenus moyens

middleman *n* intermédiaire *mf*

◇ *middleman's business* commerce *m* intermédiaire

◇ *middleman's market* marché *m* intermédiaire

MIS *n (abbr* **marketing information system)** système *m* d'information marketing

misleading advertising *n* publicité *f* mensongère

missionary selling *n* ventes *fpl* de prospection

MLM *n (abbr* **multi-level marketing)** VRC *f*

model *n* (**a**) *(small version)* maquette *f* (**b**) *(example)* modèle *m*; **we plan to bring out a new model for the millennium** nous projetons de sortir un nouveau modèle pour le nouveau millénaire

moderator *n (of group meeting)* animateur(trice) *m,f*

modified rebuy *n* réachat *m* modifié

monadic *adj*

◇ *monadic test* test *m* monadique

◇ *monadic testing* tests *mpl* monadiques

money-back *adj*
◇ *money-back guarantee* garantie *f* de remboursement
◇ *money-back offer* offre *f* de remboursement

money-off *adj*
◇ *money-off deal* offre *f* de remboursement
◇ *money-off voucher* bon *m* de remboursement

monitor *vt* surveiller, contrôler

monitoring *n* surveillance *f*, contrôle *m* continu

monopolize *vt (market)* monopoliser

monopoly *n* monopole *m* ; **to have a monopoly of** *or* **on sth** avoir le monopole de qch
◇ *monopoly control* contrôle *m* monopolistique
◇ *monopoly market* marché *m* monopolistique

motivation *n* motivation *f*
◇ *motivation research* recherche *f* de motivation
◇ *motivation study* étude *f* de motivation

motivational *adj*
◇ *motivational research* recherche *f* de motivation
◇ *motivational study* étude *f* de motivation

motive *n (intention)* motif *m*

move 1 *vt (sell)* vendre ; **we must move these goods quickly** nous devons vendre ces marchandises rapidement
2 *vi (sell)* se vendre ; **the new model isn't moving very quickly** le nouveau modèle ne se vend pas très vite

mrp *n (abbr* **manufacturer's recommended price)** prix *m* conseillé par le fabricant

MRS *n (abbr* **Market Research Society)** = société d'étude de marché britannique

multibrand *n* marque *f* multiple, multimarque *f*
◇ *multibrand store* point *m* de vente multimarque

> 66
>
> The importance of flexibility is also important for brands sold into department stores and **multibrand stores** - where fashion brands have to negotiate internal politics and the disparate approaches taken by different outlets to the degree of autonomy granted to each brand.
>
> 99

multi-level marketing *n* marketing *m* de réseau, vente *f* par réseau coopté

multinational 1 *n* multinationale *f*
2 *adj* multinational(e)
◇ *multinational company* entreprise *f* multinationale
◇ *multinational marketing* marketing *m* multinational

multiple-choice *adj (question, questionnaire, survey)* à choix multiples

mystery *n*
◇ *mystery shopper* client(e) *m,f* mystère
◇ *mystery shopping* pseudo-achat *m*

name *n (of person)* nom *m*; *(of company)* raison *f* sociale; **Cannon Gait are a huge name in the publishing business** Cannon Gait est une entreprise très importante dans le monde de l'édition

◇ *name brand* marque *f*
◇ *name licensing* cession *f* de licence de nom
◇ *name product* marque *f*

national *adj* national(e)

◇ *national market* marché *m* national
◇ *national press* presse *f* nationale

NBA *n* (*abbr* **net book agreement**) = accord entre maisons d'édition et libraires stipulant que ces derniers n'ont le droit de vendre aucun ouvrage à un prix inférieur à celui fixé par l'éditeur

need *n* besoin *m*; **needs and wants** besoins *mpl* et désirs *mpl*

◇ *needs analysis* analyse *f* des besoins
◇ *needs assessment* estimation *f* des besoins
◇ *need identification* identification *f* des besoins
◇ *need level* niveau *m* des besoins
◇ *need market* marché *m* des besoins
◇ *need recognition* reconnaissance *f* des besoins
◇ *need set* ensemble *m* de besoins
◇ *needs study* étude *f* des besoins

needs-and-wants exploration *n* exploration *f* des besoins et des désirs

needs-based *adj* fondé(e) sur les besoins

net *adj* net (nette)

◇ *net book agreement* = accord entre maisons d'édition et libraires stipulant que ces derniers n'ont le droit de vendre aucun ouvrage à un prix inférieur à celui fixé par l'éditeur
◇ *net margin* marge *f* nette
◇ *net profit* bénéfice *m* net
◇ *net profit margin* marge *f* commerciale nette

network *n (for distribution, sales)* réseau *m*

new *adj* nouveau(elle); *(not used)* neuf (neuve)

◇ *new buy situation* situation *f* de nouvel achat

◇ *new product* nouveau produit *m*

◇ *new product development* développement *m* de nouveaux produits

◇ *new product marketing* marketing *m* de nouveaux produits

> As the UK economy teeters on the brink of another recession, there is strong suspicion that **new product development** will be the first casualty of slashed marketing budgets. This was certainly the case when NPD was left in disarray by risk-averse managements.

news agency *n* agence *f* de presse

newspaper *n* journal *m*

◇ *newspaper advertisement* publicité *f* presse

◇ *newspaper advertising* publicité *f* presse

new-to-the-company product *n* produit *m* nouveau dans la société

new-to-the-world product *n* produit *m* nouveau dans le monde

next-day delivery *n* livraison *f* lendemain

niche *n* (in market) créneau *m*, niche *f*

◇ *niche market* niche *f*

◇ *niche marketing* marketing *m* ciblé

◇ *niche player* acteur *m* sur un segment de marché

◇ *niche product* produit *m* ciblé

non-adopter *n* = consommateur qui n'essaie jamais de nouveaux produits

no-name product *n* produit *m* sans nom

non-business marketing *n* marketing *m* non-commercial

non-delivery *n* (of goods) non-livraison *f*; **in the event of non-delivery** dans l'éventualité où les marchandises ne seraient pas livrées

non-probability *adj*

◇ *non-probability sample* échantillon *m* non probabiliste

◇ *non-probability sampling* échantillonnage *m* non probabiliste

non-random *adj*

◇ *non-random sample* échantillon *m* empirique

◇ *non-random sampling* échantillonnage *m* empirique

non-refundable *adj* (packaging) perdu(e)

non-returnable *adj* sans réserve de retour; (container) non consigné(e); (packaging) non consigné(e), perdu(e)

NPD *n* (abbr new product development) développement *m* de nouveaux produits

numerical distribution *n* distribution *f* numérique

objective *n (goal)* objectif *m*; **our objective for this year is to increase sales by 10%** nous avons pour objectif d'augmenter nos ventes de 10% au cours de l'année prochaine

observation *n* observation *f*

observational research *n* étude *f* par observation

obsolescence *n* obsolescence *f*

odd-even *adj*
◊ *odd-even price* prix *m* magique
◊ *odd-even pricing* fixation *f* des prix magiques

odd lot *n (of goods)* lot *m* dépareillé

odd-numbers *adj*
◊ *odd-numbers price* prix *m* magique
◊ *odd-numbers pricing* fixation *f* des prix magiques

offer 1 *n* offre *f*; **to make sb an offer (for sth)** faire une offre à qn (pour qch)
   2 *vt* offrir; **to offer goods for sale** mettre des marchandises en vente
◊ *offer price* prix *m* vendeur, prix *m* offert

off-the-peg research *n* = étude de marché utilisant des données déjà rassemblées

off-the-shelf *adj (goods)* prêt(e) à l'usage

oligopoly *n* oligopole *m*

omnibus survey *adj* enquête *f* omnibus

one-level distribution channel *n* canal *m* de distribution court

one-stop *adj*
◊ *one-stop buying* achats *mpl* regroupés
◊ *one-stop shop* magasin *m* où l'on trouve de tout
◊ *one-stop shopping* achats *mpl* regroupés

one-to-one marketing *n* marketing *m* one to one

one-way *adj (packaging)* perdu(e)

on-line, online *adj Comptr* en ligne
◊ *on-line catalogue* catalogue *m* en ligne
◊ *on-line marketing* marketing *m* électronique
◊ *on-line retailer* société *f* de commerce en ligne
◊ *on-line retailing* commerce

m électronique

◇ **on-line selling** vente *f* en ligne, vente *f* électronique

◇ **on-line shop** magasin *m* électronique

◇ **on-line shopping** achats *mpl* par Internet

◇ **on-line terminal** terminal *m* de paiement connecté

> 🙶
>
> UK-based Interactive Music & Video Shop is an **online retailer** selling 230,000 music and video products. As well as selling through its site (*invs.com*), it handles **online retailing** for partners that include Sony.
>
> 🙷

on-pack *adj*

◇ **on-pack offer** prime *f* différée

◇ **on-pack promotion** promotion *f* on-pack

on-target earnings *npl (of salesperson)* salaire *m* de base plus commissions

open-ended *adj (question)* ouvert(e)

opening *n (in market)* débouché *m*, ouverture *f*; **we have exploited an opening in the market** nous avons exploité une ouverture sur le marché

operation *n (campaign)* opération *f*

operational *adj* opérationnel(elle)

◇ **operational marketing** marketing *m* opérationnel

◇ **operational planning** pla-

nification *f* des opérations

◇ **operational research** recherche *f* opérationnelle

opinion *n*

◇ **opinion former, opinion leader** leader *m* d'opinion, préconisateur *m*

◇ **opinion measurement** sondage *m* d'opinion

◇ **opinion measurement technique** technique *f* de sondage d'opinion

◇ **opinion poll, opinion survey** sondage *m* (d'opinion), enquête *f* (d'opinion)

opportunity *n* opportunité *f*; **opportunities and threats** opportunités *fpl* et menaces *fpl*

◇ **opportunity to hear** occasion *f* d'entendre

◇ **opportunity to see** occasion *f* de voir

◇ **opportunity and threat analysis** analyse *f* des opportunités et des menaces

> 🙶
>
> As if economic turmoil, fickle consumers, the rival popularity of computer games and rising music piracy were not enough, the music industry is now faced with **opportunities and threats** presented by the Internet.
>
> 🙷

optimal *adj* optimal(e), optimum

◇ **optimal price** prix *m* optimum

◇ **optimal psychological price** prix *m* psychologique optimum

optional-feature pricing n fixation f du prix en fonction des options

order 1 n (request for goods) commande f; **to place an order (with sb/for sth)** passer une commande (à qn/de qch); **to make sth to order** faire qch sur commande; **to fill an order** exécuter une commande; **as per order** conformément à votre commande

2 vt (goods) commander

◇ **order cycle** cycle m de commande

◇ **order cycle time** durée f du cycle de commande

order-to-remittance cycle n cycle m commande-livraison-facturation

organigram n organigramme m

organization(al) chart n organigramme m

origin n origine f

◇ **origin of goods label** marque f d'origine

original packaging n emballage m d'origine

OTE npl (abbr **on-target earnings**) (of salesperson) salaire m de base plus commissions

OTH n (abbr **opportunity to hear**) ODE f

OTS n (abbr **opportunity to see**) ODV f

outdoor n

◇ **outdoor advertising** publicité f extérieure

◇ **outdoor network** réseau m d'affichage

outgoing inventory inventaire m de sortie

outlet n (market) débouché m (point of sale) point m de vente **there are not many sales outlet in Japan** le Japon offre peu de débouchés commerciaux

out-of-town adj (shopping centre, retail park) = situé à la périphérie d'une ville

outsell vt (of goods) se vendre mieux que; (of retailer) vendre plus que

overall adj global(e); **she has overall responsibility for sales** elle est responsable de l'ensemble du service des ventes

◇ **overall consumption** consommation f totale

◇ **overall demand** demande f globale

overcharge 1 vt (person) faire payer trop cher à; (goods) survendre

2 vi faire payer trop cher

overdemand n demande f excédentaire

overlap n débordement m

overload vt (market) surcharger

over-position vt surpositionner

over-positioning n surpositionnement m

overprice vt vendre trop cher

overpriced adj trop cher (chère)

overseas 1 adj d'outremer, étranger(ère)

2 adv à l'étranger

◇ *overseas market* marché *m* étranger, marché *m* extérieur, marché *m* d'outremer

overstock *vt (market)* encombrer; *(warehouse)* trop approvisionner (**with** de)

overstocked *adj (market)* encombré(e); *(warehouse)* trop approvisionné(e); **the market is overstocked with foreign goods** le marché regorge de marchandises étrangères

own brand *n* marque *f* de distributeur

own-brand *adj*

◇ *own-brand label* marque *f* de distributeur

◇ *own-brand product* produit *m* à marque de distributeur

own-branding *n* apposition *f* de la marque de distributeur

own-label *adj* à marque de distributeur

P *n* **the four Ps** les quatre P, le marketing mix

pack 1 *n* paquet *m*
  2 *vt (goods)* emballer

package 1 *n* (**a**) *(set of proposals)* ensemble *m* (**b**) *(parcel)* paquet *m*, colis *m*
  2 *vt* emballer, conditionner

packaging *n* emballage *m*

◇ **packaging charges, packaging costs** frais *mpl* d'emballage

packing *n* emballage *m*

◇ **packing charges, packing costs** frais *mpl* d'emballage
◇ **packing list** liste *f* de colisage
◇ **packing slip** bon *m* de livraison

paired comparison *n* comparaison *f* par paire

P & L *n* (**a**) *(abbr* **profit and loss***)* pertes *fpl* et profits *mpl* (**b**) *(abbr* **profit and loss form***)* compte *m* d'exploitation; **we can see from the P&L that developing the product is not a viable option** le compte d'exploitation montre clairement qu'il ne serait pas rentable de développer ce produit

p & p *n Br (abbr* **postage and packing***)* frais *mpl* de port et d'emballage

panel *n (for market research)* panel *m*

◇ **panel discussion** débat *m*
◇ **panel member** panéliste *mf*
◇ **panel research** recherches *fpl* par panel

parallel *adj*

◇ **parallel importing** importations *fpl* parallèles
◇ **parallel market** marché *m* parallèle
◇ **parallel selling** vente *f* parallèle

parcel *n* paquet *m*, colis *m*

partnership *n* association *f*

◇ **partnership agreement** accord *m* de partenariat

party-plan selling *n* vente *f* domiciliaire

passing *adj*

◇ **passing customer** client(e) *m,f* de passage

The four Ps
Les quatre P

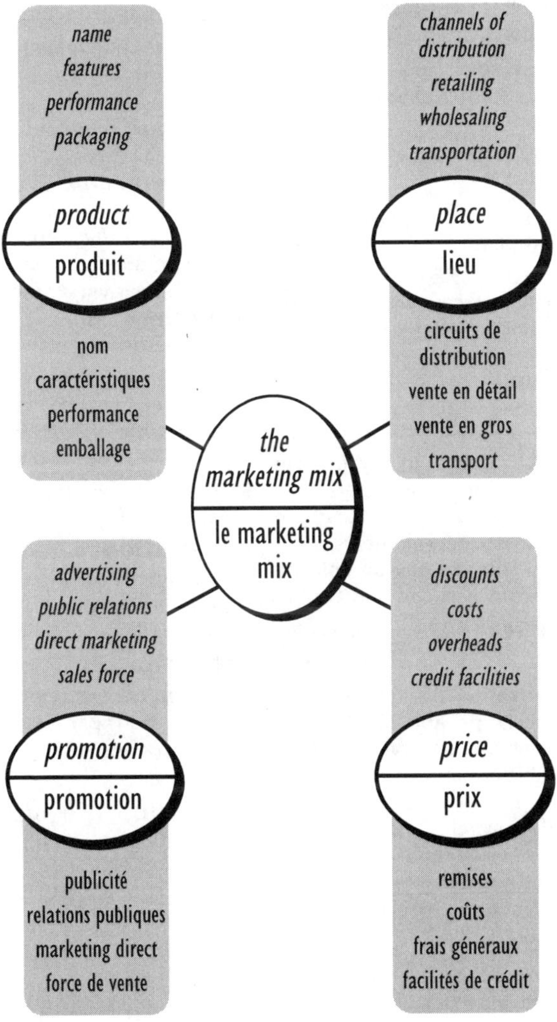

product / produit
- name / nom
- features / caractéristiques
- performance / performance
- packaging / emballage

place / lieu
- channels of distribution / circuits de distribution
- retailing / vente en détail
- wholesaling / vente en gros
- transportation / transport

the marketing mix / le marketing mix

promotion / promotion
- advertising / publicité
- public relations / relations publiques
- direct marketing / marketing direct
- sales force / force de vente

price / prix
- discounts / remises
- costs / coûts
- overheads / frais généraux
- credit facilities / facilités de crédit

◊ *passing trade* clients *mpl* de passage

patch *n (of sales representative)* secteur *m*

patron *n (of shop)* client(e) *m,f*

patronage *n* (**a**) *(custom)* clientèle *f* (**b**) *(sponsorship)* mécénat *m*

pattern *n (sample)* échantillon *m*

◊ *pattern book* livre *m* d'échantillons

pay 1 *vt (person, bill, sum of money)* payer; **you pay £500 now, the rest later** vous payez 500 livres maintenant, le solde plus tard

2 *vi* payer; **to pay by cheque/ credit card** payer par chèque/ carte de crédit; **to pay (in) cash** payer comptant, payer en liquide *ou* en espèces; **to pay in full** payer intégralement, payer en totalité; **to pay on delivery** payer à la livraison

▸ **pay for** *vt insep (item, goods)* payer

payable *adj* payable; **payable in cash** payable comptant; **payable on delivery/with order** payable à la livraison/à la commande; **cheques should be made payable to J&B Ltd** les chèques devraient être libellés *ou* établis à l'ordre de J&B Ltd

payment *n* paiement *m*, versement *m*

◊ *payment on account* paiement *m* partiel

◊ *payment in advance* paiement *m* par anticipation

◊ *payment in arrears* paiement *m* arriéré

◊ *payment in cash* paiement *m* en espèces

◊ *payment by cheque* paiement *m* par chèque

◊ *payment on delivery* livraison *f* contre remboursement

◊ *payment facilities* facilités *fpl* de paiement

◊ *payment in full* paiement *m* intégral

◊ *payment by instalments* paiement *m* échelonné, paiement *m* par versements

peak time *n Br (on TV)* prime time *m*

◊ *peak time advertisement* publicité *f* au prime time

◊ *peak time advertising* publicité *f* au prime time

penetrate *vt (market)* pénétrer

penetration *n (of market)* pénétration *f*

◊ *penetration price* prix *m* de pénétration

per capita *adj* par tête

◊ *per capita consumption* consommation *f* par tête

perceive *vt (product, brand)* percevoir

perceived *adj* perçu(e)

◊ *perceived performance* résultats *mpl* perçus

◊ *perceived quality* qualité *f* perçue

◊ *perceived risk* risque *m* perçu

◊ *perceived service* service *m* perçu

◊ *perceived value* valeur *f* perçue

◇ *perceived value pricing* tarification *f* en fonction de la valeur perçue

percent 1 *n* pourcentage *m*
2 *adv* pour cent; **prices went up ten percent** les prix ont augmenté de dix pour cent

percentage *n* pourcentage *m*; **to get a percentage on sth** *(commission)* toucher un pourcentage sur qch

perception *n* *(of product, brand)* perception *f*

> **❝**
> Editorial will target women with health and beauty themes harmonised with the Advantage proposition of treating yourself. The aim is to shift **perception** of the Boots brand from something worthy to something inspirational.
> **❞**

perceptual *adj* perceptuel (elle)

◇ *perceptual map* carte *f* perceptuelle

perfect competition *n* concurrence *f* parfaite

performance *n* *(of company, product)* performance *f*

◇ *performance test* test *m* de performance

perimeter *n*

◇ *perimeter advertising* publicité *f* périphérique

◇ *perimeter board* panneau *m* publicitaire *(autour d'un terrain de sport)*

> **❝**
> A new sponsorship package launches in January, following deals with all 72 clubs in the Premier and Nationwide football leagues. Associated partners will have access to all of the clubs' marketing communications, including databases for direct-mail campaigns, football programmes, merchandise, posters, **perimeter boards** and websites.
> **❞**

perishable 1 *n* **perishables** denrées *fpl* périssables
2 *adj* *(goods)* périssable

personal *adj*

◇ *personal observation* observation *f* en situation

◇ *personal selling* ventes *fpl* personnelles

personality promotion *n* promotion *f* par une personnalité

person-to-person approach *n* approche *f* personnalisée

persuasion *n* persuasion *f*

PEST *n* *(abbr* **political, economic, sociological, technological)** = facteurs politiques, économiques, sociaux et technologiques

physical *adj*

◇ *physical distribution* distribution *f* physique

◇ *physical distribution management* gestion *f* de la distribution physique

picture completion *n (in market research)* images *fpl* à compléter

pie chart *n* graphique *m* circulaire, camembert *m*

pilot *vt (study, scheme)* piloter
◇ **pilot questionnaire** questionnaire *m* pilote
◇ **pilot study** étude *f* pilote, pré-étude *f*
◇ **pilot survey** enquête *f* pilote

PIMS *n (abbr profit impact of marketing strategy)* IRSM *m*

pitch **1** *n (of product)* promotion *f*; *(of idea)* présentation *f*, soumission *f*
2 *vt (product)* promouvoir; *(idea)* présenter, soumettre
3 *vi* faire une soumission; **to pitch for sth** faire une soumission pour qch

> 44
> KFC originally invited five agencies to **pitch**. Apart from Zenith, Initiative and Optimedia, New PHD and Motive were also asked to present but were knocked out after the first round.
> 77

place **1** *n* lieu *m*
2 *vt (order)* passer (**with** à); *(contract)* passer (**with** à); *(advertisement)* insérer (**in** dans)
◇ **place of delivery** lieu *m* de livraison

placement *n (of product)* placement *m*

plan *n (project)* plan *m*

player *n (participant)* acteur *m*; **who are the key players in this market?** qui sont les acteurs principaux sur ce marché?

> 44
> But Lexus would be wise to consider the fortunes of Audi. It has taken many years for VW to turn the brand, which already had a long history, into a major **player** in the premium market.
> 77

PLC *n (abbr product lifecycle)* cycle *m* de vie du produit

plinth *n (for displaying goods)* plinthe *f*

plug *Fam* **1** *n (publicity)* pub *f*; **their products got another plug on TV** on a encore fait du battage *ou* de la pub pour leurs produits à la télé
2 *vt (product)* faire du battage *ou* de la pub pour

point *n* (**a**) *(place)* lieu *m* (**b**) *(on loyalty card)* point *m*
◇ **point of delivery** lieu *m* de livraison
◇ **point of purchase** lieu *m* d'achat, lieu *m* de vente
◇ **point of sale** lieu *m* de vente, point *m* de vente; **at the point of sale** sur le lieu de vente

point-of-purchase *adj*
◇ **point-of-purchase advertising** publicité *f* sur le lieu de vente, PLV *f*
◇ **point-of-purchase display** exposition *f* sur le lieu de vente
◇ **point-of-purchase information** informations *fpl* sur le

lieu de vente

◇ **point-of-purchase material** matériel *m* de publicité sur le lieu de vente, matériel *m* de PLV

◇ **point-of-purchase promotion** promotion *f* sur le lieu de vente

point-of-sale *adj*

◇ **point-of-sale advertising** publicité *f* sur le lieu de vente, PLV *f*

◇ **point-of-sale display** exposition *f* sur le lieu de vente

◇ **point-of-sale information** informations *fpl* sur le lieu de vente

◇ **point-of-sale material** matériel *m* de publicité sur le lieu de vente, matériel *m* de PLV

◇ **point-of-sale promotion** promotion *f* sur le lieu de vente

◇ **point-of-sale terminal** terminal *m* point de vente

policy *n (strategy)* politique *f*; **the company's success is essentially down to their inspired marketing policy** le succès de l'entreprise est dû en grande partie à l'intelligence de leur politique de commercialisation

poll **1** *n (survey)* sondage *m* (d'opinion); **to carry out a poll (on sth)** faire un sondage (sur qch)

2 *vt (person)* sonder; **most of those polled were in favour of the plan** la plupart des personnes sondées étaient favorables au projet

polling *n* sondage *m*

◇ **polling company** institut *m* de sondage

pollster *n* enquêteur(trice) *m,f*

POP *n (abbr* **point of purchase)** lieu *m* d'achat, lieu *m* de vente

population *n* population *f*

◇ **population growth** croissance *f* démographique

portfolio *n* portefeuille *m*

◇ **portfolio mix** portefeuille *m* d'activités

POS *n (abbr* **point of sale)** PDV *m*

position **1** *n (of company, of product on market)* position *f*
2 *vt (product)* positionner

positioning *n (of product)* positionnement *m*

◇ **positioning map** carte *f* de positionnement

◇ **positioning strategy** stratégie *f* de positionnement

◇ **positioning study** étude *f* de positionnement

post *Br* **1** *n (mail)* courrier *m*
2 *vt (letter, parcel)* poster

postage *n* affranchissement *m*; *Br* **postage and packing** frais *mpl* de port et d'emballage; **postage included** port compris; **postage paid** port payé

postal *adj* postal(e)

◇ **postal survey** enquête *f* postale

postcode *n Br* code *m* postal

posted price *n* prix *m* public

poster *n* affiche *f*

◇ **poster advertising** publicité *f* par affichage, publicité *f* par voie d'affiches

⋄ **poster campaign** campagne *f* d'affichage

> 66
>
> They point to the **poster campaign** it launched last September, through Ogilvy & Mather, which effectively re-launched Wisk as a main-stream colour care detergent, and the new label design as evidence of Lever's determin-ation to boost its sales.
>
> 99

post-paid 1 *adj* port payé
  2 *adv* en port payé

post-purchase *adj* post-achat

⋄ **post-purchase behaviour** comportement *m* post-achat
⋄ **post-purchase evaluation** évaluation *f* post-achat

post-test 1 *n* post-test *m*
  2 *vt* post-tester

potential *adj* (*buyer, custom-er*) éventuel(elle), potentiel (elle)

power brand *n* marque *f* forte

> 66
>
> United Biscuits has moved all advertising for its McVitie's and KP brands into Publicis. The change is part of the food giant's desire to cost-effectively market its **power brands** – such as Go Ahead and McVitie's Jaffa Cakes.
>
> 99

PR *n* (*abbr* **public relations**) RP *f*; **who does their PR?** qui est-ce qui s'occupe de leurs relations publiques?

⋄ **PR agency, PR consultancy** agence *f* conseil en com-munication
⋄ **PR consultant** conseil *m* en communication

predatory *adj*

⋄ **predatory price** prix *m* prédateur
⋄ **predatory pricing** fixation *f* des prix prédateurs

preference test *n* test *m* de préférence

preferential price *n* prix *m* préférentiel

preliminary *adj* (*study, re-search*) préliminaire

pre-marketing *n* pré-com-mercialisation *f*, pré-marke-ting *m*

premium *adj*

⋄ **premium price** prix *m* de prestige
⋄ **premium product** produit *m* de prestige
⋄ **premium selling** vente *f* avec prime
⋄ **premium service** service *m* premier

> 66
>
> Scrumpy Jack branding will appear on perimeter boards. New ads highlighting the sponsorship are also planned, as well as on-pack promotions. New packaging, which stresses the brand as a **premium product**, launches in May and will incorporate the cricket logo.
>
> 99

pre-pack *vt* préconditionner, préemballer

pre-package *vt* préconditionner, préemballer

pre-packaged *adj* préconditionné(e), préemballé(e)

pre-packed *adj* préconditionné(e), préemballé(e)

presentation pack *n* paquet *m* de présentation

press *n* (*newspapers*) **the press** la presse

◇ **press agency** agence *f* de presse

◇ **press attaché** attaché(e) *m,f* de presse

◇ **press campaign** campagne *f* de presse

◇ **press card** carte *f* de presse

◇ **press conference** conférence *f* de presse

◇ **press insert** encart *m* presse

◇ **press kit** dossier *m* de presse

◇ **press office** service *m* de presse

◇ **press officer** responsable *mf* des relations avec la presse

◇ **press pack** dossier *m* de presse

◇ **press release** communiqué *m* de presse

prestige *n*

◇ **prestige advertising** publicité *f* de prestige

◇ **prestige price** prix *m* de prestige

◇ **prestige product** produit *m* de prestige

◇ **prestige promotion** promotion *f* de prestige

pre-test 1 *n* pré-test *m*

2 *vt* pré-tester

price 1 *n* prix *m*; **to rise** *or* **increase** *or* **go up in price** augmenter

2 *vt* (**a**) (*decide cost of*) déterminer *ou* fixer le prix de; **the book is priced at £17** le livre coûte 17 livres

(**b**) (*indicate cost of*) mettre le prix sur; **these goods haven't been priced** ces articles n'ont pas reçu de prix *ou* n'ont pas été étiquetés

(**c**) (*ascertain cost of*) s'informer du prix de; (*estimate value of*) évaluer qch, estimer la valeur de qch; **she priced it in several shops before buying it** elle a vérifié le prix dans plusieurs magasins avant de l'acheter

(**d**) **to price competitors out of the market** éliminer la concurrence en pratiquant des prix déloyaux; **to price oneself out of the market** perdre sa clientèle en pratiquant des prix trop élevés; **we've been priced out of the Japanese market** nous avons perdu le marché japonais à cause de nos prix

◇ **price agreement** accord *m* sur les prix

◇ **price ceiling** plafond *m* de prix

◇ **price control** contrôle *m* des prix

◇ **price cut** réduction *f* (des prix), baisse *f* des prix

◇ **price differential** écart *m* de prix

◇ **price fixing** (*control*) contrôle *m* des prix

◇ **price freeze** gel *m* des prix

◇ *price increase* hausse *f* des prix, augmentation *f* des prix

◇ *price index* indice *m* des prix

◇ *price inflation* inflation *f* des prix

◇ *price label* étiquette *f* de prix

◇ *price leader* prix *m* directeur

◇ *price leadership* = position dominante en matière de fixation des prix

◇ *price level* niveau *m* de prix

◇ *price list* tarif *m*, liste *f* des prix

◇ *price mark-up* majoration *f* de prix

◇ *price plan* plan *m* prix

◇ *price point* point *m* prix

◇ *price policy* politique *f* de prix

◇ *price positioning* positionnement *m* de prix

◇ *price promotion* promotion *f*

◇ *price proposal* proposition *f* de prix

◇ *price range* gamme *f* des prix, échelle *f* des prix

◇ *price reduction* réduction *f* (des prix)

◇ *price regulation* réglementation *f* des prix

◇ *price ring* monopole *m* des prix

◇ *price scale* barème *m* des prix, échelle *f* des prix

◇ *price sensitivity* sensibilité *f* aux prix

◇ *price setting* détermination *f* des prix, fixation *f* des prix

◇ *price stability* stabilité *f* des prix

◇ *price survey* enquête *f* sur les prix

◇ *price tag, price ticket* étiquette *f* de prix

◇ *price undercutting* gâchage

m des prix

◇ *price war* guerre *f* des prix

▸ **price down** *vt sep* baisser le prix de, démarquer; **all items have been priced down by 10%** tous les articles ont été démarqués de 10%

▸ **price up** *vt sep* augmenter le prix de

price-elastic *adj* au prix élastique

price-inelastic *adj* au prix stable

price-sensitive *adj* sensible aux prix

pricing *n* détermination *f* du prix, fixation *f* du prix

◇ *pricing policy* politique *f* de prix

primary *adj Econ* primaire

◇ *primary data* informations *fpl* primaires, données *fpl* primaires

◇ *primary demand* demande *f* primaire

◇ *primary market* marché *m* primaire

◇ *primary sector* secteur *m* primaire

prime time *n (on TV)* prime time *m*

◇ *prime time advertisement* publicité *f* au prime time

◇ *prime time advertising* publicité *f* au prime time

print *n (printed matter)* texte *m*

◇ *print ad, print advertisement* publicité *f* presse

◇ *print advertising* publicité *f* presse

> This will be backed up by **print ads** in local and regional papers, radio ads, ads on tube cars and taxi sides. The £250,000 campaign will be run through the summer.

private-label brand n marque f de distributeur

probability n

◇ **probability sample** échantillon m probabiliste

◇ **probability sampling** échantillonnage m probabiliste

problem child n *(company, product)* dilemme m

> Long a **problem child**, Granada Computer Services is now thriving and as of April 15, it restructured its customer support functions into two separate divisions with the aim of providing a more focussed and efficient service.

process vt *(data)* traiter

producer n *(of raw materials, goods)* producteur(trice) m,f; **this region is Europe's biggest wine producer** cette région est la plus grande productrice de vin d'Europe

◇ **producer goods** biens mpl de production

product n produit m

◇ **product advertising** publicité f de produit

◇ **product analysis** analyse f de produit

◇ **product attribute** attribut m du produit

◇ **product augmentation** amélioration f du produit

◇ **product awareness** notoriété f du produit, mémorisation f du produit

◇ **product bundling** groupage m de produits

◇ **product bundling pricing** fixation f des prix par lot

◇ **product category** catégorie f de produit

◇ **product design** conception f du produit

◇ **product development** élaboration f du produit

◇ **product development cost** coût m de l'élaboration du produit

◇ **product differentiation** différenciation f du produit

◇ **product display** présentation f du produit

◇ **product diversification** diversification f des produits

◇ **product features** caractéristiques fpl du produit

◇ **product image** image f de produit

◇ **product improvement** amélioration f du produit

◇ **product information sheet** fiche f technique

◇ **product innovation** innovation f de produit

◇ **product liability** responsabilité f du produit

◇ **product liability insurance** assurance f de responsabilité du produit

Product lifecycle
Cycle de vie du produit

sales and profit/ventes et profit

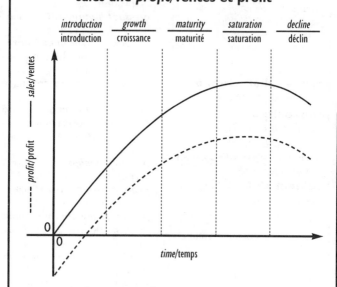

| introduction | growth | maturity | saturation | decline |
| introduction | croissance | maturité | saturation | déclin |

types of consumer/types de consommateur

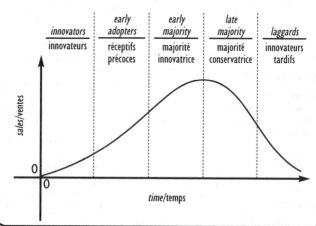

| innovators | early adopters | early majority | late majority | laggards |
| innovateurs | réceptifs précoces | majorité innovatrice | majorité conservatrice | innovateurs tardifs |

⬦ *product lifecycle* cycle *m* de vie du produit

⬦ *product lifecycle curve* courbe *f* du cycle de vie du produit

⬦ *product line* ligne *f* de produits

⬦ *product management* gestion *f* de produits

⬦ *product manager* chef *m* de produit, directeur(trice) *m,f* de produit

⬦ *product mix* assortiment *m* de produits, mix *m* de produits

⬦ *product orientation* optique *f* produit

⬦ *product placement* placement *m* de produit

⬦ *product planning* plan *m* de développement des produits

⬦ *product policy* politique *f* de lancement de produit

⬦ *product portfolio* portefeuille *m* de produits

⬦ *product positioning* positionnement *m* du produit

⬦ *product profile* profil *m* du produit

⬦ *product promotion* communication *f* produit

⬦ *product range* gamme *f* de produits

⬦ *product specialist* spécialiste *mf* produit

⬦ *product test* essai *m* de produits

⬦ *product testing* essais *mpl* de produits

⬦ *product testing panel* panel *m* d'essayeurs de produits

production *n* production *f*, fabrication *f*; **to go into/out of** **production** être/ne plus être fabriqué(e)

⬦ *production capacity* capacité *f* de production

⬦ *production cost* coût *m* de production

product/market pair *n* couple *m* produit/marché

product/price policy *n* politique *f* de produit/prix

profile *n* (of product, consumer, market) profil *m*

profit *n* bénéfice *m*, profit *m*; **profits were down/up this year** les bénéfices ont diminué/augmenté cette année; **to make a profit** faire un bénéfice *ou* des bénéfices; **to sell sth at a profit** faire un bénéfice sur une vente; **profit and loss** pertes *fpl* et profits *mpl*; **profit and loss form** compte *m* d'exploitation

⬦ *profit margin* marge *f* bénéficiaire

⬦ *profit motive* motivation *f* par le profit

profitability *n* rentabilité *f*

66

When it comes to price-cutting, Thomson can compete easily, protecting its number one position by ruthlessly squeezing margins when necessary. But for long-term **profitability** it needs to talk up brand values over savings.

99

profitable *adj* rentable

programme n (plan) programme m; **to draw up a programme** arrêter un programme

project 1 n projet m
  2 vt (forecast) prévoir; **he's projecting a 40% slide in May** il prévoit une baisse de 40% au mois de mai; **we have attempted to project next year's sales figures** nous avons tenté de prévoir les chiffres de vente pour l'année prochaine

projected adj (forecast) prévu(e); **the projected growth of sales** la croissance prévue des ventes

projection n (forecast) projection f, prévision f; **here are my projections for the next ten years** voici mes prévisions pour les dix années à venir

promo n Fam promo f

promote vt (product) promouvoir, faire la promotion de

promoter n promoteur(trice) m,f

promotion n (marketing, special offer) promotion f; **this week's promotion** la promotion de la semaine

◇ **promotions agency** agence f de promotion
◇ **promotion budget** budget m promotionnel
◇ **promotion campaign** campagne f de promotion
◇ **promotion team** équipe f promotionnelle

promotional adj promotionnel(elle)

◇ **promotional campaign** campagne f de promotion
◇ **promotional costs** coûts mpl de promotion
◇ **promotional discount** remise f promotionnelle
◇ **promotional literature** prospectus mpl promotionnels
◇ **promotional material** matériel m de promotion
◇ **promotional offer** offre f promotionnelle
◇ **promotional policy** politique f de communication, politique f de promotion
◇ **promotional price** prix m promotionnel
◇ **promotional sample** échantillon m promotionnel
◇ **promotional target** cible f de communication
◇ **promotional video** (cassette f) vidéo f promotionnelle

proprietary adj

◇ **proprietary article** article m de marque (déposée)
◇ **proprietary brand** marque f déposée
◇ **proprietary name** nom m déposé

prospect 1 n (prospective customer) client(e) m,f éventuel(elle), client(e) m,f potentiel(elle)
  2 vi prospecter; **to prospect for new customers** prospecter la clientèle

◇ **prospect pool** groupe m de prospects

❝

It helps to develop the brand world that the customer has bought into … by presenting

> relevant lifestyle editorial … and incentives targeted at the needs of the reader. It's important to remember that often this reader will be a **prospect** rather than an exisiting customer.
>
> **"**

prospective *adj (buyer, client)* éventuel(elle), potentiel(elle)

prospectus *n (about company, product)* prospectus *m*

psychographic *adj (data, profile, segment)* psychographique

psychological *adj*
◇ *psychological price* prix *m* psychologique
◇ *psychological profile* profil *m* psychologique

publicity *n* publicité *f*; **it'll give us free publicity for the product** ça fera de la publicité gratuite pour notre produit
◇ *publicity agent* agent *m* publicitaire, agent *m* de publicité
◇ *publicity budget* budget *m* publicitaire
◇ *publicity brochure* brochure *f* publicitaire
◇ *publicity campaign* campagne *f* publicitaire, campagne *f* de publicité
◇ *publicity department* service *m* de publicité
◇ *publicity expenses* dépenses *fpl* de la publicité
◇ *publicity manager* chef *m* de (la) publicité

publicize *vt (product, event)* faire de la publicité pour; **the launch of their new product has been widely publicized** leur nouveau produit a été lancé à grand renfort de publicité

public relations *npl* relations *fpl* publiques; **it was a good public relations exercise** ce fut une réussite pour ce qui est des relations publiques
◇ *public relations agency, public relations consultancy* agence *f* conseil en communication
◇ *public relations consultant* conseil *m* en communication
◇ *public relations manager* directeur(trice) *m,f* des relations publiques
◇ *public relations officer* responsable *mf* des relations publiques

pull strategy *n* stratégie *f* pull

punter *n Fam (customer)* client(e) *m,f*

purchase **1** *n (act of buying, thing bought)* achat *m*; **to make a purchase** faire un achat

2 *vt* acheter, acquérir; **to purchase sth from sb** acheter qch à qn; **to purchase sth on credit** acheter qch à crédit

3 *vi* acheter; **now is the time to purchase** c'est maintenant qu'il faut acheter
◇ *purchase behaviour* comportement *m* d'achat
◇ *purchase cost* coût *m* d'achat
◇ *purchase decision* décision *f* d'achat
◇ *purchase diary* relevé *m* d'achat journalier

◇ *purchase environment* environnement *m* d'achat

◇ *purchase frequency* fréquence *f* d'achat

◇ *purchase invoice* facture *f* d'achat

◇ *purchase note* bordereau *m* d'achat

◇ *purchase order* (for goods, service) bon *m* de commande

◇ *purchase price* prix *m* d'achat

◇ *purchase volume* volume *m* d'achat

> Those involved in the design of fashion stores stress that the key to making the **purchase environment** appealing to the consumer is to develop an integrated strategy that reflects the advertising that has brought people to the store.

purchaser *n* acheteur(euse) *m,f*

◇ *purchaser behaviour* comportement *m* de l'acheteur

purchasing *n* achat *m*

◇ *Am purchasing agent* acheteur(euse) *m,f*

◇ *purchasing behaviour* comportement *m* d'achat

◇ *purchasing behaviour model* modèle *m* de comportement d'achat

◇ *purchasing decision* décision *f* d'achat

◇ *purchasing department* service *m* des achats

◇ *purchasing manager* chef *m* des achats

◇ *purchasing motivator* mobile *m* d'achat

◇ *Econ purchasing power* pouvoir *m* d'achat

◇ *purchasing process* processus *m* d'achat

◇ *purchasing rights* droits *mp* d'achat

> Although information on them from the four database companies correctly suggests that they enjoy luxuries like good food and foreign holidays, it doesn't tell us anything about the real life factors that influence their **purchasing decisions**.

pure competition *n* concurrence *f* pure

purposive *adj*

◇ *purposive sample* échantillon *m* empirique

◇ *purposive sampling* échantillonnage *m* empirique

push strategy *n* stratégie push

pyramid selling *n* vente pyramidale

qualitative *adj* qualitatif(ive)

◇ *qualitative forecasting* prévisions *fpl* qualitatives

◇ *qualitative research* études *fpl* qualitatives

◇ *qualitative study* étude *f* qualitative

quality *n (standard)* qualité *f*; **of good/poor quality** de bonne/mauvaise qualité

◇ *quality control* contrôle *m* de (la) qualité

◇ *quality goods* marchandises *fpl* de qualité

◇ *quality label* label *m* de qualité

◇ *quality management* gestion *f* qualité

◇ *quality positioning* positionnement *m* par la qualité

quality-price ratio *n* rapport *m* qualité-prix

quantitative *adj* quantitatif(ive)

◇ *quantitative forecasting* prévisions *fpl* quantitatives

◇ *quantitative research* études *fpl* quantitatives

◇ *quantitative study* étude *f* quantitative

quantity *n* quantité *f*; **to buy sth in large quantities** acheter qch en grande quantité

◇ *quantity discount* remise *f* ou escompte *m* sur la quantité ou sur les achats en gros

question 1 *n (in survey)* question *f*

2 *vt (consumer)* interroger

◇ *question mark (product)* point *m* d'interrogation, dilemme *m*

questionnaire *n* questionnaire *m*

◇ *questionnaire survey* enquête *f* par questionnaire

quota *n* (**a**) *(limited quantity)* quota *m* (**b**) *(share)* part *f*, quota *m*

◇ *quota sample* échantillon *m* par quotas

◇ *quota sampling* échantillonnage *m* par quotas

radio advertising n publicité f à la radio

raise vt *(price, rate)* augmenter

rake-off n *Fam* pourcentage m, commission f; **to get a rake-off on each sale** toucher un pourcentage *ou* une commission sur chaque vente

R&D, R and D n *(abbr research and development)* R-D f

random adj

◇ *random check* contrôle m par sondage(s)

◇ *random sample* échantillon m aléatoire

◇ *random sampling* échantillonnage m aléatoire

◇ *random selection* sélection f au hasard

range 1 n *(of prices, colours, products)* gamme f; *(of advertising campaign)* rayon m d'action; **we stock a wide range of office materials** nous avons en stock une large gamme de matériels de bureau; **this product is the top/bottom of the range** ce produit est le modèle haut/bas de gamme

2 vi **to range from … to …** aller de … à …; **prices range from**

£15 to £150 les prix vont de 15 livres à 150 livres

◇ *range addition* ajout m à la gamme

◇ *range stretching* extension de la gamme

rate n **(a)** *(percentage)* taux m **(b)** *(price, charge)* tarif m; **the going rate** le tarif courant

◇ *rate of adoption* taux m d'adoption

◇ *rate of awareness* taux m de notoriété

◇ *rate of churn* taux m de clients passés à la concurrence

◇ *Econ rate of inflation* taux m d'inflation

◇ *rate of penetration* taux m de pénétration

rating scale n échelle f de classement

ratio n rapport m

reach n *(of campaign, advertisement)* portée f

reaction n *(of consumer to product)* réaction f

real repositioning n repositionnement m réel

rebrand vt *(product)* changer la marque de

rebranding *n* changement *m* de marque

rebuy *n* réachat *m*
◇ *rebuy rate* taux *m* de réachat

recall 1 *n* (a) *(of brand name)* mémorisation *f* (b) *(of faulty goods)* rappel *m*
  2 *vt (faulty goods)* rappeler
◇ *recall rate* taux *m* de mémorisation
◇ *recall score* score *m* de mémorisation
◇ *recall test* test *m* de rappel, test *m* de mémorisation

receipt *n* (a) *(act of receiving)* réception *f*; **to be in receipt of sth** avoir reçu qch; **to pay on receipt** payer à la réception (b) *(proof of payment)* reçu *m* (**for** de); *(in supermarket)* ticket *m* de caisse (**for** de)

reciprocal relationships **model** *n* modèle *m* de relations réciproques

recognition *n* reconnaissance *f*
◇ *recognition score* score *m* de reconnaissance
◇ *recognition test* test *m* de reconnaissance

recommended retail price *n* prix *m* recommandé, prix *m* conseillé

reduce *vt* réduire; *(price)* baisser

reduced *adj* réduit(e); *(goods)* soldé(e), en solde
◇ *reduced price* prix *m* réduit; **to buy sth at a reduced price** acheter qch à prix réduit

reduced-price offer *n* offre *f* à prix réduit

reduction *n* réduction *f*; *(of prices)* baisse *f*; *(discount)* rabais *m*, remise *f*; **to make a reduction (on sth)** faire un rabais *ou* une remise (sur qch)

reference *n*
◇ *reference customer* client(e) *m,f* de référence
◇ *reference group* groupe *m* de référence
◇ *reference sale* vente *f* de référence

refund 1 *n* remboursement *m*; **to get a refund** se faire rembourser
  2 *vt (person, money)* rembourser; **to refund sb sth, to refund sth to sb** rembourser qch à qn; **they refunded me the postage** ils m'ont remboursé les frais de port

refundable *adj* remboursable

refusal rate *n* taux *m* de refus

registered *adj*
◇ *registered design* modèle *m* déposé
◇ *registered trademark* marque *f* déposée

regular customer *n* client(e) *m,f* habitué(e)

reject 1 *n (object)* (article *m* de) rebut *m*
2 *vt (goods)* refuser

relationship marketing *n* marketing *m* relationnel

> *"*
> In a bid to capitalise on the growth of **relationship marketing**, AT&T is preparing to launch a managed loyalty programme linking the functions of a loyalty card, call centre, customer database analysis and campaign management.
> *"*

relative *adj* relatif(ive)
◇ *relative market share* part *f* de marché relative

relaunch 1 *n (of product)* relancement *m*, relance *f*
2 *vt (product)* relancer

remarket *vt* recommercialiser

remarketing *n* marketing *m* de relance

repackage *vt (goods)* reconditionner, repenser l'emballage de ; *(company, image)* redorer

repayment *n* remboursement *m* ; **repayments can b spread over 12 months** le remboursements peuven être échelonnés sur 12 mois
◇ *repayment options* formule *fpl* de remboursement

repeat 1 *vt (order, offer* renouveler
2 *n*
◇ *repeat order* commande renouvelée
◇ *repeat purchase* achat *n* renouvelé
◇ *repeat sale* vente *f* répétée

reply 1 *n* réponse *f* ; **reply pai** réponse *f* payée
2 *vi* répondre (**to** à)
◇ *reply card* carte-réponse *f*
◇ *reply coupon* coupon-réponse *m*

reply-paid card *n* carte *f* T

report 1 *n (account, review,* rapport *m* (**on** sur) ; *(of meeting, speech)* compte-rendu *m* **to draw up** *or* **make a report or sth** faire *ou* rédiger un rapport sur qch
2 *vt (give account of)* rendre compte de ; **to report one's findings (to sb)** faire un rapport (à qn)
3 *vi (give account)* faire un rapport (**to sb** à qn ; **on sth** sur qch)

reposition *vt (brand, product)* repositionner

> *"*
> Sales, independent for each of the four brands, operate out of new design studios, showrooms and offices. The brands have been **reposit-**

ioned with relevant distribution and marketing changes. The team is now in place but the total reorganisation task has been expensive and operational efficiency has suffered during the process of change.

"

repositioning n (of brand, product) repositionnement m

representative 1 n (of group, company, organization) représentant(e) m,f
    2 adj représentatif(ive)

◇ *representative sample* échantillon m type

repurchase 1 n réachat m
    2 vt réacheter

◇ *repurchase market* marché m de renouvellement

◇ *repurchase rate* taux m de réachat

resale n revente f

◇ *resale price maintenance* prix m de vente imposé

◇ *resale value* valeur f à la revente

resaleable adj revendable

research 1 n recherche f; **to do research (into sth)** faire des recherches (sur qch); **research and development** recherche f et développement m
    2 vt faire des recherches sur
    3 vi faire des recherches (**into** sur)

◇ *research and development manager* directeur(trice) m,f de recherche et développement

resell vt revendre

respondent n répondant(e) m,f

response n (to question in survey) réponse f

◇ *response rate* taux m de réponse

restock vt (shop) réassortir

restocking n (of shop) réassortiment m

retail 1 n (vente f au) détail m; **a wholesale and retail business** un commerce de gros et de détail
    2 vt vendre au détail
    3 vi se vendre (au détail); **they retail at \$50 each** ils se vendent à 50 dollars la pièce

◇ *retail audit* audit m des détaillants

◇ *retail auditor* audit m des détaillants, auditeur(trice) m,f des détaillants

◇ *retail chain* chaîne f de détail

◇ *retail customer* client(e) m,f qui achète au détail

◇ *retail dealer* détaillant(e) m,f

◇ *retail goods* marchandises fpl au détail

◇ *retail outlet* magasin m de (vente au) détail, point m de (vente au) détail

◇ *retail panel* panel m de détaillants

◇ *retail park* zone f commerciale

◇ *retail price* prix m de détail

◇ Br *retail price index* indice m des prix de détail

◇ *retail price maintenance* prix m imposé

◇ *retail sales* ventes *fpl* au détail

◇ *retail shop* magasin *m* de (vente au) détail

◇ *retail trade* (commerce *m* de) détail *m*

> Warner Brothers has struck a licensing deal with Swedish fashion retailer H&M to supply Warner-branded crèches. Industry insiders say that Warner Bros is planning similar deals with larger **retail chains** across Europe.

retailer *n* détaillant(e) *m,f*

◇ *retailer co-operative* groupe *m* de détaillants

◇ *retailer margin* marge *f* du détaillant

retailing mix *n* marchéage *m* de distribution

return 1 *n* (**a**) *(of goods)* renvoi *m*; *(article)* rendu *m*; **on sale or return** *(goods)* vendu(e) avec possibilité de retour (**b**) **returns** *(profit)* bénéfices *mpl* **2** *vt (goods)* renvoyer

revenue *n (from sales)* recettes *fpl*

rise 1 *n (in price, cost of living)* hausse *f*, augmentation *f*; **the rise in the price of consumer goods** la hausse du prix des biens de consommation **2** *vi* monter, augmenter; **prices are rising steadily** les prix augmentent régulièrement

rising star *n* produit *m* d'avenir

rival *adj & n* rival(e) *m,f*

road *n* **to be on the road** *(of salesman)* être sur la route

roadshow *n* tournée *f* de présentation

> Maritz did not carry out the BA launch in isolation; all staff were briefed face to face on the strategy behind the new identity before it was unveiled to them at a high-tech mobile **roadshow**. Attendance was not compulsory — staff had to feel they were there through choice.

rock-bottom *adj (price)* sacrifié(e)

▸ **roll out** *vt sep (product)* lancer

roll-out *n (of product)* lancement *m*

rough *n (of design)* crayonné *m*, esquisse *f*

RPI *n Br (abbr* **retail price index***)* indice *m* des prix de détail

RPM *n (abbr* **retail price maintenance***)* prix *m* imposé

RRP *n (abbr* **recommended retail price***)* prix *m* recommandé, prix *m* conseillé

RTM *n (abbr* **registered trademark***)* marque *f* déposée

▸ **rush out** *vt sep (new product, advertisement)* sortir rapidement

sale *n* (**a**) *(act, event)* vente *f*; **sales** *(turnover)* chiffre *m* d'affaires; *(sector)* la vente; **to work in sales** travailler dans la vente; **for sale** à vendre; **to put sth up for sale** mettre qch en vente; **on sale** en vente; **sales and marketing** vente-marketing *f*; **sales and marketing department** service *m* vente-marketing; **sale or return** vente *f* avec faculté de retour; **sale as seen** vente *f* en l'état; **sale by description** vente *f* sur description; **sale by sample** vente *f* sur échantillon

(**b**) *(at reduced prices)* soldes *mpl*; *Br* **in the sale**, *Am* **on sale** *(article)* en solde; **the sales** les soldes; **I got it in a sale** je l'ai acheté en solde

◇ *sales account* compte *m* des ventes

◇ *sales acumen* sens *m* du commerce

◇ *sales analysis* analyse *f* des ventes

◇ *sales area (in store)* surface *f* de vente, espace *m* de vente; *(district)* région *f* desservie

◇ *Br sales assistant* vendeur (euse) *m,f*

◇ *sales audit* audit *m* de vente

◇ *sales budget* budget *m* commercial, budget *m* des ventes

◇ *sales campaign* campagne *f* de vente

◇ *sales chart* courbe *f* des ventes

◇ *Am sales clerk* vendeur (euse) *m,f*

◇ *sales commission* commission *f* de vente

◇ *sales consultant* conseiller (ère) *m,f* commercial(e)

◇ *sales contract* contrat *m* de vente

◇ *sales counter* comptoir *m* de vente

◇ *sales coverage* couverture *f* du marché

◇ *sales department* service *m* des ventes

◇ *sales drive* campagne *f* de vente

◇ *sales effectiveness* efficacité *f* des ventes

◇ *sales engineer* agent *m* technico-commercial

◇ *sales equation* équation *f* de vente

◇ *sales executive* cadre *m* commercial

◇ *sales expansion* développement *m* des ventes

◇ *sales figures* chiffre *m* de ventes

The sales and marketing department

Le service vente-marketing

sales and marketing director

directeur de marketing

sales manager

directeur de ventes

advertising manager

directeur de la publicité

distribution manager

directeur de la distribution

market research manager

responsable des études de marché

sales promotion manager

directeur de la promotion des ventes

marketing manager

directeur du marketing

area sales representative

représentant commercial régional

market researcher

enquêteur

brand manager

chef de produit

sales representative

représentant commercial

◇ *sales floor* surface *f* de vente

◇ *sales force* force *f* de vente

◇ *sales forecast* prévision *f* des ventes

◇ *sales invoice* facture *f* de vente

◇ *sales letter* lettre *f* de vente

◇ *sales management* direction *f* des ventes, direction *f* commerciale

◇ *sales manager* directeur (trice) *m,f* commercial(e), chef *m* des ventes

◇ *sales meeting* réunion *f* de représentants

◇ *sales network* réseau *m* de vente

◇ *sales objective* objectif *m* de vente

◇ *sales outlet* point *m* de vente

◇ *sales pitch* arguments *mpl* de vente

◇ *sales policy* politique *f* de vente

◇ *sales potential* potentiel *m* de vente

◇ *sale price* (selling price) prix *m* de vente; (reduced price) prix *m* soldé

◇ *sales projection* prévision *f* des ventes

◇ *sales promoter* promoteur (trice) *m,f* des ventes

◇ *sales promotion* promotion *f* des ventes

◇ *sales promotion agency* agence *f* de promotion des ventes

◇ *sales promotion manager* directeur(trice) *m,f* de la promotion des ventes

◇ *sales quota* quota *m* de ventes

◇ *sales report* rapport *m* de vente

◇ *sales representative* représentant(e) *m,f*, agent *m* commercial

◇ *sales research* études *fpl* sur les ventes

◇ *Am sales slip* ticket *m* de caisse

◇ *sales staff* personnel *m* de vente

◇ *sales support* soutien *m* commercial

◇ *sales target* objectif *m* de vente

◇ *Am sales tax* TVA *f*

◇ *sales team* équipe *f* de vente

◇ *sales technician* agent *m* technico-commercial

◇ *sales technique* technique *f* de vente

◇ *sales territory* territoire *m* de vente

◇ *sales tool* instrument *m* de vente

◇ *sales volume* volume *m* des ventes

>
> Thus it has been shown that with professional pre-planning and management, exhibitions can be a powerful **sales tool** and not the expensive luxury that many companies regard them to be.
>

saleability *n* facilité *f* de vente, facilité *f* d'écoulement

saleable *adj* vendable

salesman *n* (for company) représentant *m*; (in shop) vendeur *m*

salesmanship *n* technique *f* de vente

salesperson n *(for company)* représentant(e) m,f; *(in shop)* vendeur(euse) m,f

saleswoman n *(for company)* représentante f; *(in shop)* vendeuse f

same-day delivery n livraison f le jour même

sample 1 n échantillon m; **up to sample** pareil à l'échantillon, conforme à l'échantillon; **to send sth as a sample** envoyer qch à titre d'échantillon; **to buy sth from sample** acheter qch d'après échantillon

  2 vt *(public opinion)* sonder

◇ **sample base** base f de sondage

◇ **sample book** catalogue m d'échantillons, livre m d'échantillons

◇ **sample card** carte f d'échantillons

◇ **sample pack** paquet m échantillon

◇ **sample survey** enquête f par sondage

sampler n *(person)* échantillonneur(euse) m,f

sampling n échantillonnage m

◇ **sampling error** erreur f d'échantillonnage

◇ **sampling method** méthode f d'échantillonnage

◇ **sampling quota** quota m d'échantillonnage

saturate vt *(market)* saturer

saturated adj *(market)* saturé(e)

saturation n *(of market)* saturation f

◇ **saturation advertising** publicité f intensive

◇ **saturation campaign** campagne f intensive, campagne f de saturation

◇ **saturation point** point m de saturation; **the market has reached saturation point** le marché est saturé

> 66
> With the main market for computer games (pre-adolescent boys) reaching **saturation point**, the big companies are casting around for ways to keep those sales figures healthy. The latest big idea is to turn girls into committed game-heads.
> 99

SBU n *(abbr strategic business unit)* DAS m, UAS f

scale n *(of prices, ratings, importance)* échelle f

schedule 1 n planning m

  2 vt prévoir; **the launch is scheduled for early next year** le lancement est prévu pour le début de l'année prochaine

score nm score m

scrambled adj

◇ **scrambled merchandising, scrambled retailing** présentation f d'articles variés

season n *(for trade)* saison f; **Christmas is our busiest season** c'est à Noël que nous travaillons le plus

seasonal adj *(demand, campaign, discount)* saisonnier(ère)

secondary *adj*

◇ **secondary data** informations *fpl* secondaires, données *fpl* secondaires

◇ **secondary market** marché *m* secondaire

◇ **secondary sector** secteur *m* secondaire

second-hand **1** *adj (goods)* d'occasion

2 *adv (buy)* d'occasion

◇ **second-hand dealer** brocanteur(euse) *m,f*, revendeur (euse) *m,f*

◇ **second-hand market** marché *m* de revente

◇ **second-hand shop** brocante *f (magasin)*

◇ **second-hand trade** brocante *f (commerce)*

second-rate *adj (goods)* de qualité inférieure

sector *n* secteur *m*; **he works in the advertising sector** il travaille dans la publicité

segment **1** *n (of market, customer base)* segment *m*

2 *vt (market, customer base)* segmenter

> **❝**
> Claims Chris Bryan of AT&T Finance Commerce: "We will be able to manage the whole process from issuing the cards to analysing and **segmenting** the customer base and designing direct mail using the loyalty scheme as a measurement mechanism."
> **❞**

segmentation *n (of market,*

customer base) segmentation *f*

select *vt* sélectionner

selection *n* sélection *f*

◇ **selection error** erreur *f* d'echantillonnage

◇ **selection method** méthode *f* de sélection

selective *adj* sélectif(ive)

◇ **selective distortion** distorsion *f* sélective

◇ **selective distribution** distribution *f* sélective

◇ **selective marketing** marketing *m* sélectif

◇ **selective perception** perception *f* sélective

◇ **selective retention** rétention *f* sélective

self-liquidating premium *n* prime *f* auto-payante

self-mailer *n* carte *f* de publicité directe *(qui est mise à la poste sans enveloppe)*

self-service *n* libre service *m*

◇ **self-service shop** libre service *m*

sell **1** *vt* vendre; **to sell sth to sb, to sell sb sth** vendre qch à qn; **to sell sth for cash** vendre qch (au) comptant; **to sell sth at a loss** vendre qch à perte

2 *vi (of product)* se vendre; *(of person)* vendre

▸ **sell off** *vt sep (at reduced price)* solder; *(to clear)* liquider

▸ **sell out** **1** *vt sep* **to be sold out** *(of item)* être épuisé(e)

2 *vi* **(a)** *(sell stock)* liquider (son stock) **(b)** *(run out)* vendre tout le stock; **to sell out of sth** ne plus avoir de qch

▶ **sell up** vt sep (goods) procéder à la liquidation de

sellable adj vendable

sell-by date n date f limite de vente

seller n (a) (person) vendeur (euse) m,f (b) (article) **to be a good/bad seller** se vendre bien/mal; **it's one of our biggest sellers** c'est un de nos articles qui se vend le mieux

◇ **seller's market** marché m à la baisse, marché m vendeur

selling n (of goods) vente f

◇ **selling costs** frais mpl commerciaux

◇ **selling licence** licence f de vente

◇ **selling point** argument m de vente

◇ **selling power** puissance f de vente

◇ **selling price** prix m de vente

```
"
    … the Guinness name,
prestige and selling power
really comes into its own.
"Anker stout has only a small
percentage of the market so
though bar owners will agree
to stock it they will usually
insist on selling Guinness as
well," he explains.
                            "
```

sell-off n (at reduced price) solde m; (to clear) liquidation f

semantic differential n différentiel m sémantique

send vt envoyer; **all customers on our mailing list will be sent a** catalogue tous les clients qui figurent sur notre liste d'adresses recevront un catalogue

▶ **send back** vt sep (goods) renvoyer

▶ **send out** vt sep (leaflets, mailing) envoyer

service n (a) (facility provided) service m (b) Econ **services** services mpl; **goods and services** biens mpl et services

SET® n Comptr (abbr **secure electronic transaction**) SET f

set 1 n (of needs, considerations) ensemble m
2 vt (prices) fixer

settle vt (account) régler; (bill) acquitter, régler

settlement n (of account) règlement m; (of bill) acquittement m, règlement m; **I enclose a cheque in settlement of your account** veuillez trouver ci-joint un chèque en règlement de votre compte

◇ **settlement discount** remise f pour règlement rapide

◇ **settlement period** délai m de règlement

sexy adj Fam (product) branché(e)

share n (of market) part f

◇ **share point** point m de part de marché

◇ **share of voice** part f de voix

shelf n (in shop) rayon m, étagère f

◇ **shelf facing** facing m, frontale f

◇ **shelf impact** impact m en

linéaire

◇ **shelf life** *(of product)* durée *f* (utile) de vie

◇ **shelf space** linéaire *m*

◇ **shelf yield** vente *f* par mètre linéaire

> **"**
>
> The package design incorporates a sunburst on each product and deep primary colors to gain **shelf impact** and identify the components of the product line.
>
> **"**

shelving *n* rayonnage *m*

shift *Fam* **1** *vt (sell)* écouler; **how can we shift this old stock?** comment écouler ces vieilles marchandises?

   2 *vi (sell)* se vendre; **those TVs just aren't shifting at all** ces télés just ne se vendent pas du tout

ship *vt (send by sea)* expédier par mer; *(send by any means)* expédier

shipment *n* (**a**) *(sending of goods) (by sea)* expédition *f* par mer, expédition *f* par bateau; *(by any means)* expédition *f* (**b**) *(cargo, goods shipped)* chargement *m*

shipper *n (of goods)* expéditeur(trice) *m,f*

shipping *n (of goods) (by sea)* expédition *f* par mer; *(by any means)* expédition *f*

◇ **shipping address** adresse *f* de livraison

◇ **shipping charges** frais *mpl* d'expédition

◇ **shipping company** entreprise *f* de transport routier

◇ **shipping costs** frais *mpl* d'expédition

◇ **shipping depot** dépôt *m* d'expédition

◇ **shipping office** bureau *m* d'expédition

shop 1 *n (for goods)* magasin *m* **2** *vi* faire ses courses; **to shop around** comparer les prix

◇ *Br* **shop front** devanture *f*

◇ *Br* **shop window** vitrine *f*, devanture *f*

shopkeeper *n* commerçant(e) *m,f*, détaillant(e) *m,f*

shopping *n* courses *fpl*; **to do one's/the shopping** faire ses/les courses

◇ **shopping basket** *Econ* panier *m* de la ménagère; *Br Comptr (for on-line purchases)* caddie® *m*

◇ *Am Comptr* **shopping cart** *(for on-line purchases)* caddie® *m*

◇ **shopping centre** centre *m* commercial

◇ *Am* **shopping mall** galerie *f* marchande

> **"**
>
> "The effects of inflation are not limited to the **shopping basket**", says Raoul Pinnell, Prudential's marketing director. "Those special events are treats that we save up for, look forward to and are also subject to the ravages of inflation."
>
> **"**

short delivery n manque m à la livraison

showcard n *(in shop)* pancarte f; *(of samples)* carte f d'échantillons

showcase 1 n vitrine f; **a showcase for British exports** une vitrine pour les exportations britanniques

2 vt exposer, présenter; **the exhibition will showcase our new product range** nous présenterons notre nouvelle gamme de produits dans le cadre de l'exposition

showroom n salle f d'exposition

shrink-wrap vt emballer sous film plastique

shrink-wrapped adj emballé(e) sous film plastique

sight n **to sell sth sight unseen** vendre qch sans inspection; **to buy sth sight unseen** acheter qch sans l'avoir vu

> **"**
>
> Five years ago companies that bought their personal computers **sight unseen** through the mail were few and far between. During the 1980s the business PC, like many other IT products, was best bought from a reputable dealer. But PCs are increasingly sold through direct channels rather than distributors, with reliable suppliers offering rapid delivery at rock bottom prices.
>
> **"**

simultaneous product development n développement m simultané de produits

site n *(for advertising)* emplacement m; *Comptr (on Internet)* site m

size n *(of market, market share, sample)* taille f

skim vt *(market)* écrémer

skimming n *(of market)* écrémage m

◇ **skimming price** prix m d'écrémage

slogan n slogan m (publicitaire)

slump 1 n *(in prices, sales, market)* effondrement m (**in** de); *(economic depression)* crise f (économique); **a slump in prices/demand** une forte baisse des prix/de la demande

2 vi *(of prices, sales, market)* s'effondrer

small adj

◇ *Br* **small ad** petite annonce f

◇ **small business** petite entreprise f

◇ **small trader** petit(e) commerçant(e) m,f

smart card n carte f à puce, carte f à mémoire

SME n *(abbr* **small and medium-sized enterprise)** PME f

soar vi *(of prices, profits, sales)* monter en flèche; **sales have soared since the advertising campaign** les ventes ont monté en flèche depuis la campagne publicitaire

sociodemographic *adj*
socio-démographique

◊ *sociodemographic data* données *fpl* socio-démographiques

◊ *sociodemographic profile* profil *m* socio-démographique

◊ *sociodemographic segment* segment *m* socio-démographique

◊ *sociodemographic segmentation* segmentation *f* socio-démographique

socio-economic classification *n* classification *f* socio-professionnelle

sociological *adj* (survey) sociologique

socio-professional group *n* catégorie *f* socio-professionnelle

soft sell *n* méthode *f* de vente non agressive

> **"**
>
> For that is the purpose of the muzak, is it not? It is a variant on the **soft sell** device of the supermarkets who have apparently demonstrated that people buy more when they are subjected to muzak. What is new is perhaps the idea that people have to be encouraged or influenced to spend.
>
> **"**

sole *adj* unique

◊ *sole agency* représentation *f* exclusive

◊ *sole agency contract* contrat *m* de représentation exclusive

◊ *sole agent* agent *m* exclusif; **to be sole agent for Rover** avoir la représentation exclusive de Rover

◊ *sole dealer* concessionnaire *m,f* exclusif(ive)

◊ *sole supplier* fournisseur (euse) *m,f* exclusif(ive)

solus *adj* isolé(e)

◊ *solus advertisement* publicité *f* isolée

◊ *solus position* emplacement *m* isolé

◊ *solus site* emplacement *m* isolé

special 1 *n* Am (special offer) offre *f* spéciale; **on special** en promotion
2 *adj*

◊ *special offer* offre *f* spéciale; **on special offer** en promotion

◊ *special price* prix *m* spécial

specialist *n* spécialiste *mf*

◊ *specialist retailer* détaillant(e) *m,f* spécialisé(e)

speciality goods, *Am* **specialty goods** *npl* produits *mpl* spécialisés

specification buying *n* achats *mpl* spécifiés

specifications *npl* (of sale) cahier *m* des charges

spend 1 *n* dépenses *fpl*; **we must decrease our marketing spend** il nous faut diminuer nos dépenses de marketing; **this year's spend has exceeded the budget by 10%** nous avons dépassé de 10% les dépenses

Socio-economic classification

Classification socio-professionnelle

It has been proposed that this scale of social classification replace the existing ABCI system, which is considered out-of-date.

Dans un avenir proche la grille de classification sociale ci-dessous pourrait remplacer la grille ABCI, que certains considèrent dépassé.

Grade Catégorie	Occupation Profession
1	*Professionals* Professions intellectuelles supérieures *Teachers, doctors, lawyers, business executives, entrepreneurs* Professeurs, médecins, avocats, cadres, chefs d'entreprise
2	*Lower managerial and professional* Professions intermédiaires supérieures *Police officers, nurses, journalists, musicians, actors* Policiers, infirmières, journalistes, musiciens, acteurs
3	*Intermediate occupations* Professions intermédiaires *Clerks, secretaries, computer technicians, dental nurses* Employés de bureau, secrétaires, techniciens en informatique, assistants dentaires
4	*Small employers and the self-employed* Chefs de PMEs et artisans *Painters, taxi drivers, publicans, farmers* Peintres, chauffeurs de taxi, tenanciers de pub, agriculteurs
5	*Lower supervisory, craft and related occupations* Tâches de supervision, artisans *Printers, plumbers, butchers, train drivers* Imprimeurs, plombiers, bouchers, conducteurs de train
6	*Semi-routine occupations* Tâches semi-répétitives *Sales assistants, hairdressers, factory workers, drivers* Vendeurs, coiffeurs, ouvriers d'usine, chauffeurs
7	*Routine occupations* Tâches répétitives *Labourers, waiters, refuse collectors, couriers* Manœuvres, serveurs, éboueurs, coursiers
8	*Never worked or long-term unemployed* Sans activité professionnelle

prévues au budget de l'année écoulée

2 vt *(money)* dépenser; **to spend money on sth** dépenser de l'argent en qch

"

The chain will spend over £2m on advertising to build its market share, representing an increase in current **spend** through incumbent agency Holder Henry Pearce and Bailey.

"

spending n dépenses *fpl*

◇ **spending money** argent m disponible

◇ *Econ* **spending power** pouvoir m d'achat

spinner n *(for displaying goods)* tourniquet m

spin-off n *(by-product)* produit m dérivé

◇ **spin-off product** produit m dérivé

spoiler campaign n = campagne lancée par une entreprise pour minimiser l'impact d'une campagne publicitaire menée par une société concurrente

"

The Kenco Coffee company is to run a **spoiler campaign** to Nescafé's 60th birthday free-coffee promotion. Kenco is rebranding High Street Kensington tube station for the next three months as High Street Kenco. It will hand

out free coffee as well as entertain commuters with mime artists, jugglers and celebrity lookalikes.

"

sponsor 1 n *(of sportsman, team, tournament)* sponsor m; *(of film, TV programme)* sponsor m, commanditaire m

2 vt sponsoriser

sponsorship n *(of sportsman, team, tournament)* sponsoring m, parrainage m; *(of film, TV programme)* parrainage m

◇ **sponsorship agreement** contrat m de sponsoring

◇ **sponsorship budget** budget m alloué au sponsoring

◇ **sponsorship deal** contrat m de sponsoring

spontaneous recall n notoriété f spontanée

spot n *(in advertising)* message m publicitaire, spot m

stability n *(of prices)* stabilité f

stable n *(prices)* stable

stage n *(of product)* phase f

stand n *(at exhibition)* stand m (d'exposition)

standard 1 n **(a)** *(level)* niveau m; **to be up to/below standard** être du/en dessous du niveau requis; **most of the goods are up to standard** la plupart de marchandises sont de qualité satisfaisante

(b) *(set requirements)* norme f; **to make a product comply with standards** adapter un produit aux normes; **to set standards for a product** fixer des normes

pour un produit
2 *adj (design, size, price)*
standard

◊ **standard deviation** écart *m*
type

◊ **standard price** prix *m* taxé

◊ **standard sample** échantillon
m modèle

star *n (product)* vedette *f*

statement *n (of expenses,
sales figures)* état *m*

statutory rights *npl (of
purchaser)* droits *mpl* statutaires

sticker *n* autocollant *m*

◊ **sticker price** prix *m* affiché,
prix *m* à la vente

stimulation marketing *n*
marketing *m* de stimulation

stimulus *n* stimulant *m*

◊ **stimulus response** réponse *f*
stimulée

stock 1 *n (of goods)* stock *m*;
stocks are low il y a peu de
marchandises en stock; **while
stocks last** jusqu'à épuisement
des stocks; **to be in stock** être
en stock; **to be out of stock** *(of
product)* être épuisé(e); **we're
out of stock** nous sommes en
rupture de stock
2 *vt* **(a)** *(supply)* approvisionner **(with** de); **this shop is well
stocked** ce magasin est bien
approvisionné
(b) *(have in stock)* avoir en
stock; **we don't stock that item
any more** nous ne vendons *ou*
faisons plus cet article

◊ **stock clearance** liquidation *f*
de stock

◊ *Br* **stock control** gestion *f* des
stocks, contrôle *m* des stocks

◊ **stock in hand** marchandises
fpl en stock, marchandises *fpl*
en magasin

◊ **stock valuation** évaluation *f*
des stocks

stocklist *n Br* inventaire *m*; **to
make a stocklist of goods**
inventorier des marchandises

stockpile 1 *n (goods)* stocks
mpl de réserve
2 *vt (goods)* stocker

stocktake *vi Br* faire *ou*
dresser un inventaire

stocktaking *n* inventaire *m*
(des stocks); **to do the stocktaking** faire l'inventaire; **stocktaking is in February** on fait
l'inventaire en février

store 1 *n* **(a)** *(supply)* provision
f, stock *m*, réserve *f*
(b) *(warehouse)* entrepôt *m*
(c) *(large shop)* grand magasin
m; *Am (shop)* magasin *m*
2 *vt (goods)* mettre en magasin, entreposer

◊ **store audit** contrôle *m* des
points de vente

◊ **store brand** marque *f* de
magasin

◊ **store card** carte *f* de crédit
(d'un magasin)

◊ *Am* **store front** devanture *f*

◊ *Am* **store window** vitrine *f*,
devanture *f*

storekeeper *n Am (shopkeeper)* commerçant(e) *m,f*,
détaillant(e) *m,f*

strapline *n* signature *f*, base
line *f*

> Gone is the exuberant 'It Could Be You' slogan that carried the Lottery through its first five years. The new 'Maybe. Just Maybe' **strapline** stresses the enjoyment of anticipation as much as the prospect of winning.

strategic *adj* stratégique

◇ **strategic business unit** domaine *m* d'activité stratégique, unité *f* d'activité stratégique

◇ **strategic marketing** marketing *m* stratégique

◇ **strategic planning** planification *f* stratégique

◇ **strategic position** position *f* stratégique

◇ **strategic positioning** positionnement *m* stratégique

◇ **strategic targeting** ciblage *m* stratégique

◇ **strategic withdrawal** *(of product, campaign)* repli *m* stratégique

strategy *n* stratégie *f*

stratified *adj*

◇ **stratified sample** échantillon *m* stratifié

◇ **stratified sampling** échantillonnage *m* stratifié

strength *n* *(of product, company)* force *f*

◇ **strengths, weaknesses, opportunities and threats** forces, faiblesses, opportunités et menaces *fpl*

structured *adj* *(interview)* structuré(e)

study *n* *(of market, feasibility)* étude *f*

stuffer *n* *(insert)* encart *m*

subliminal advertising *n* publicité *f* subliminale

sub-standard *adj* *(goods)* de qualité inférieure

substitute *n* *(product)* substitut *m*

◇ **substitute product** produit *m* substitut

supermarket *n* supermarché *m*

superstore *n* hypermarché *m*, grande surface *f*

supplier *n* fournisseur(euse) *m,f*

◇ **supplier's credit** crédit *m* fournisseur

◇ **supplier file** fiche *f* fournisseur

supply **1** *n* **(a)** *Econ* offre *f*; **supply and demand** l'offre et la demande

(b) *(stock)* provision *f*, réserve *f*; *(act of supplying)* approvisionnement *m*; **supplies** provisions *fpl*; **we are expecting a new supply of microchips** nous espérons recevoir bientôt un nouveau stock de microprocesseurs

2 *vt* *(goods, services)* fournir; **to supply sb with sth, to supply sth to sb** fournir qn de qch, fournir qch à qn; **they supply all the local retailers** ils fournissent tous les détaillants du coin

◇ **supply curve** courbe *f* de l'offre

◇ **supply price** prix *m* de l'offre

surfeit *n* surabondance *f*; **there is a surfeit of imported goods** il y a trop d'importations

survey 1 *n* (**a**) *(study, investigation)* étude *f*, enquête *f*; **they carried out a survey of retail prices** ils ont fait une enquête sur les prix au détail (**b**) *(opinion poll)* sondage *m*
2 *vt* (**a**) *(study, investigate)* faire une étude de, étudier (**b**) *(poll)* sonder; **65% of women surveyed say that they are happy with their current brand** 65% des femmes interrogées se déclarent satisfaites de la marque qu'elles utilisent

◇ **survey research** recherche *f* par sondage

suspect *n* client(e) *m,f* potentiel(elle)

◇ **suspect pool** clients *mpl* potentiels

SWOT *n* (*abbr* **strengths, weaknesses, opportunities and threats**) forces, faiblesses, opportunités et menaces *fpl*

◇ **SWOT analysis** analyse *f* des forces, faiblesses, opportunités et menaces

system *n* système *m*

◇ **systems buying** achat *m* de système

takings *npl* recette(s) *f(pl)*

target 1 *n (objective)* objectif *m*; **to be on target** respecter les objectifs; **to meet sales targets** atteindre les objectifs de vente **2** *vt (market)* cibler; *(advertising campaign)* diriger

◊ **target audience** audience *f* cible

◊ **target buyer** acheteur(euse) *m,f* cible

◊ **target consumer** consommateur(trice) *m,f* cible

◊ **target cost** coût *m* ciblé

◊ **target group** groupe *m* cible

◊ **Target Group Index** indice *m* des groupes cibles

◊ **target market** marché *m* cible

◊ **target marketing** marketing *m* ciblé

◊ **target population** population *f* cible

◊ **target price** prix *m* d'équilibre

◊ **target pricing** fixation *f* du prix en fonction de l'objectif

> **"**
> Gary Twelvetree, *Heat* marketing manager, said: "We looked at our **target** audience and saw they were avid consumers of entertainment products, so it made sense to tie in with Virgin."
> **"**

targeting *n* ciblage *m*

TAT *n (abbr* **thematic apperception test)** TAT *m*

tax 1 *n (on goods, imports)* taxe *f*; **to put a 10% tax on sth** imposer *ou* taxer qch à 10%; **there is a high tax on whisky** le whisky est fortement taxé **2** *vt (goods, imports)* taxer, frapper d'un taxe; **luxury goods are taxed at 28%** les articles de luxe sont taxés à 28%

tax-exempt *adj (goods)* exonéré(e) de taxes

tax-free *adj (goods)* exonéré(e) de taxes

◊ **tax-free shopping** achats *mpl* hors taxes

team *n (of workers)* équipe *f*

teaser *n* aguiche *f*

◊ **teaser ad** aguiche *f*

◊ **teaser campaign** campagne *f* teasing

> **"**
> Based on the theme 'It's what your TV has been crying out

> for', the campaign kicked off with a short **teaser** burst, followed by a 90-second launch film and two 40 second follow-ups.
>
> **"**

telemarketing *n* télémarketing *m*

teleorder 1 *n* commande *f* par ordinateur

2 *vt* commander par ordinateur

telephone *n* téléphone *m*

◇ **telephone canvassing** prospection *f* téléphonique, démarchage *m* à distance, télédémarchage *m*

◇ **telephone follow-up** relance *f* téléphonique

◇ **telephone interview** entretien *m* téléphonique, entretien *m* par téléphone

◇ **telephone order** commande *f* téléphonique, commande *f* par téléphone

◇ **telephone selling** télévente *f*, vente *f* par téléphone

◇ **telephone survey** enquête *f* téléphonique, enquête *f* par téléphone

telesales *n* téléventes *fpl*, phoning *m*

teleshopping *n* achats *mpl* à domicile, téléachat *m*

television *n* télévision *f*

◇ **television advertisement** publicité *f* télévisée

◇ **television advertising** publicité *f* télévisée

◇ **television audience** (reached by advertising) audience *f* télévisuelle

◇ **television campaign** campagne *f* télévisuelle

◇ **television commercial** sp m

◇ **television viewer** téléspectateur(trice) *m,f*

◇ **television viewing pan** panel *m* de téléspectateurs

terminal *n* (for paymen terminal *m*

terms *npl* (of sale, agreemen repayment) conditions *fp* termes *mpl*

territory *n* (of salesperso territoire *m*

tertiary sector *n* secteur tertiaire

test 1 *n* (**a**) (of quality) contrô *m* (**b**) (of reaction, popularit évaluation *f* (**c**) (of produc essai *m*

2 *vt* (**a**) (quality) contrôler ((reaction, popularity) mesure évaluer (**c**) (product) essayer

◇ **test area** région *f* test

◇ **test city** ville *f* test

◇ **test market** marché *m* te moin, marché *m* test

◇ **test site** site *m* témoin

testimonial advertising témoignage *m*, publicité testimoniale

test-market *vt* tester sur marché

test-shop *n* magasin *m* labo ratoire

thematic apperceptio test *n* test *m* d'apercepti thématique

tied outlet *n* concession

exclusive, magasin *m* sous franchise exclusive

tie-in *n* = livre, cassette etc lié à un film ou une émission

◊ *tie-in promotion* promotion *f* collective

◊ *tie-in sale* vente *f* jumelée

till *n* (*cash register*) caisse *f*

◊ *till receipt* ticket *m* de caisse

time pricing *n* fixation *f* des prix en fonction du moment

TM (*abbr* **trademark**) marque *f* (de fabrique)

top-of-the-range *adj* haut de gamme

total 1 *n* total *m*

2 *adj* total(e); **marketing the product accounts for 20% of the total costs** le coût de commercialisation du produit revient à 20% du coût total

trade 1 *n* (**a**) (*commerce*) commerce *m*, affaires *fpl*; **it's good for trade** cela fait marcher le commerce

(**b**) *Am* (*transaction*) marché *m*, affaire *f*

2 *vi* (*do business*) faire du commerce, commercer; **he trades in clothing** il est négociant en confection

◊ *trade agreement* accord *m* commercial

◊ *trade credit* crédit *m* fournisseur

◊ *trade cycle* cycle *m* de commercialisation

◊ *Br Trade Descriptions Act* = loi qui empêche la publicité mensongère

◊ *trade discount* (*to customer*)

escompte *m* commercial, escompte *m* d'usage; (*to retailer*) escompte *m* professionnel

◊ *trade exhibition* foire-exposition *f*, exposition *f* commerciale

◊ *trade fair* foire *f* commerciale, salon *m*

◊ *trade figures* chiffre *m* d'affaires

◊ *trade marketing* marketing *m* commercial, trade marketing *m*

◊ *trade press* presse *f* professionnelle

◊ *trade price* prix *m* marchand

trademark *n* marque *f* (de fabrique)

trade-off analysis *n* analyse *f* conjointe

trader *n* commerçant(e) *m,f*, marchand(e) *m,f* (**in** en); (*on large scale*) négociant(e) *m,f* (**in** en)

traffic 1 *n* (*trade*) commerce *m*

2 *vi* **to traffic in sth** faire le commerce de qch

◊ *traffic builder* article *m* d'appel

transaction *n* (*deal*) opération *f* (commerciale), affaire *f*

transport 1 *n* (*of goods*) transport *m*

2 *vt* (*goods*) transporter

◊ *transport advertising* affichage *m* transport

◊ *transport company* société *f* de transport

◊ *transport costs* frais *mpl* de transport

◊ *transport facilities* moyens

mpl de transport

trend *n* tendance *f*; **the general trend of the market** les tendances *fpl* du marché

◇ *trend analysis* analyse *f* des tendances

◇ *trend reversal* renversement *m* de tendance

trial *n*

◇ *trial order* commande *f* d'essai

◇ *trial period* période *f* d'essai

true sample *n* échantillon *m* représentatif

trusted third party *n* Comptr *(for Internet transactions)* tierce partie *f* de confiance

try *vt (product)* essayer

TTP *n* Comptr *(abbr* **trusted third party)** TPC *f*

turbomarketing *n* turbomarketing *m*

turnover *n* (a) *(of company)* chiffre *m* d'affaires; **his turnover is £100,000 per annum** il fait 100 000 livres d'affaires par an (b) *(of stock)* écoulement *m*,

rotation *f*

◇ *turnover rate* taux *m* de rotation

turnround *n (of stock)* rotation *f*

TV *n (television)* télé *f*

◇ *TV advertisement* publicité *f* télévisée

◇ *TV advertising* publicité *f* télévisée

◇ *TV campaign* campagne *f* télévisuelle

◇ *TV commercial* spot *m*

◇ *TV viewing panel* panel *m* de téléspectateurs

“

Simon Carter, head of residential marketing at London Electricity, said: "This is our first exposure on TV and we're hoping to take the brand to new areas. TV is a great medium but we're putting our toes in the water to see if it's successful for us. If this works for us we'll look at developing full **TV campaigns**."

”

ultimate consumer *n* utilisateur(trice) *m,f* final(e)

umbrella trademark *n* marque *f* ombrelle

unbonded warehouse *n* entrepôt *m* fictif

unbranded *adj* sans marque

undercut *vt (competitor)* vendre moins cher que

undersell *vt (person, company)* vendre moins cher que ; *(goods)* vendre au-dessous de la valeur de

undifferentiated marketing *n* marketing *m* indifférencié

unfair competition *n* concurrence *f* déloyale

unique *adj*

◊ *unique proposition* proposition *f* unique

◊ *unique selling point, unique selling proposition* proposition *f* unique de vente

unit *n* unité *f*; **each lot contains a hundred units** chaque lot contient cent unités

◊ *unit cost* coût *m* unitaire

◊ *unit price* prix *m* unitaire, prix *m* à l'unité

universe *n (number of people in group or segment)* univers *m*

unlimited *adj (guarantee, warranty)* illimité(e)

unload *vi Am (flood market)* inonder le marché

unmarketable *adj (goods)* invendable

unpack *vt (goods)* déballer

unsaleable *adj (goods)* invendable

unstructured *adj (interview)* non structuré(e), libre

untaxed *adj (goods)* non imposé(e), non taxé(e)

UP *n (abbr unit price)* PU *m*

upmarket 1 *adj* haut de gamme

2 *adv* **to move upmarket** se repositionner à la hausse

use *vt (product)* utiliser

use-by date *n* date *f* de péremption

user *n (of product)* utilisateur (trice) *m,f*

◇ *user panel* panel *f* d'utilisateurs

USP *n* (*abbr* **unique selling point** *or* **proposition**) proposition *f* unique de vente

"

In its extreme form, this is an expression of the Unique Selling Proposition, or **USP**. Very simply, the theory behind this is that any product has some characteristic which can be developed so as to make it unique in its class.

"

vacuum pack *n* emballage *m* sous vide

vacuum-packed *adj* emballé(e) sous vide

value *n* valeur *f*; **to be of value** avoir de la valeur; **to be of no value** être sans valeur; **to be good/poor value (for money)** être d'un bon/mauvais rapport qualité-prix; **to go up/down in value** prendre/perdre de la valeur; **to set** *or* **put a value on sth** estimer la valeur de qch

◇ **value brand** marque *f* de valeur

◇ **value chain** chaîne *f* de valeur

value-added tax *n Br* taxe *f* à la valeur ajoutée

VAT *n Br* (*abbr* **value-added tax**) TVA *f*; **exclusive of** *or* **excluding VAT** hors TVA; **subject to VAT** soumis(e) à la TVA

vertical integration *n Econ* intégration *f* verticale

volume *n* volume *m*

◇ **volume of exports** volume *m* d'exportations

◇ **volume of imports** volume *m* d'importations

◇ **volume of purchases** volume *m* d'achats

◇ **volume mailing** multipostage *m*, publipostage *m* groupé

◇ **volume of sales** volume *m* de ventes, chiffre *m* d'affaires

> **"**
>
> Although it was a **volume mailing**, we incorporated specific targeted messages, propositions and tones in order to enable us to evaluate and analyse our targeting methods.
>
> **"**

voluntary *adj*

◇ **voluntary chain** chaîne *f* volontaire

◇ **voluntary export restraint** quotas *mpl* volontaires à l'export

◇ **voluntary retailer chain** chaîne *f* volontaire de détaillants

voucher *n* (**a**) *(for purchase)* bon *m* (**b**) *(receipt)* reçu *m*, récépissé *m*

want ad *n Am* petite annonce *f*

warehouse 1 *n* entrepôt *m*, dépôt *m* de marchandises
　2 *vt* entreposer, mettre en entrepôt
◇ **warehouse charges** frais *mpl* d'entreposage
◇ **warehouse club** club *m* de gros
◇ **warehouse receipt** récépissé *m* d'entrepôt

warehousing *n (of goods)* entreposage *m*, magasinage *m*
◇ **warehousing charges** frais *mpl* d'entreposage, frais *mpl* de magasinage

warranty *n* garantie *f*; **under warranty** sous garantie
◇ **warranty certificate** certificat *m* de garantie

wealth *n* richesse *f*

wealthy *adj* riche

Web *n Comptr* the Web le Web, la Toile
◇ **Web site** site *m* Web

weighted distribution *n* distribution *f* valeur

white goods *npl* appareils *mpl* ménagers

wholesale 1 *n* (vente *f* en) gros *m*; **wholesale and retail** gros et le détail
　2 *adj* de gros
　3 *adv (buy, sell)* en gros
◇ **wholesale customer** client(e) *m,f* qui achète en gros
◇ **wholesale dealer** grossiste *mf*
◇ **wholesale distribution** distribution *f* en gros
◇ **wholesale goods** marchandises *fpl* de gros
◇ **wholesale price** prix *m* de gros
◇ **wholesale price index** indice *m* des prix de gros
◇ **wholesale trade** commerce *m* de gros

wholesaler *n* grossiste *m*, commerçant(e) *m,f* en gros
◇ **wholesaler margin** marge *f* du grossiste

wildcat *n Am (product, company)* dilemme *m*

window *n (of shop)* vitrine *f*
◇ **window display** étalage *m*

with-pack premium *n* prime *f* directe

word-of-mouth advertising *n* publicité *f* de bouche à oreille

world *n* monde *m*

◇ *world market* marché *m* mondial

◇ *Comptr* **the World Wide Web** le World Wide Web

worldwide 1 *adj* mondial(e), global(e)

2 *adv* dans le monde entier; **this product is now sold** **worldwide** ce produit se vend maintenant dans le monde entier

wrap *vt (goods)* emballer

WWW *n Comptr* (*abbr* **World Wide Web**) WWW

yes/no question *n (in survey)* question *f* fermée

youth *n*

◇ **youth market** marché *m* de la jeunesse

◇ **youth marketing** marketing *m* de la classe des jeunes, marketing *m* des juniors

zero *n*

◇ **zero defects** zéro défaut *m*

◇ **zero defects purchasing** achats *mpl* zéro défaut

◇ *Econ* **zero growth** croissance *f* zéro

zero-rated *adj (for VAT)* exempt(e) *ou* exonéré(e) de TVA; **in Britain, books are zero-rated** en Grande-Bretagne, les livres sont exempts *ou* exonérés de TVA

zero-rating *n* franchise *f* de TVA, taux *m* zero

zip code *n Am* code *m* postal

SAMPLE MARKETING CORRESPONDENCE

i. General layout and style – Ordering a catalogue

SOCIÉTÉ LE GROS ET CIE

PB 34
ZI La Cadanelle
03000 Moulins

sender's address (centred at the top of the page)

Madame Simone Dubreuil,
TECHNO-MEDIA,
25, avenue du Mont Blanc,
67000 Strasbourg

address of the person/company to whom the letter is being sent

reference number

Réf: KLB/14762

purpose of the letter

Objet: Commande de catalogue

Moulins, le 10 avril 2000

date follows place where writing from

do not use name person whom you writing

Madame,

opening paragraph

Suite à notre conversation téléphonique d'hier, je souhaiterais recevoir votre dernier catalogue ainsi qu'une liste de vos tarifs.

Comme je vous l'ai déjà précisé, notre système informatique vient d'être modernisé et nous envisageons avec vous un contrat annuel pour la fourniture de bandes, de disquettes et de cartouches ainsi que pour l'entretien de notre matériel. Je vous remercie donc de bien vouloir me communiquer ces renseignements afin que nous puissions poursuivre nos négociations.

development

formal letter ending

Je vous prie de croire, Madame, en l'expression de mes sentiments les meilleurs.

S. Moreau   *signature*

name

title

p.o. Gérard Lefèvre
la secrétaire
Stéphanie Moreau

P.J.: enveloppe timbrée

ii. Letter of inquiry and answer

Note use of conditional tense to convey polite tone

Monsieur,

Auriez-vous l'obligeance de bien vouloir nous envoyer votre dernier catalogue présentant les nouveaux produits de votre gamme NENUTAM?

Nous vous saurions gré de nous préciser également vos tarifs actuels ainsi que vos conditions et délais de livraison à l'étranger.

Veuillez agréer, Monsieur, l'expression de nos sentiments distingués.

Le Directeur
Jean Martin
Jean Martin

Answer

Monsieur,

Nous avons bien reçu votre demande de renseignements du 30 août au sujet de la gamme NENUTAM, présentée dans notre nouveau catalogue ci-joint. Monsieur François Dupont, notre directeur régional des ventes, vous contactera prochainement pour prendre rendez-vous et il sera en mesure de vous renseigner de manière plus détaillée et de vous conseiller sur les acquisitions que vous souhaiteriez faire. Nous sommes convaincus que la gamme NENUTAM conviendra parfaitement à vos besoins.

Nous vous prions d'agréer, Monsieur, l'expression de nos sentiments les meilleurs.

Le Directeur commercial

Jean-Pierre LeGoff
Jean-Pierre LeGoff

business@harrap.eng

iii. Order placed by a customer and answer

Madame,

Suite à notre entretien téléphonique du 3 octobre dernier, nous vous confirmons notre commande de 300 mallettes de jeux, référence 12345.

Nous vous rappelons que ces articles doivent impérativement nous être parvenus pour le 15 novembre, les courses de Noël commençant de plus en plus tôt.

Nous vous prions de croire, Madame, à l'expression de nos sentiments distingués.

Jacques Dupont

Jacques Dupont
Directeur des achats

Answer

Monsieur,

Nous avons bien reçu votre commande du 9 octobre.

Nous avons le plaisir de vous informer que les 300 mallettes de jeux vous ont été expédiées ce jour selon vos instructions.

Nous vous rappelons que nos délais de livraison sont de 10 jours minimum et que si vous désirez un nouvel envoi avant Noël, il serait prudent de nous prévenir par fax.

Nous vous prions d'agréer, Monsieur, l'expression de nos sentiments dévoués.

Marie-Françoise Durand

Marie-Françoise Durand
Directrice des ventes

If it is necessary to cancel or alter an order, one can use th
following sentences:

Veuillez annuler la première partie de notre ordre (We must as
you to cancel the first part of our order)

Nous vous serions obligés de remettre la livraison à… (We woul
be obliged if you would delay delivery until…)

iv. Invoicing and payment

date etc

> Messieurs,
>
> Nous vous adressons votre relevé trimestriel pour la
> période du 1.1.99 au 30.03.99.
>
> Nous vous serions obligés de bien vouloir nous couvrir de
> cette somme dans les meilleurs délais.
>
> Veuillez agréer, Messieurs, nos salutations distinguées.
>
> Le Chef comptable
>
> *Eric Leblanc*
>
> Eric Leblanc

Payment

date etc

> Monsieur,
>
> Veuillez trouver ci-joint notre traite bancaire de FF7 590
> comme paiement de la facture No 1949.
>
> Nous vous prions d'agréer, Monsieur, l'expression de nos
> salutations distinguées.   ← formal letter ending
>
> *Cécile Dupont*
>
> Cécile Dupont
> Service de la Comptabilité
>
> P.J.: traite bancaire   ← indicates enclosed documents

business@harrap.eng

Please note that "business@harrap.eng" is **not** an e-mail address but simply a device to identify that
this supplement is for English speakers.

v. Mailing

When writing to clients, it is possible to use various terms of address.

The most common ones are: "Cher(s) client(s)/Chère(s) cliente(s)", "Cher Monsieur/Chère Madame" and – for example in the case of a newpaper or trade journal writing to a reader – "Cher Lecteur/Chère Lectrice".

Cher client,

En raison d'un changement dans notre politique des ventes, notre catalogue ne comportera plus de prix et ces derniers seront fournis sur demande.

Sentiments dévoués

La Direction

---

vi. Memo

The title of a French memo ("note de service") is usually centred. The purpose of the memo is outlined below the heading with specific indications like "pour affichage" (for circulation), "pour information" (for information) etc.

The sender, the recipient, the subject, the date and the signature are then mentioned successively.

vii. Faxes

Faxes, which are by definition a form of rapid communication, can generally be drafted in a more casual and concise way than letters.

When handwritten, the endings of faxes correspond to the short ones used for letters.

A l'attention de : Nicolas Roche
Date : mardi le 16 mai
Numéro de télécopie : 01 40 92 97 35
De la part de : Pierre Lenoir
Nombre de pages (y compris cette page) : 1
Message : La réunion de représentants a été reportée au lundi 24 juin. Nous nous chargeons de la réservation de votre billet d'avion ainsi que de votre chambre d'hôtel.

Cordialement,
P. Lenoir

---

viii. E-mails

E-mail addresses are made up of two parts, the first being the user's name and the second being the domain name. The two parts are separated by the symbol @ (pronounced "arrobase" in French).

- Because of the nature of the medium, e-mails are not subject to the formal code of letter-writing that is prevalent in French.

- E-mail is becoming more and more widely used in the French working environment, although it is probably not yet as established a method of business correspondence as it is in English.

- E-mails in French are often written in a slightly less telegraphic style than tends to be the case in English, this being mainly due to the fact that French contains fewer of the abbreviated forms that characterize so much of this type of communication in English. Endings are usually rather informal.

- The same rules of "netiquette" apply as in English, so avoid typing entire words in capital letters as this is equivalent to shouting.

- Note that in the model e-mail below, the headings are in English as most French firms use American-manufactured software.

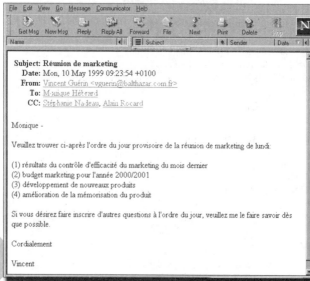

Please note that "business@harrap.eng" is **not** an e-mail address but simply a device to identify that this supplement is for English speakers.

abordable *adj* affordable

AC *nf* (*abrév* **audience cumulée**) cumulative audience

accaparer *vt* (*marché*) to corner; *Écon* **accaparer des marchandises** (*pour contrôler le marché*) to withhold goods from the market

acceptabilité de la marque *nf* brand acceptability, brand acceptance

accord *nm* (*convention*) agreement; **signer un accord** to sign an agreement; **conclure un accord** to come to *or* reach an agreement

◇ *accord commercial* trade agreement
◇ *accord de commercialisation* marketing agreement
◇ *accord de distribution exclusive* exclusive distribution agreement
◇ *accord d'exclusivité* exclusivity agreement
◇ *accord de franchise* franchise agreement
◇ *accord de licence* licensing agreement
◇ *accord de partenariat* partnership agreement
◇ *accord de représentation* agency agreement
◇ *accord de reprise* buyback agreement

> Sitôt réélu pour un mandat de trois ans, Jean-Paul Cluzel, Pdg de RF1, ambitionne de réaliser une seconde implantation à Marseille. Le 15 janvier, il prévoit de se rendre dans cette ville pour présenter un **accord de partenariat** avec deux stations associatives.

accrédité, -e *adj* (*représentant*) accredited; **notre représentant dûment accrédité** our duly authorized agent

accréditer *vt* (*représentant*) to accredit

accroche *nf* slogan

accumulation *nf* (*de marchandises*) (*action*) stockpiling; (*résultat*) stockpile; (*de stocks*) accumulation, build-up

accumuler *vt* (*marchandises*) to stockpile; (*stocks*) to accumulate, to build up

achalandage *nm (clientèle)* custom, clientele

achalandé, -e *adj* **bien achalandé** *(qui compte de nombreux clients)* with a large clientele; *(bien approvisionné)* well-stocked; **mal achalandé** *(qui compte peu de clients)* with a small clientele; *(mal approvisionné)* poorly-stocked

achat *nm (action)* purchase, purchasing; *(chose achetée)* purchase; **faire un achat** to make a purchase; **faire l'achat de qch** to purchase sth; **un bon/mauvais achat** a good/bad buy

◇ **achat sur catalogue** mail-order purchasing

◇ **achats centralisés** centralized purchasing

◇ **achats comparatifs** comparison shopping

◇ **achat au comptant** cash purchase

◇ **achat à crédit** credit purchase; *(location-achat)* buying on hire purchase *or Am* on the installment plan

◇ **achats directs** direct purchasing

◇ **achats à domicile** teleshopping

◇ **achat d'émotion** emotional purchase

◇ **achat d'espace** media buying

◇ **achat en espèces** cash purchase

◇ **achats hors taxe** tax-free shopping

◇ **achat impulsif, achat d'impulsion** impulse buy

◇ **achat juste à temps** just-in-time purchasing

◇ *Ordinat* **achat en ligne** online purchase

◇ **achat à petits prix** low-cost purchase

◇ **achat prévu** destination purchase

◇ **achats regroupés** one-stop buying

◇ **achat renouvelé** repeat purchase

◇ **achat spontané** impulse buy

◇ **achat de système** systems buying

"

En 1997, les ventes de bonbons en sachet reculent, la confiserie de chocolat aussi. Tous les fabricants se plaignent d'une organisation du linéaire trop floue, parfois désordonnée, ce qui limiterait la découverte de nouveaux produits et les **achats d'impulsion**.

"

achetable *adj* purchasable

acheter *vt (acquérir)* to buy, to purchase; **acheter qch à qn** *(faire une transaction)* to buy sth from sb; *(en cadeau)* to buy sth for sb; **acheter qch en gros/au détail** to buy sth wholesale/retail; **acheter qch à crédit** to buy sth on credit; **acheter qch à tempérament** to buy sth on hire purchase *or Am* on the installment plan; **acheter qch par correspondance** to buy sth by mail order

acheteur, -euse *nm,f (a)* *(acquéreur)* buyer, purchaser

on n'a pas pu trouver acheteur pour ce produit there are no buyers for *or* there is no market for this product **(b)** *(pour un magasin)* buyer

◇ *acheteur anonyme* anonymous buyer

◇ *acheteur cible* target buyer

◇ *acheteur éventuel* potential buyer

◇ *acheteur impulsif* impulse buyer

◇ *acheteur industriel* business buyer

◇ *acheteur non-identifié* anonymous buyer

◇ *acheteur potentiel* potential buyer

◇ *acheteur principal* head buyer

acompte *nm (versement régulier)* instalment; *(premier versement)* down payment, deposit; **payer par acomptes** to pay by *or* in instalments; **payer** *ou* **verser un acompte de 4 000 francs** *ou* **4 000 francs en acompte (sur qch)** to make a down payment of 4,000 francs (on sth), to pay a deposit of 4,000 francs (on sth)

acquéreur, -euse *nm,f* purchaser, buyer

acquérir *vt (acheter)* to buy, to purchase

acquisition *nf (action)* purchasing; *(chose achetée)* purchase; **faire l'acquisition de qch** to purchase sth

acte de vente *nm* bill of sale

acteur *nm (participant)* player

◇ *acteur du marché, acteur*

sur le marché market participant, market player

> Le Web est devenu un autre canal de vente qui va bouleverser la manière de travailler des **acteurs** de la communication et du marketing.

actif, -ive *adj (marché)* active

action *nf (campagne)* campaign

◇ *action commerciale* marketing campaign

◇ *action promotionnelle* promotional campaign

◇ *action de vente* sales campaign, sales drive

activité *nf (du marché, d'une entreprise)* activity

administration *nf (gestion)* administration, direction, management

◇ *administration des ventes* sales management

adopter *vt (produit)* to adopt

adopteur *nm (d'un produit)* adopter

◇ *adopteur précoce* early adopter; **les adopteurs précoces de notre nouveau produit représentent 5% du marché potentiel** the early adopters of our new product make up 5% of the potential market

adoption *nf (d'un produit)* adoption

adresse *nf* address

◇ *adresse de facturation* invoicing address, address for invoicing

◇ *adresse de livraison* delivery address; *(d'objets volumineux)* shipping address

adresser *vt (courrier, colis)* to address; **adresser qch à qn** to send sth to sb

affaire *nf* (**a**) *(transaction)* deal, transaction; **faire affaire (avec qn)** to do a deal (with sb); **conclure une affaire (avec qn)** to clinch a deal (with sb)
(**b**) *(achat à bon marché)* bargain; **faire une (bonne) affaire** to get a (good) bargain

◇ *affaire blanche* break-even deal

affichage *nm (activité)* bill-sticking, bill-posting; *(ensemble d'affiches)* posters; *(publicité)* poster advertising, display advertising

◇ *affichage transport* transport advertising

> **"**
>
> "Cette marque communique quasiment tous les jours et représente pour nous un énorme potentiel créatif," se réjouit B. Lacoste. "La campagne se déclinera en **affichage**, en radio, en presse et en TV."
>
> **"**

affiche *nf* poster, advertisement

◇ *affiche publicitaire* poster, advertisement

afficher *vt (mettre en évidence)* to put up, to display

afficheur *nm* bill-sticker, bill-poster

◇ *afficheur publicitaire* bill-sticker, bill-poster

affranchir *vt (lettre, colis)* to put a stamp/stamps on; *(avec une machine)* to frank

affranchissement *nm (coût)* postage

AFNOR *nf (abrév* **Association française de normalisation***)* French industrial standard authority, *Br* ≃ BSI, *Am* ≃ AS

agence *nf (bureau)* agency, bureau

◇ *agence conseil en communication* public relations agency, PR agency

◇ *agence de design* design agency

◇ *agence de distribution* distribution agency

◇ *agence maritime* shipping agency, forwarding agency

◇ *agence de marketing direct* direct marketing agency

◇ *agence de notation* credit (rating) agency, *Am* credit bureau

◇ *agence de presse* press agency, news agency

◇ *agence de promotion* promotions agency

◇ *agence de promotion de ventes* sales promotion agency

◇ *agence de publicité* advertising agency

agencement *nm (d'un magasin)* layout

agent *nm* agent

◇ *agent attitré* appointed agent

◇ *agent commercial* sales representative

◇ *agent commercial exclusif* sole agent, sole representative

◇ *agent commissionnaire* commission agent

◇ *agent direct* commission agent

◇ *agent de distribution* distribution agent

◇ *agent exclusif* sole agent

◇ *agent exportateur* export agent

◇ *agent de fret* freight forwarder, forwarding agent

◇ *agent importateur* import agent

◇ *agent indépendant* free agent

◇ *agent intermédiaire* middleman

◇ *agent de ligne* forwarding agent

◇ *agent mandataire* authorized agent

◇ *agent publicitaire, agent de publicité* advertising agent, publicity agent

◇ *agent technico-commercial* sales technician, sales engineer

agrandir s'agrandir *vpr (marché)* to expand; **le marché des logiciels s'agrandit** the software market is expanding

agréé, -e *adj* authorized; *(échantillon)* approved

agrément *nm (du consommateur, du client)* approval

> **"**
>
> Pendant dix semaines, Ipsos a mesuré **l'agrément** des lecteurs: 70% des sondés ont apprécié cette nouvelle formule, plébiscitant notamment les nouveaux outils de sélection des programmes.
>
> **"**

aguiche *nf* teaser (ad)

AIDA *nm (abrév **attention-intérêt-désir-action**)* AIDA

AIO *nm (abrév **activités, intérêts et opinions**)* AIO

ajout *nm*

◇ *ajout à la gamme* range addition

◇ *ajout à la ligne* line addition

aléatoire *adj (sondage, échantillon, échantillonnage)* random

allée *nf (dans un magasin)* aisle

alliance de marque *nf* cobranding

amélioration du produit *nf* product augmentation, product improvement

AMM *nf (abrév **autorisation de mise sur le marché**)* = official authorization for marketing a pharmaceutical product

analyse *nf* analysis

◇ *analyse des besoins* needs analysis

◇ *analyse conjointe* conjoint analysis, trade-off analysis

◇ *analyse des coûts* cost analysis

◇ *analyse coût-profit* cost-benefit analysis

◇ *analyse des coûts et rendements* cost-benefit analysis

◇ *analyse économique* economic analysis

◇ *analyse des forces et faiblesses* strengths and weaknesses analysis

◇ *analyse des forces, faiblesses, opportunités et menaces* SWOT analysis

◇ *analyse du marché* market analysis

◇ *analyse des marchés* market research

◇ *analyse des médias* media analysis

◇ *analyse des opportunités et des menaces* opportunity and threat analysis

◇ *analyse du prix de revient* cost analysis

◇ *analyse de produit* product analysis

◇ *analyse par segment* cluster analysis

◇ *analyse du style de vie* lifestyle analysis

◇ *analyse des tendances* trend analysis

◇ *analyse des ventes* sales analysis

analyste *nmf* analyst

◇ *analyste du marché* market analyst

◇ *analyste des médias* media analyst

animateur, -trice *nm,f (d'une réunion de groupe)* leader, moderator

◇ *animateur des ventes* marketing executive

animation *nf (promotion)* promotion; **faire des animations dans les supermarchés** to promote products in supermarkets

◇ *animation commerciale* marketing campaign

◇ *animation des ventes* sales drive, sales promotion

annonce *nf (texte publicitaire)* advert, advertisement; **mettre** *ou* **insérer une annonce dans un journal** to put an advertisement in a newspaper

◇ *annonces classées* classified ads

◇ *annonce publicitaire* advert, advertisement

annonceur *nm (de publicité)* advertiser

" ─────────────

Par ce biais, ils espèrent surtout attirer de nouveaux **annonceurs**, dont le nombre reste stable depuis 1994.

───────────── "

annuel, -elle *adj (chiffre d'affaires, budget, ventes)* annual

AOC *nf (abrév* **appellation d'origine contrôlée)** = guarantee of quality

appel à froid *nm* cold call

appellation d'origine contrôlée *nf* = guarantee of quality

apprentissage *nm (expérience de consommation)* learning

approche *nf*

◇ *approche directe* cold calling

◇ *approche personnalisée* person-to-person approach

approuver *vt* **approuver et contre-argumenter** to agree and counter

approvisionnement *nm (a)* *(action)* supply (**en** with); *(d'un* *magasin)* stocking (**en** with) (**b**) *(réserve)* supply, stock; **faire un approvisionnement de qch** to stock up with sth

◊ *approvisionnements de réserve* reserve stocks

approvisionner 1 *vt (fournir)* to supply (**en** with)

2 s'approvisionner *vpr* to get in supplies (**en** of); **s'approvisionner chez qn** to get one's supplies from sb

après-vente *adj* after-sales

arbre de décision *nm* decision tree

argent *nm (richesse)* money; **payer en argent** to pay (in) cash

◊ *argent comptant* cash

◊ *Ordinat argent électronique* e-cash

◊ *Ordinat argent virtuel* e-cash

argumentaire *nm* promotion leaflet; **l'argumentaire est très convaincant** the sales pitch is very convincing

argument de vente *nm* selling point

arrivage *nm (marchandises)* consignment; **nous venons d'avoir un arrivage** we've just had a fresh consignment in

article *nm (produit)* article, item; **faire l'article (pour qch)** to make a sales pitch (for sth); **nous ne suivons** *ou* **faisons plus cet article** we don't stock that item any more

◊ *article d'appel* loss leader, traffic builder

◊ *article bas de gamme* bottom-of-the-range item

◊ *articles de consommation courante* consumer goods

◊ *article démarqué* mark-down

◊ *articles d'exportation* export goods, exports

◊ *article en fin de série* discontinued item

◊ *article à forte rotation* fast mover

◊ *articles de grande consommation* consumables, consumer goods

◊ *article haut de gamme* top-of-the-range item

◊ *articles de luxe* luxury goods

◊ *article de marque* branded article

◊ *article de première nécessité* basic commodity

◊ *article de rebut* reject

◊ *article en réclame* special offer

asile *nm (document publicitaire)* stuffer, insert

association *nf (organisation)* association

◊ *association de consommateurs* consumer association

assorti, -e *adj* **bien/mal assorti** *(magasin)* well-/poorly-stocked

assortiment *nm (de marchandises)* assortment, selection, range

◊ *assortiment de produits* product mix

> **“**
>
> Notre culture, le point fort de l'enseigne, c'est le discount … Toute notre stratégie vise à

conserver cette compétitivité sur les prix pour la totalité de l'**assortiment**, y compris les frais.

"

assortir 1 *vt (magasin)* to stock, to supply
2 s'assortir *vpr* to buy one's stock; **il s'assortit dans les magasins de gros** he buys his stock wholesale

assurance *nf* insurance
◇ **assurance de responsabilité du produit** product liability insurance

atmosphère *nf (d'un point de vente)* atmosphere

attaché, -e *nm,f* attaché
◇ **attaché commercial** *(d'une entreprise)* sales representative
◇ **attaché de presse** press attaché

attachement à la marque *nm* brand bonding

attaque *nf (sur un marché)* attack
◇ **attaque frontale** head-on attack
◇ **attaque latérale** flank attack

attaquer *vt (marché)* to attack

attitude *nf (du consommateur)* attitude; **l'attitude du consommateur à l'égard du produit est décevante** the consumer attitude towards the product is disappointing

attraction *nf (pour un produit)* attraction, appeal; **les automobiles allemandes suscitent une**

attraction très marquée chez le Britanniques German cars are very popular with the British

attrait *nm (d'un produit,* attraction, appeal
◇ **attrait commercial** marke appeal; **ce produit présente un attrait commercial certai** this product has definite market appeal

attribut *nm (d'un produit,* attribute

attribution *nf* attribution

audience *nf* audience
◇ **audience captive** captive audience
◇ **audience cible** target audience
◇ **audience cumulée** cumulative audience
◇ **audience globale** global audience
◇ **audience instantanée** instantaneous audience
◇ **audience télévisuelle** television audience
◇ **audience utile** addressable audience

"
Selon lui, avec 1,7% d'**audience cumulée** en Île-de-France, la fréquence parisienne de RF1, qui permet d'avoir des intervenants de très grande qualité, a déjà renforcé la notoriété de la radio internationale en France.
"

audimètre *nm* = device placed in selected households to measure television audience ratings

audimétrie *nf* audience measurement

audit *nm* (a) *(service)* audit; **être chargé de l'audit d'une société** to audit a company (b) *(personne)* auditor

◇ *audit consommateur* consumer audit

◇ *audit des détaillants* retail audit; *(personne)* retail auditor

◇ *audit externe* external audit; *(personne)* external auditor

◇ *audit interne* internal audit; *(personne)* internal auditor

◇ *audit marketing* marketing audit; *(personne)* marketing auditor

◇ *audit de vente* sales audit

auditeur, -trice *nm,f (chargé de l'audit)* auditor

◇ *auditeur des détaillants* retail auditor

◇ *auditeur externe* external auditor

◇ *auditeur interne* internal auditor

◇ *auditeur marketing* marketing auditor

augmentation *nf* increase (**de** in)

◇ *augmentation de prix* price increase

◇ *augmentation du prix de vente* mark-up

augmenter **1** *vt (taux d'intérêt, prix)* to increase, to put up, to raise; *(dépenses)* to in-crease; **augmenter les ventes de 10%** to increase sales by 10% **2** *vi (taux d'intérêt, prix)* to increase, to go up, to rise; *(dépenses)* to increase; **augmenter de valeur** to increase in value; **tout a augmenté de prix** everything has gone up in price; **le chiffre d'affaires a augmenté de 10% par rapport à l'année dernière** the turnover has increased by 10% *or* is 10% up on last year

autorisation *nf* (a) *(permission)* authorization; **avoir l'autorisation de vendre qch** to be licensed to sell sth (b) *(document)* licence, permit

◇ *autorisation d'exporter* export permit

avance *nf (avantage)* lead; **conserver son avance sur ses concurrents** to retain one's lead over one's competitors; **être en avance sur la concurrence** to be ahead of the competition

avantage *nm* advantage

◇ *avantage comparatif* comparative advantage

◇ *avantage concurrentiel* competitive advantage; **l'avantage concurrentiel de notre offre réside dans l'excellence de notre service** the competitive advantage of what we have to offer lies in the excellence of our service

avoir *nm (attestation de crédit)* credit note

baisse *nf (des prix, des ventes, de la demande)* fall, drop (**de** in); **être en baisse** *ou* **à la baisse** to be falling

baisser 1 *vt (prix)* to lower, to reduce, to bring down; **faire baisser le coût de la vie** to lower *or* reduce *or* bring down the cost of living; **la concurrence fait baisser les prix** competition brings prices down
2 *vi (prix)* to fall

bandeau *nm (espace publicitaire)* advertising space *(in the shape of a band around a vehicle)*; *Ordinat (dans un site web)* banner

banque de données *nf* data bank

baratin *nm Fam* sales pitch

◇ **baratin publicitaire** sales pitch

baratiner *vt Fam* **baratiner qn** *(sujet: vendeur)* to give sb the sales pitch

baromètre *nm* barometer

◇ **baromètre de clientèle** customer barometer

◇ **baromètre d'image** image barometer

◇ **baromètre de marque** brand barometer

bas, basse 1 *adj (prix)* low; **acheter/vendre qch à bas prix** to buy/sell sth cheap
2 *nm (du marché)* low end

base *nf*

◇ **base de clientèle** customer base

◇ **base de consommateurs** customer base

◇ *Ordinat* **base de données** database

◇ *Ordinat* **base de données de consommateurs** customer database

◇ **base de sondage** sample base

battage *nm (publicité)* hype; **faire du battage autour de qch** to hype sth up

◇ **battage médiatique** media hype

◇ **battage publicitaire** hype

benchmarking *nm* benchmarking

bénéfice *nm* **(a)** *(gain)* profit; **donner** *ou* **enregistrer un bénéfice** to show a profit; **réaliser** *ou* **dégager un bénéfice** to make a profit; **vendre qch à bénéfice** to sell sth at a profit (**b**) *(avantage)* benefit

◊ *bénéfice brut* gross profit

◊ *bénéfice consommateur (d'un produit)* consumer benefit

◊ *bénéfice net* net profit

besoin *nm (du consommateur)* need; **notre produit répond au besoin fondamental du consommateur** our product meets the consumer's basic need

bien *nm* biens goods; **biens et services** goods and services

◊ *bien de consommation* consumer product, consumer good

◊ *bien de consommation durable* consumer durable

◊ *biens durables* consumer durables, durable goods

bilan commercial *nm* market report

blister *nm* blister pack

bon *nm (papier)* voucher, coupon

◊ *bon d'achat* discount voucher *(for future purchases)*

◊ *bon de commande* order form, purchase order

◊ *bon à délivrer* freight release

◊ *bon d'expédition* dispatch note, consignment note

◊ *bon de garantie* guarantee, guarantee slip

◊ *bon de livraison* delivery note

◊ *bon de réduction* money-off coupon *or* voucher

◊ *bon de remboursement* money-off coupon *or* voucher

> En janvier, le cercle Gaultier proposera aux consommateurs de recevoir des E mail sur les produits qui les intéressent, des réductions sous forme de **bons d'achat** d'une valeur de 10% de ce que le client a déjà acheté à compter de 5 000F.

bonus *nm* bonus

◊ *bonus produit* product bonus

bordereau *nm* note, slip; *(de marchandises)* invoice, account

◊ *bordereau d'achat* purchase note

◊ *bordereau de débit* debit note

◊ *bordereau d'envoi* dispatch note, consignment note

◊ *bordereau d'expédition* dispatch note, consignment note

◊ *bordereau de livraison* delivery note

◊ *bordereau (des) prix* price list

bouche à oreille *nm* word-of-mouth advertising

boutique *nf* shop, store

◊ *boutique franchisée* franchise outlet

◊ *boutique hors taxe* duty-free shop

brainstorming *nm (activité)* brainstorming; *(séance)* brainstorming session

brief *nm* brief

briefing *nm* briefing

brocante *nf* *(commerce)* second-hand trade; *(magasin)* second-hand shop

brocanteur, -euse *nm,f* second-hand dealer

brochure *nf* brochure

◊ *brochure publicitaire* publicity brochure

brut, -e *adj (bénéfice, marge, valeur)* gross

budget *nm* **(a)** *(plan financier)* budget **(b)** *(dans la publicité, dans le marketing)* account; **l'agence s'est assuré le budget Brook** the agency has secured the Brook account

◊ *budget commercial* sales budget

◊ *budget marketing* marketing budget

◊ *budget promotionnelle* promotion *or* publicity budget

◊ *budget publicitaire, budget de publicité* advertising budget, publicity budget

◊ *budget de trésorerie* cash budget

◊ *budget des ventes* sales budget

> «
>
> L'enseigne de réparation automobile Midas a confié ses 40 millions de francs de **budget publicitaire** à l'agence CLM/BBDO, après compétition contre Hémisphère droit, FCB et Faure Vadon, qui était l'agence de Midas depuis environ 20 ans.
>
> »

budgétisation *nf* budgeting

budgétiser *vt* to include in the budget, to budget for

bulletin *nm* *(communiqué)* bulletin; *(d'entreprise)* newsletter; *(formulaire)* form

◊ *bulletin d'expédition* dispatch note, consignment note

◊ *bulletin de garantie* guarantee (certificate)

◊ *bulletin de vente* sales note

bureau *nm* **(a)** *(agence)* office **(b)** *(service)* department

◊ *bureau d'achat* purchase department

◊ *bureau d'expédition* forwarding office, shipping office

◊ *bureau d'exportation* export office

◊ *bureau de publicité* advertising agency

◊ *Bureau de vérification de la publicité* = French advertising standards authority, *Br* ≃ ASA

BVP *nm* *(abrév* **Bureau de vérification de la publicité***)* = French advertising standards authority, *Br* ≃ ASA

CA nm (abrév **chiffre d'affaires**) turnover

cabinet d'études nm market research company

cachet de fabrique nm maker's trademark

caddie® nm Ordinat (pour achats en ligne) Br shopping basket, Am shopping cart

cadeau nm free gift
◊ **cadeau gratuit, cadeau publicitaire** free gift

cadre nm (dans une entreprise) executive, manager; **les cadres** the managerial staff, the management
◊ **cadre commercial** sales executive
◊ **cadre d'entreprise** company executive, company manager

CAF adj (abrév **coût, assurance, fret**) CIF

cahier des charges nm (d'une vente) specifications

CAHT nm (abrév **chiffre d'affaires hors taxe**) pre-tax turnover

caisse nf (dans un magasin) cash desk; (dans un supermarché) check-out; **tenir la caisse** to be in charge of the cash; **passer à la caisse** to go to the cash desk; (dans un supermarché) to go through the check-out
◊ **caisse comptable** cash register, till
◊ **caisse enregistreuse** cash register, till

caissier, -ère nm,f (dans un magasin) cashier; (dans un supermarché) check-out operator

calendrier nm schedule
◊ **calendrier de campagne** media schedule

camembert nm Fam pie chart

campagne nf campaign; **lancer une campagne** to launch a campaign
◊ **campagne d'affichage** poster campaign
◊ **campagne commerciale** marketing campaign

⋄ *campagne de dénigrement* countermarketing campaign

⋄ *campagne d'image de marque* branding campaign

⋄ *campagne intensive* saturation campaign

⋄ *campagne de presse* press campaign

⋄ *campagne de promotion* promotion campaign, promotional campaign

⋄ *campagne publicitaire, campagne de publicité* advertising campaign, publicity campaign

⋄ *campagne de publicité directe* direct mail campaign

⋄ *campagne de saturation* saturation campaign

⋄ *campagne télévisuelle* television campaign

⋄ *campagne de vente* sales drive

> **"**
>
> Aux heureux élus, l'État offre les services des meilleures firmes de marketing, et paie des **campagnes de promotion** dans les médias nationaux.
>
> **"**

canal *nm* channel

⋄ *canal de communication* communications channel

⋄ *canal de communication commerciale* marketing communications channel

⋄ *canal de distribution* distribution channel, channel of distribution

cannibaliser *vt (produit)* to cannibalize

cannibalisme *nm (d'un produit)* cannibalization

capacité *nf (possibilité)* capacity

⋄ *Écon capacité d'achat* purchasing power

⋄ *capacité linéaire* shelf space

⋄ *capacité de production* production capacity

capital-marque *nm* brand equity; **le succès de notre produit s'explique par la valeur de son capital-marque** the success of our product is down to the value of its brand equity

captif, -ive *adj (marché, audience, clientèle)* captive

caractéristique *nf (d'un produit)* characteristic, feature

⋄ *caractéristiques techniques* specifications

carte *nf (document)* card

⋄ *carte de crédit* credit card

⋄ *carte de débit* debit card

⋄ *carte d'échantillons* sample card, showcard

⋄ *carte de fidélité* loyalty card

⋄ *carte à mémoire* smart card

⋄ *carte de paiement* debit card

⋄ *carte perceptuelle* perceptual map

⋄ *carte de positionnement* positioning map

⋄ *carte de presse* press card

⋄ *carte de publicité* mailing card

⋄ *carte de publicité directe* self-mailer

⋄ *carte à puce* smart card

⋄ *carte de réduction* discount card

Canaux de distribution

Channels of distribution

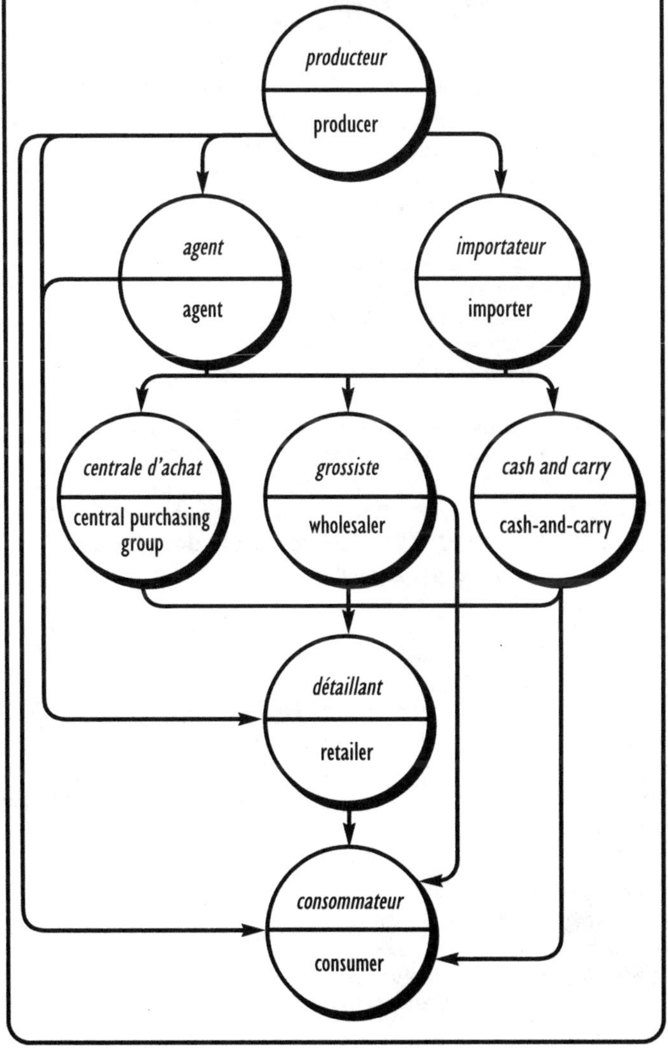

producteur / producer

agent / agent

importateur / importer

centrale d'achat / central purchasing group

grossiste / wholesaler

cash and carry / cash-and-carry

détaillant / retailer

consommateur / consumer

◇ *carte de représentant* = sales representative's official identity card

◇ *carte T* reply-paid card

carte-réponse *nf* reply card

cash and carry 1 *adj* cash-and-carry

  2 *nm* cash-and-carry (store)

catalogue *nm* catalogue; **acheter qch sur catalogue** to buy sth from a catalogue

◇ *catalogue d'échantillons* sample book

◇ *Ordinat* *catalogue électronique* electronic catalogue

◇ *Ordinat* *catalogue en ligne* on-line catalogue

◇ *catalogue illustré* illustrated catalogue

◇ *catalogue des prix* price list

◇ *catalogue de vente par correspondance* mail-order catalogue

> **"**
>
> En juillet 1997, le **catalogue électronique** de La Redoute ne comptait que 600 connexions par jour. Depuis le début de l'année, ils sont plus de 1 300 à se brancher quotidiennement sur le site.
>
> **"**

cataloguer *vt* (*produits*) to catalogue

catégorie *nf* category

◇ *catégorie de produits* product category

◇ *catégorie socio-professionnelle* socio-professional group

CCI *nf* (a) (*abrév* **Chambre de commerce et d'industrie**) Chamber of Commerce and Industry (b) (*abrév* **Chambre de commerce internationale**) ICC

CEN *nm* (*abrév* **Comité européen de normalisation**) European Standards Commission

centrale d'achat(s) *nf* central purchasing office; (*au sein d'une entreprise*) central purchasing department

centre *nm* (*organisme, lieu*) centre

◇ *centre commercial* *Br* shopping centre, *Am* shopping mall

certificat *nm* certificate

◇ *certificat de garantie* guarantee (certificate), warranty

◇ *certificat d'origine* certificate of origin

◇ *certificat de qualité* certificate of quality

cession de licence *nf* licensing

◇ *cession de licence de marque* corporate licensing

◇ *cession de licence de nom* name licensing

chaîne *nf* (*de magasins, de restaurants*) chain

◇ *chaîne de détail* retail chain

◇ *chaîne de valeur* value chain

◇ *chaîne volontaire* voluntary chain

◇ *chaîne volontaire de détaillants* voluntary retailer chain

challengeur *nm* (*market*) challenger

chambre *nf* (*organisation*)

◇ *Chambre de commerce*

Catégories socio-professionnelles
French social classification system

Catégorie Social Grade	Profession du chef de famille Chief income earner's occupation
1	*Agriculteurs exploitants* Farmers
2	*Artisans, commerçants et chefs d'entreprise* Self-employed craftsmen, traders and company managers
3	*Cadres et professions intellectuelles supérieures* Higher managerial and professional
4	*Professions intermédiaires* Intermediate professional
5	*Employés et personnel de service* Ancillary staff
6	*Ouvriers qualifiés* Skilled manual workers
7	*Manœuvres et ouvriers spécialisés* Semi-skilled and unskilled manual workers
8	*Personnes sans activité professionnelle* Unemployed

Chamber of Commerce

◇ **Chambre de commerce et d'industrie** Chamber of Commerce and Industry

◇ **Chambre de commerce internationale** International Chamber of Commerce

champ concurrentiel nm competitive scope

changement de marque nm brand switching

chargé nm

◇ **chargé de budget** account executive

◇ **chargé de clientèle** account manager

◇ **chargé de comptes** account executive

◇ **chargé d'étude de marché** market research manager

◇ **chargé de relations clients** customer relations manager

chargement nm (marchandises) consignment, shipment

chef nm (responsable) head

◇ **chef des achats** purchasing manager

◇ **chef de file** (produit) leader

◇ **chef de marque** brand manager

◇ **chef de produit** product manager

◇ **chef de (la) publicité** publicity manager

◇ **chef de rayon** (d'un magasin) department manager, floor manager

◇ **chef de service** department manager

◇ **chef des ventes** sales manager

chèque-cadeau nm gift token, gift voucher

chiffre nm (total) amount, total; **le budget marketing atteint un chiffre de deux millions de francs** the marketing budget has reached a figure of two million francs

◇ **chiffre d'affaires** turnover

◇ **chiffre d'affaires global** total sales

◇ **chiffre d'affaires prévisionnel** projected turnover, projected sales revenue

◇ **chiffre de vente** sales figures; **ils ont augmenté leur chiffre de vente** they have increased their sales

choix nm (a) (sélection) choice, selection; **à choix multiples** (question, questionnaire, enquête) multiple-choice (b) (qualité) **de choix** choice, selected; **de premier choix** top-quality; **de second choix** second grade

◇ **choix du marché** market choice

ciblage nm targeting

◇ **ciblage stratégique** strategic targeting

cible nf target

◇ **cible commerciale** marketing target

◇ **cible de communication** promotional target

◇ **cible marketing** marketing target

◇ **cible média** media target

◇ **cible publicitaire** advertising target

cibler vt to target; **notre campagne publicitaire cible en priorité les jeunes** our advertising campaign is targeted principally at young people

> Il est complété par un questionnaire sur les habitudes de consommation des nouveaux emménagés, qui va permettre de constituer une BBD qualifiée et, ainsi, de mieux **cibler** les offres commerciales.

circuit *nm* channel

◊ *circuit commercial* commercial channel

◊ *circuit de commercialisation* marketing channel

◊ *circuit de distribution* distribution network

◊ *circuits de vente* commercial channels

clause d'exclusivité *nf* exclusivity clause

client, -e *nm,f* client, customer; *(dans la publicité)* account; **c'est un bon client** he's a good customer

◊ *client actuel* existing customer

◊ *client éventuel* prospective customer, prospect

◊ *client habitué* regular customer

◊ *client imprévu* chance customer

◊ *client mystère* mystery shopper

◊ *client de passage* passing customer

◊ *client potentiel* potential customer, prospect

◊ *client de référence* reference customer

◊ *client régulier* regular customer

clientèle *nf (clients)* customers, clientele; *(fait d'acheter)* custom; **attirer la clientèle** to attract custom; **avoir une grosse clientèle** to have a large clientele *or* customer base; **accorder sa clientèle à qn** to give sb one's custom

◊ *clientèle de passage* passing trade

climat économique *nm* economic climate

club de gros *nm* warehouse club

CNC *nm (abrév* **Comité national de la consommation***)* = French consumer protection organization

co-branding *nm* co-branding

code-barre *nm* bar code

code postal *nm Br* postcode, *Am* zip code

cœur de cible *nm* core market, core audience

> … Avec ce reformatage, la station s'inscrit pleinement dans le pôle radio de la CLT, en totale complémentarité commerciale avec RTL2, également dirigée par Axel Duroux dont le **cœur de cible** est les 25-34 ans.

colis *nm* parcel, package

◊ *colis contre remboursement* *Br* cash on delivery parcel, *Am* collect on delivery parcel

collecte *nf*

◊ *collecte de données, collecte d'informations* data collection; **la collecte d'informations est une des phases fondamentales des études de marché** data collection is one of the basic stages of market research

comestibles *nmpl* foodstuffs, food products

comité *nm* committee

◊ *Comité européen de normalisation* European Standards Commission

commande *nf (de produit)* order; **faire** *ou* **passer une commande (à qn/de qch)** to put in *or* place an order (with sb/for sth); **exécuter/livrer une commande** to fill/deliver an order; **fait sur commande** made to order; **payable à la commande** payment with order, cash with order; **conformément à votre commande** as per (your) order

◊ *commande d'essai* trial order

◊ *commande export, commande pour l'exportation* export order

◊ *commande ferme* firm order

◊ *Ordinat* **commande par ordinateur** teleorder

◊ *commande par quantité* bulk order

◊ *commande renouvelée* repeat order

◊ *commande téléphonique, commande par téléphone* telephone order

commander *vt (marchandises)* to order; **commander qch chez qn** to order sth from sb; **commander qch par téléphone** to order sth by telephone; **commander qch par ordinateur** to teleorder sth

commanditaire *nm (d'un tournoi, d'un spectacle)* sponsor

commanditer *vt (tournoi, spectacle)* to sponsor

commerçant, -e *nm,f* trader; *(qui tient un magasin)* shopkeeper

◊ *commerçant en détail* retailer

◊ *commerçant en gros* wholesaler

commerce *nm* **(a)** *(activité, secteur)* commerce, trade; **être dans le commerce, faire du commerce** to be in trade, to run a business; **faire du commerce avec qn** to do business with sb; **faire le commerce de qch** to trade in sth **(b)** *(circuit de distribution)* market; **on ne trouve pas encore ce produit dans le commerce** this item is not yet available on the market; **cela ne se trouve plus dans le commerce** it's gone off the market **(c)** *(magasin)* shop, store

◊ *commerce de demi-gros* cash-and-carry

◊ *commerce de détail* retail trade

◊ *Ordinat* **commerce élec-**

tronique e-commerce

◇ *commerce d'exportation* export trade

◇ *commerce de gros* wholesale trade

◇ *commerce d'importation* import trade

◇ *commerce intérieur* domestic trade, home trade

◇ *commerce intermédiaire* middleman's business

commercer *vi* to trade, to deal (**avec** with)

commercial, -e 1 *adj (activité, attaché)* commercial; *(délégué, direction, service)* sales 2 *nm,f (personne)* salesman, *f* saleswoman

commercialement *adv* commercially

commercialisable *adj* marketable

commercialisation *nf* marketing

commercialiser *vt* to market; **le produit sera commercialisé en janvier** the product will be coming onto the market in January

❝

La branche internationale du groupe Télé Images a créé, en septembre, un département chargé de **commercialiser** la banque d'images constituée des rushes non exploités des documentaires animaliers produits par XL Production et Télé Images Nature.

❞

commis *nm (dans un magasin)* *Br* sales assistant, *Am* sales clerk

commission *nf* (a) *(comité)* commission, committee (b) *(pourcentage)* commission, percentage; **3% de commission** 3% commission; **il reçoit** *ou* **touche une commission de 5% sur chaque vente** he gets a commission of 5% on each sale; **être payé à la commission** to be paid on a commission basis

◇ *commission de gestion* agency fee

◇ *commission de normalisation* standards commission

◇ *commission de vente* sales commission

commissionnaire *nm (commission)* agent, broker

◇ *commissionnaire d'achat* buyer

◇ *commissionnaire expéditeur* forwarding agent, carrier

◇ *commissionnaire à l'export, commissionnaire exportateur* export agent

◇ *commissionnaire à l'import, commissionnaire importateur* import agent

◇ *commissionnaire de transport* forwarding agent, carrier

communication *nf (publicité)* promotion

◇ *communication événementielle* event promotion

◇ *communication institutionnelle* corporate promotion

◇ *communication sur le lieu de vente* point-of-sale promotion

◇ *communication produit* product promotion

"
La marque X de parfums pour femmes a décidé de développer une **communication événementielle** autour de la fête des mères (30 mai 1999). Pour répondre à cette problématique marketing spécifique, elle entend mettre en œuvre une opération de parrainage TV.
"

communiqué de presse *nm* press release

comparaison par paire *nf* paired comparison

compétitif, -ive *adj (société, prix)* competitive; **leurs produits sont très compétitifs** *ou* **sont à des prix très compétitifs** their products are very competitively priced

compétitivité *nf (de société, de prix)* competitiveness

comportement *nm* behaviour

◇ *comportement d'achat* buying behaviour, purchasing behaviour

◇ *comportement d'achat habituel* habitual buying *or* purchasing behaviour

◇ *comportement de l'acheteur* buyer behaviour, purchaser behaviour

◇ *comportement du consommateur* consumer behaviour

◇ *comportement post-achat* post-purchase behaviour

"
Le **comportement** de plus en plus capricieux des consommateurs et la raréfaction des grands projets immobiliers conduisent les gestionnaires des centres commerciaux à multiplier les études clientèle.
"

comptant 1 *adv* **payer comptant** to pay (in) cash; **payer cent francs comptant** to pay a hundred francs in cash; **acheter/vendre qch comptant** to buy/sell sth for cash

2 *nm* cash; **acheter/vendre qch au comptant** to buy/sell sth for cash; **payable au comptant** *Br* cash *or Am* collect on delivery; **comptant contre documents** cash against documents

compte *nm (en comptabilité, chez un commerçant)* account; **avoir un compte chez qn** to have an account with sb; **(se faire) ouvrir un compte chez qn** to open an account with sb; **mettre** *ou* **inscrire qch sur le compte de qn** to enter sth to sb's account; **mettez-le** *ou* **inscrivez-le à mon compte** charge it to my account; **régler un compte** to settle an account; **pour règlement de tout compte** *(sur facture)* in full settlement

◇ *compte d'abonnement* budget account

◊ *compte agence* agency account

◊ *compte client* customer account

◊ *compte crédit* budget account

◊ *compte d'exploitation* profit and loss form, P&L

◊ *compte permanent* *Br* credit account, *Am* charge account

◊ *compte de pertes et profits* profit and loss account

compte-clé *nm* key account

compte-rendu *nm* report

comptoir de vente *nm* sales counter

concentration *nf Écon* integration

◊ *concentration horizontale* horizontal integration

◊ *concentration verticale* vertical integration

concept *nm* concept

◊ *concept de marketing* marketing concept

◊ *concept de marque* brand concept

◊ *concept publicitaire* advertising concept

concepteur, -trice *nm,f* designer

◊ *concepteur rédacteur* copywriter

conception *nf (d'un produit)* design; **un produit de conception française** a French-designed product

◊ *conception du produit* product design

concession *nf* concession

◊ *concession exclusive* tied outlet

concessionnaire *nmf* agent, dealer; *(de licence)* licensee; *(de contrat de franchisage)* franchisee

◊ *concessionnaire agréé* approved dealer, authorized dealer

◊ *concessionnaire exclusif* sole agent, sole dealer

◊ *concessionnaire export* export agent

concevoir *vt (produit)* to design

concurrence *nf Écon (concept)* competition; **la concurrence** *(les entreprises concurrentes)* the competition; **faire (de la) concurrence à qn/qch** to compete with sb/sth; **être en concurrence avec qn** to be in competition with sb; **entrer en concurrence avec qn** to compete with sb; **nos prix défient toute concurrence** our prices are unbeatable

◊ *concurrence déloyale* unfair competition

◊ *concurrence directe* direct competition

◊ *concurrence parfaite* perfect competition

◊ *concurrence pure* pure competition

concurrencer *vt* to compete with; **leur nouvelle gamme ne peut concurrencer la nôtre** their new line can't compete with ours; **ils nous concurrencent dangereusement** they're very dangerous competitors

concurrent, -e **1** *adj (sociétés,*

produits) competing, rival
2 *nm,f* competitor, rival

◇ **concurrent principal** major competitor

◇ **concurrent tardif** late entrant

concurrentiel, -elle *adj* competitive; **ces marchandises sont vendues à des prix concurrentiels** these goods are competitively priced

condition *nf* (a) *(stipulation)* condition, stipulation; **sans condition** *(offre)* unconditional; **acheter des marchandises sous condition** to buy goods on sale or return; **envoyer des marchandises à condition** to send goods on approval; **conditions** *(d'une vente, d'un accord)* terms
(b) *(état)* condition; **les marchandises nous sont parvenues en bonne condition** the goods arrived in good condition

◇ **conditions de livraison** terms of delivery

◇ **conditions du marché** market conditions

◇ **conditions de paiement** terms (of payment)

conditionné, -e *adj (emballé)* prepacked, prepackaged

conditionnement *nm (action, emballage)* packaging

conditionner *vt (emballer)* to package

conférence de presse *nf* press conference

conforme *adj* **conforme à la demande** as per order; **conforme à la description** as represented

conjoncture *nf Écon* **conjoncture (économique)** economic situation, economic circumstances; **on assiste à une dégradation de la conjoncture économique** the economic situation is deteriorating

connaissance de la marque *nf* brand familiarity

conquérir *vt (marché, part de marché)* to conquer; **l'entreprise a réussi à conquérir de nouvelles parts de marché en dépit de la récession** the company has managed to conquer new market shares despite the recession

conquête *nf (d'un marché, d'une part de marché)* conquest; **la conquête de nouveaux marchés en Asie est une des priorités de l'entreprise** conquering new Asian markets is one of the company's priorities

conseil *nm (personne)* consultant

◇ **conseil en communication** media consultant, PR consultant

◇ **conseil en marketing** marketing consultant

◇ **conseil en promotion, conseil en publicité** advertising consultant

conseiller, -ère *nm,f (spécialiste)* adviser, consultant

◇ **conseiller de clientèle** consumer adviser

◇ **conseiller commercial** marketing consultant, sales consultant

◇ *conseiller en marketing* marketing consultant

consignataire *nmf* consignee

consignateur, -trice *nm,f* consigner, consignor

consignation *nf (de marchandises)* consignment; **en consignation** on consignment; **envoyer qch à qn en consignation** to consign sth to sb, to send sth to sb on consignment

consolidation de ligne *nf* line filling

consommateur, -trice *nm,f* consumer

◇ *consommateur cible* target consumer

◇ *consommateur final* end-user

consommation *nf* consumption

◇ *consommation intérieure* home consumption

◇ *consommation de masse* mass consumption

◇ *consommation des ménages* household consumption

◇ *consommation par tête* per capita consumption

consommatique *nf* consumer research

consommatisme *nm* consumerism

consommer *vt* to consume

consomptible *adj* consumable

consumérisme *nm* consumerism

contrat *nm (accord)* contract, agreement

◇ *contrat d'agence* agency contract

◇ *contrat de concession* licence agreement

◇ *contrat de location-vente* hire purchase agreement, *Am* installment plan agreement

◇ *contrat de représentation exclusive* sole agency contract

◇ *contrat de sponsoring* sponsorship deal

◇ *contrat de vente* bill of sale, sales contract

contrôle *nm (des marchandises)* inspection; *(d'un magasin)* audit

◇ *contrôle continu* monitoring

◇ *contrôle d'efficacité du marketing* marketing efficiency study

◇ *contrôles à l'importation* import controls

◇ *contrôle monopolistique* monopoly control

◇ *contrôle des points de vente* store audit

◇ *contrôle des prix* price control

◇ *contrôle de (la) qualité* quality control

◇ *contrôle de la qualité totale* total quality control

◇ *contrôle par sondage(s)* random check

◇ *contrôle des stocks* *Br* stock control, *Am* inventory control

contrôler *vt (marchandises)* to inspect; *(magasin)* to audit; *(qualité)* to control

co-opérative *nf* co-operative

copy stratégie *nf* copy strategy

◇ *copy stratégie créative* creative copy strategy

couple produit/marché *nm* product/market pair

coupon *nm* coupon, voucher

couponing *nm* couponing

couponnage *nm* couponing

coupon-prime *nm* gift voucher, gift token

coupon-réponse *nm* reply coupon

courbe *nf* curve; *(graphe)* graph

◇ *courbe des coûts* cost curve

◇ *courbe de croissance* growth curve

◇ *courbe du cycle de vie (d'un produit)* lifecycle curve

◇ *courbe de la demande* demand curve

◇ *courbe d'expérience* experience curve

◇ *courbe de l'offre* supply curve

◇ *courbe des prix* price curve

◇ *courbe des ventes* sales chart

cours du change *nm* exchange rate

courses *nfpl* shopping; **faire ses/les courses** to do one's/the shopping

courtage *nm (profession)* brokerage; *(commission)* brokerage, commission; **être vendu par courtage** to be sold on commission; **faire le courtage** to be a broker

courtier, -ère *nm,f* broker

coût *nm* cost; **coût et fret** cost and freight; **coût par mille** cost per thousand

◇ *coût d'achat* purchase cost

◇ *coût ciblé* target cost

◇ *coût de distribution* distribution cost

◇ *coût de l'élaboration du produit* product development cost

◇ *coûts hors-média* below-the-line costs

◇ *coût de production* production cost

◇ *coûts de promotion* promotional costs

◇ *coût de revient* cost price

◇ *coût unitaire* unit cost

◇ *coût unitaire moyen* average cost per unit

◇ *le coût de la vie* the cost of living

coûter *vi* to cost; **combien ça coûte?** how much does it cost? **cela coûte mille francs** it costs a thousand francs; **coûter cher** to be expensive

couverture *nf* coverage, exposure

◇ *couverture du marché* sales coverage

◇ *couverture médiatique* media coverage, media exposure

> Le logiciel réunit les données d'audience de la télévision, de la radio et de la presse quotidienne nationale et magazine. L'une des tâches du logiciel est de définir le

point maximum de **couverture** atteint par chaque média.

"

CPM nm (abrév **coût par mille**) cost per thousand

crayonné nm rough, rough layout

créancier, -ère nm,f creditor

créatif, -ive nm,f (de publicité) designer, creative

création nf (département) creation, creative

créativité nf creativity

crédit nm (prêt) credit; **acheter/vendre qch à crédit** to buy/ to sell sth on credit or on hire purchase or Am on the installment plan; **faire crédit à qn** to give sb credit; **ouvrir un crédit à qn/chez qn** to open a credit account in sb's name/with sb

◊ **crédit à la consommation, crédit au consommateur** consumer credit

◊ **crédit fournisseur** supplier's credit, trade credit

◊ **crédit gratuit** interest-free credit

créneau nm (market) niche, gap in the market; **exploiter un nouveau créneau** to fill a new gap or niche in the market

◊ **créneau porteur** big gap in the market

critère nm criterion; **quels sont les critères de segmentation les plus importants?** what are the most important criteria for segmentation?

croissance nf growth; **notre entreprise est en pleine croissance** our company is growing rapidly

◊ **croissance démographique** demographic growth, population growth

◊ **croissance économique** economic growth

◊ **croissance du marché** market growth

cycle nm cycle

◊ **cycle commande-livraison-facturation** order-to-remittance cycle

◊ **cycle de commercialisation** trade cycle

◊ **cycle de la distribution** distribution cycle

◊ **cycle de vie** lifecycle

◊ **cycle de vie familial** family lifecycle

◊ **cycle de vie de la marque** brand lifecycle

◊ **cycle de vie du produit** product lifecycle, PLC

Cycle de vie du produit
Product lifecycle

ventes et profit/sales and profit

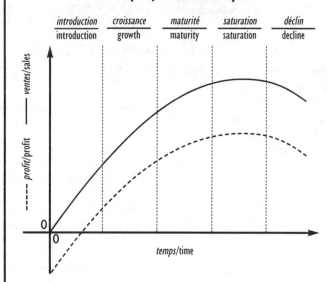

types de consommateur/types of consumer

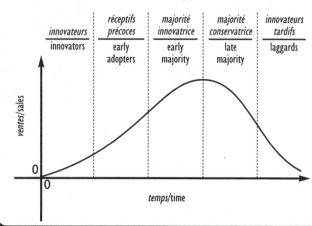

DAS *nm* (*abrév* **domaine d'activité stratégique**) SBU

date *nf* date
◇ *date d'exécution* completion date
◇ *date de facturation* invoice date
◇ *date limite de consommation* best-before date
◇ *date limite de vente* sell-by date
◇ *date de livraison* delivery date
◇ *date de péremption* use-by date

DC *nm Fam* (*abrév* **directeur de la création**) creative director

déballage *nm* (*de marchandises*) unpacking; (*exposition*) display

déballer *vt* (*marchandises*) to unpack; (*exposer*) to display

débiteur, -trice *nm,f* debtor

débordement *nm* (*d'une annonce*) overlap

débouché *nm* (*marché*) outlet, market, opening; **créer de nouveaux débouchés pour un produit** to open up new markets *or* to create new outlets for a product

debriefing *nm* debriefing

décision *nf* (*choix*) decision
◇ *décision d'achat* buying decision, purchasing decision

déclin *nm* decline; **être en déclin** to be on the decline

défense *nf*
◇ *défense du consommateur, défense des consommateurs* consumer protection, consumerism

déficit *nm* deficit, loss; **être en déficit** to be in deficit

degré de solvabilité *nm* credit rating

dégressif *nm* discount
◇ *dégressif sur le volume* bulk discount

dégriffé, -e 1 *adj* = with its designer label removed and reduced in price

2 *nm* = reduced-price designer item with its label removed

délai *nm* time allowed

◇ **délai de commercialisation** (d'un produit) launching period

◇ **délai de crédit** credit period

◇ **délai d'exécution** deadline; (de livraison, de production) lead time

◇ **délai garanti de livraison** guaranteed delivery period

◇ **délai de garantie** guarantee period, term of guarantee

◇ **délai de livraison** delivery time, lead time

◇ **délai de réachat** repurchase period

◇ **délai de réflexion** cooling-off period

◇ **délai de règlement** settlement period

délégué, -e *nm,f* delegate, representative

◇ **délégué commercial** sales representative

demande *nf* Écon demand; **l'offre et la demande** supply and demand; **répondre à la demande** to meet demand; **la demande est en hausse/en baisse** demand is up/down; **la demande croissante de produits biologiques** the increasing demand for organic products

◇ **demande des consommateurs** consumer demand

◇ **demande excédentaire** ove demand

◇ **demande du marché** marke demand

◇ **demande primaire** primar demand

◇ **demande soutenue** fu demand

démarchage *nm* (porte-à porte) door-to-door sellin (prospection) canvassing; **fair du démarchage** to do door-to door selling, to sell door-to-doo

◇ **démarchage à distanc** telephone canvassing

démarche *nf* (initiative) step (approche) approach

◇ **démarche marketing** mar keting approach

démarcher 1 *vt* (client, entre prise) to visit

2 *vi* (faire du porte-à-porte) t do door-to-door selling, to se door-to-door

démarcheur, -euse *nm,f* (a (représentant) door-to-doo salesman, *f* saleswoman (b (prospecteur) canvasser

◇ **démarcheur en publicit** advertisement canvasser

démarketing *nm* demarket ing; **la consommation d'alcoo requiert la mise en œuvr d'une politique de démarketing** alcohol consumption require a policy of demarketing to be implemented

démarque *nf* mark-down

démarquer *vt* to mark down

demi-gros *nm* cash-and-carry

démographie *nf* demography

démographique *adj* demographic

démonstration *nf (d'article)* demonstration; **faire la démonstration de qch** to demonstrate sth

◊ *démonstration sur le lieu de vente* in-store demonstration

denrée *nf* commodity; *(aliment)* foodstuff

◊ *denrées alimentaires* food products, foodstuffs

◊ *denrées de consommation courante* basic consumer goods

◊ *denrées du pays* home produce

◊ *denrées périssables* perishable goods

dépense *nf* expenditure, expense; **dépenses** expenses

◊ Écon *dépenses de consommation* consumer spending

◊ Écon *dépenses des ménages* household expenditure

◊ *dépenses publicitaires, dépenses de la publicité* publicity expenses

dépenser *vt (argent)* to spend; **dépenser de l'argent en qch** to spend money on sth

dépliant *nm* leaflet

◊ *dépliant publicitaire* advertising leaflet

dépositaire *nmf (de produits)* agent

◊ *dépositaire agréé* authorized agent

◊ *dépositaire exclusif* sole agent

dépositionner *vt (produit)* to deposition

dépôt *nm (entrepôt)* depot

◊ *dépôt de distribution* distribution depot

◊ *dépôt d'expédition* shipping depot

◊ *dépôt de marchandises* goods depot, warehouse

DEPS *(abrév* **dernier entré, premier sorti)** LIFO

déréférencement *nm (d'un produit)* delisting

déréférencer *vt (produit)* to delist; **certains produits ont été déréférencés par le distributeur** some products have been delisted by the distributor

dérivé *nm (sous-produit)* by-product

désir *nm (de l'acheteur)* desire

destinataire *nmf (de marchandises)* consignee

détail *nm (dans la vente)* retail; **vendre qch au détail** to sell sth retail

détaillant, -e *nm,f* retailer, shopkeeper

◊ *détaillant indépendant* independent retailer

◊ *détaillant spécialisé* specialist retailer

détailler *vt (marchandises)* to retail, to sell retail

détaxe *nf (suppression)* lifting of tax *or* duty; *(diminution)* reduction of tax *or* duty; **vendus en détaxe** duty-free; **la**

détaxe des marchandises à l'exportation the lifting of duty on exports

détaxé, -e adj (produits, articles) duty-free

détaxer vt (supprimer) to lift the tax or duty on; (diminuer) to reduce the tax or duty on

détermination nf (des prix) fixing, setting

déterminer vt (prix) to fix

dette nf debt; **avoir des dettes** to be in debt

deuxième adj second; **de deuxième choix, de deuxième qualité** (marchandises, articles) inferior

dévalorisation nf (de marchandises) mark-down

dévaloriser 1 vt (marchandises) to mark down
2 **se dévaloriser** vpr (marchandises) to lose value

devancer vt (concurrence) to get ahead of; **sur ce marché, nous ne sommes plus devancés que par les Japonais** now only the Japanese are ahead of us in this market

devant de caisse nm checkout display

devanture nf (a) (vitrine) shop window, store window (b) (façade) shop front, store front (c) (étalage) window display

développement nm (d'un produit, d'une idée) development; **ce produit n'est qu'au stade de son développement** this product is only at the development stage
◇ **développement du marché** market development
◇ **développement des ventes** sales expansion

développer 1 vt (produit, idée) to develop
2 **se développer** vpr (produit) to develop

diagramme nm diagram; (graphique) graph, chart
◇ **diagramme à bâtons** bar chart
◇ **diagramme de circulation** flow chart
◇ **diagramme à secteurs** pie chart

différenciation nf differentiation
◇ **différenciation de ligne** line differentiation
◇ **différenciation du produit** product differentiation

differencié, -e adj (marketing) differentiated

différentiel nm differential
◇ Écon **différentiel d'inflation** inflation differential
◇ **différentiel de prix** price differential
◇ **différentiel sémantique** semantic differential

diffuser vt *(produits)* to distribute; *(publicité, émission)* to broadcast; **leurs produits sont diffusés sur une grande échelle** their products are widely available

diffusion nf *(de produits)* distribution; *(d'une publicité, d'une émission)* broadcast; **ce sont des articles de grande diffusion** they are widely-available products

> 〝
> Au dernier trimestre 1997, les rotations de Petit Cadeau étaient le double de celles réalisées par les autres confiseries de chocolat aux devants de caisse. ... Ces performances nous conduisent donc à étendre la **diffusion** de Petit Cadeau au plan national.
> 〞

dilemme nm *(produit)* problem child

diminuer vi *(profits, ventes, recettes)* to decline, to fall off

directeur, -trice nm,f *(qui fait partie du conseil d'administration)* director; *(d'un magasin, d'un service)* manager

◇ **directeur des achats** purchasing manager

◇ **directeur de la clientèle** customer relations manager

◇ **directeur commercial** sales director/manager

◇ **directeur des comptes-clients** account director

◇ **directeur de la création** creative director

◇ **directeur des exportations** export manager

◇ **directeur de marché** market manager

◇ **directeur du marketing** marketing director/manager

◇ **directeur de marque** brand manager

◇ **directeur de produit** product manager

◇ **directeur de la promotion des ventes** sales promotion manager

◇ **directeur de la publicité** advertising director/manager

◇ **directeur de recherche et développement** research and development director/manager

◇ **directeur de recherche marketing** marketing research director/manager

◇ **directeur des relations publiques** public relations director/manager

◇ **directeur des ventes** sales director/manager

◇ **directeur de la vente-marketing** sales and marketing director/manager

direction nf **(a)** *(d'une entreprise, d'un magasin, d'un service)* management **(b)** *(service)* department

◇ **direction commerciale** sales management

◇ **direction export** export management

◇ **direction marketing** marketing department

◇ *direction des ventes* sales management

discount *nm* discount; **un discount de 20%** a 20% discount

discounter¹ *nm* discounter

discounter² *vt & vi* to sell at a discount

disponibilités du stock *nfpl* items available in stock

disponible 1 *adj (article)* available; **ces articles sont disponibles en magasin** these items can be supplied from stock
2 *nm* **le disponible** *(articles)* items available in stock

dissonance cognitive *nf (de l'acheteur)* cognitive dissonance

distorsion sélective *nf* selective distortion

distribuer *vt (produits, marchandises)* to distribute

distributeur, -trice *nm,f (vendeur)* distributor, dealer

◇ *distributeur agréé* authorized distributor, authorized dealer

◇ *distributeur en gros* wholesaler

distribution *nf (de produits, de mailings)* distribution; **la grande distribution** mass distribution

◇ *distribution à domicile* door drop

◇ *distribution d'échantillons* sampling

◇ *distribution exclusive* exclusive distribution

◇ *distribution à flux tendus* just-in-time distribution

◇ *distribution en gros* wholesale distribution

◇ *distribution juste à temps* just-in-time distribution

◇ *distribution numérique* numerical distribution

◇ *distribution physique* physical distribution

◇ *distribution sélective* selective distribution

◇ *distribution valeur* weighted distribution

diversification *nf* diversification

◇ *diversification des produits* product diversification

"

… IGS est un exemple de **diversification** réussie. … Elle développe aujourd'hui plusieurs métiers, de la gravure à la composition programmée, le traitement de l'image, la création de packaging, la coloration numérique et le multimédia.

"

diversifier 1 *vt* to diversify
2 se diversifier *vpr (entreprise)* to diversify; *(produits)* to become diversified

DLC *nf (abrév **date limite de consommation**)* best-before date

DN *nf (abrév **distribution numérique**)* numerical distribution

documentation *nf (publicités)* literature, documentation

document de publicité directe nm direct mail

domaine nm
◇ **domaine d'activité stratégique** strategic business unit
◇ **domaine concurrentiel** competitive scope

donnée nf piece of data; **données** data
◇ **données démographiques** demographic data
◇ **données géodémographiques** geodemographic data
◇ **données primaires** primary data
◇ **données secondaires** secondary data
◇ **données socio-démographiques** sociodemographic data
◇ **données de style de vie** lifestyle data

doper vt (exportations, ventes) to boost; **la dépréciation de la lire a dopé les ventes à l'étranger** the depreciation in the value of the lira has boosted export sales

dossier nm file
◇ **dossier client** client file
◇ **dossier de presse** press pack or kit

droit nm (a) (prérogative) right (b) (en argent) fee; (imposition) duty; (taxe) tax; **droits à la charge du vendeur/de** l'acheteur duty to be paid by the seller/purchaser
◇ **droits d'achat** purchasing rights
◇ **droit de courtage** brokerage (fee)
◇ **droits de diffusion, droits de distribution** distribution rights
◇ **droit d'entrée** import duty
◇ **droits étrangers** foreign rights
◇ **droits exclusifs** sole rights, exclusive rights
◇ **droits d'exclusivité** exclusive rights
◇ **droit d'exportation** export duty
◇ **droits de fabrication** manufacturing rights
◇ **droit d'importation** import duty
◇ **droit de sortie** export duty
◇ **droits statutaires** statutory rights
◇ **droits de vente exclusifs** exclusive selling rights

duopole nm duopoly

duplication nf duplication
◇ **duplication d'audience** audience duplication

durée (utile) de vie nf (d'un produit) life expectancy, shelf life

DV nf (abrév **distribution valeur**) weighted distribution

écart *nm* gap
◇ *écart de performance* gap level
◇ *écart de prix* price differential
◇ *écart type* standard deviation

e-cash *nm Ordinat* e-cash

échange standard *nm (de produit)* replacement

échantillon *nm* (**a**) *(pour un sondage)* sample (**b**) *(d'un produit)* sample; **pareil** *ou* **conforme à l'échantillon** up to sample; **envoyer qch à titre d'échantillon** to send sth as a sample
◇ *échantillon aléatoire* random sample
◇ *échantillon aréolaire* cluster sample
◇ *échantillon de convenance* convenience sample
◇ *échantillon discrétionnaire* judgement sample
◇ *échantillon empirique* purposive sample, non-random sample
◇ *échantillon gratuit* free sample
◇ *échantillon modèle* standard sample

◇ *échantillon non probabiliste* non-probability sample
◇ *échantillon normal* average sample
◇ *échantillon probabiliste* probability sample
◇ *échantillon promotionnel* promotional sample
◇ *échantillon publicitaire* free sample
◇ *échantillon par quotas* quota sample
◇ *échantillon représentatif* true sample
◇ *échantillon stratifié* stratified sample
◇ *échantillon témoin* check sample
◇ *échantillon type* representative sample

échantillonnage *nm* (**a**) *(action)* sampling; *(groupe de personnes)* sample; **l'échantillonnage se fait sur un produit sur cent** one product in a hundred is sampled *or* tested (**b**) *(série d'échantillons)* range of samples
◇ *échantillonnage aléatoire* random sampling
◇ *échantillonnage aréolaire* cluster sampling

◇ *échantillonnage empirique* purposive sampling, non-random sampling

◇ *échantillonnage non probabiliste* non-probability sampling

◇ *échantillonnage probabiliste* probability sampling

◇ *échantillonnage par quotas* quota sampling

◇ *échantillonnage stratifié* stratified sampling

◇ *échantillonnage par zone* area sampling

échantillonner *vt* (**a**) *(population)* to sample (**b**) *(préparer des échantillons de)* to prepare samples of (**c**) *(comparer)* to verify *or* to check by the samples

échantillonneur, -euse *nm,f (personne)* sampler

échelle *nf (mesure)* scale

◇ *échelle d'attitudes* attitude scale

◇ *échelle de classement* rating scale

◇ *échelle d'importance* scale of importance

◇ *échelle des prix* price scale

échos *nmpl (des clients, des consommateurs)* feedback

économie *nf (système)* economy

◇ *économies d'échelle* economies of scale

◇ *économie parallèle, économie souterraine* black economy

économique *adj* (**a**) *(relatif à l'économie)* economic (**b**) *(avantageux)* economical

économiquement *adv* (**a**) *(du point de vue de l'économie)* economically (**b**) *(à moindre frais)* inexpensively; **économiquement viable** economically viable

écoulement *nm (de marchandises, d'un surplus, des stocks)* sale; **d'écoulement facile/difficile** fast-/slow-moving

écouler **1** *vt (marchandises, surplus, stocks)* to sell (off); **écouler qch à bas prix** to sell sth off cheaply; **écouler qch à perte** to sell sth at a loss; **écouler entièrement son stock** to clear one's stock; **facile/difficile à écouler** easy/difficult to sell

2 s'écouler *vpr (marchandises, surplus, stocks)* to sell; **notre stock s'écoule rapidement** our stock is selling fast

écran *nm*

◇ *écran publicitaire, écran de publicité, écran de pub* commercial break

> **❝**
>
> C'est un coup dur pour les ménagères de moins de 50 ans. Partant du principe qu'il ne suffit plus aux annonceurs de les atteindre pour émerger dans les **écrans de pub** à la télévision, Universal Média met en place une base de données sur la consommation de médias, l'attention aux médias et les habitudes d'achat.
>
> **❞**

écrémage nm (du marché) skimming

écrémer vt (marché) to skim

effectuer vt (étude de marché) to carry out; (commande) to place

effet nm effect
◇ **effet d'expérience** experience effect
◇ **effet de halo** halo effect

efficace adj (méthode, campagne) effective

efficacité nf (d'une méthode, d'une campagne) effectiveness
◇ **efficacité du coût** cost-effectiveness
◇ **efficacité promotionnelle** promotional effectiveness
◇ **efficacité publicitaire** advertising effectiveness
◇ **efficacité des ventes** sales effectiveness

effondrement nm (des prix, du marché, de la demande) slump (**de** in)

❝

L'effondrement de la demande dans la plupart des grands secteurs impose des restructurations, qui contraignent à licencier.

❞

effondrer s'effondrer vpr (prix, marché, demande) to slump; **le marché s'est effondré** the bottom has fallen out of the market

effort nm effort
◇ **effort de commercialisation** marketing effort

◇ **effort de marketing** marketing effort
◇ **effort de promotion** promotional campaign
◇ **effort publicitaire** advertising campaign

élaboration nf (d'un plan, d'une stratégie) development (d'un budget) drawing up
◇ **élaboration de concept** concept development
◇ **élaboration de produit** product development

élasticité nf (du prix, de la demande) elasticity; **quelle est l'élasticité de la demande par rapport au prix du produit?** how elastic is the demand in relation to the price of the product?

élastique adj (prix, demande) elastic

électronique adj (point de vente) electronic

emballage nm (a) (contenant) packaging; **l'emballage est consigné** there is a deposit on the packaging; **emballage compris** packaging included; **emballage gratuit** packaging free of charge (b) (action) packing, packaging
◇ **emballage factice** dummy pack
◇ **emballage géant** giant-sized pack
◇ **emballage d'origine** original packaging
◇ **emballage perdu** non-returnable packaging
◇ **emballage de présentation, emballage présentoir** display pack

◇ *emballage réutilisable* recyclable packaging

◇ *emballage transparent* blister pack

◇ *emballage sous vide* vacuum pack

emballage-bulle *nm* blister pack

emballer *vt (dans une boîte)* to pack; *(dans du papier)* to wrap up; **emballé sous vide** vacuum-packed

emblème de marque *nm* brand mark

emplacement *nm (site)* site, location; *(dans un journal, à la télé)* space

◇ *emplacement d'affichage* billboard site, *Br* hoarding site

◇ *emplacement isolé* solus position, solus site

◇ *emplacement publicitaire* advertising space

> **"**
>
> Les annonceurs sont aujourd'hui à la recherche d'une efficacité qui dépasse la simple demande d'un coût GRP et d'audiences élevées lorsqu'ils achètent des **emplacements** à la télé.
>
> **"**

encart *nm* insert

◇ *encart publicitaire* advertising insert

encombré, -e *adj (marché)* glutted, flooded

encombrement *nm (de marchandises)* glut, surplus

encombrer *vt (marché)* to glut, to flood; **les logiciels encombrent le marché** there is a glut *or* surplus of software packages on the market

encouragements *nmpl* incentives

◇ *encouragements à l'exportation* export incentives

enquête *nf* survey

◇ *enquête d'attitude* attitude survey

◇ *enquête auprès des consommateurs* consumer survey

◇ *enquête de marché* market survey

◇ *enquête omnibus* omnibus survey

◇ *enquête d'opinion* opinion poll

◇ *enquête pilote* pilot survey

◇ *enquête postale* postal survey

◇ *enquête sur les prix* price survey

◇ *enquête par questionnaire* questionnaire survey

◇ *enquête sociologique* sociological survey

◇ *enquête par sondage* opinion poll, sample survey

◇ *enquête par téléphone, enquête téléphonique* telephone survey

◇ *enquête sur le terrain* field study

enquêté, -e *nm,f* interviewee

enquêter *vi (faire un sondage)* to conduct a survey (**sur** into)

enquêteur, -trice *nm,f* interviewer

enregistrer *vt (commande)* to

enter (up); *(bénéfice)* to show; **les meilleures ventes enregistrées depuis des mois** the best recorded sales for months

enseigne *nf* brand name

> En fait, avec 975 points de vente, les deux premières **enseignes** allemandes (Lidl et Aldi) représentent à elles seules près de la moitié du parc total et pèsent pour 90% dans l'augmentation du nombre de Hard Discount en 1997.

ensemble *nm (groupe)* set

◇ **ensemble de besoins** need set

◇ **ensemble de considérations** consideration set, product choice set

◇ **ensemble évoqué** evoked set

entrée *nf (de marchandises)* import

◇ **entrée en franchise** free import

entrepreneur, -euse *nm,f (de travaux)* contractor

◇ **entrepreneur de roulage, entrepreneur de transport** haulage contractor, carrier

entreprise *nf (firme)* company, business

◇ **entreprise exportatrice** export company

◇ **entreprise innovatrice** innovator, innovating company

◇ **entreprise multinationale** multinational company

◇ **entreprise novatrice** innovator, innovating company

◇ **entreprise de vente par correspondance** mail-order company

entrer *vi (marchandises)* to enter, to be imported; **entrer dans un marché** to enter a market; **les marchandises qui entrent en France sont soumises à des droits de douane** goods entering France are subject to customs duty

entretien *nm* interview

◇ **entretien assisté par ordinateur** computer-assisted interview

◇ **entretien directif** guided interview

◇ **entretien de groupe** group interview

◇ **entretien libre** unstructured interview

◇ **entretien non directif** unguided interview

◇ **entretien non structuré** unstructured interview

◇ **entretien organisé** arranged interview

◇ **entretien en profondeur** depth interview

◇ **entretien spontané** intercept interview

◇ **entretien structuré** structured interview

◇ **entretien par téléphone, entretien téléphonique** telephone interview

enveloppe *nf (budget)* budget; **nous disposons d'une enveloppe de 70 000 francs pour la commercialisation du produit** we have a budget of

70,000 francs to market the product

◊ **enveloppe budgétaire** budget (allocation)

environnement nm (milieu) environment

◊ **environnement d'achat** purchase environment

◊ **environnement commercial** marketing environment

◊ **environnement du marché** market environment

◊ **environnement marketing** marketing environment

envoi nm (a) (action) sending; **faire un envoi tous les mois** to send goods every month (b) (marchandises) consignment (de of); **nous avons bien reçu votre envoi du 10 octobre** we acknowledge receipt of your consignment of 10 October

◊ **envoi exprès** express delivery

◊ **envoi en groupage, envoi groupé** grouped consignment

◊ **envoi en nombre** mass mailing

◊ **envoi contre paiement** cash with order

◊ **envoi contre remboursement** Br cash on delivery, Am collect on delivery

◊ **envoi à titre d'essai** goods sent on approval

envoyer vt to send; (marchandises) to send, to consign

épuisé, -e adj (marchandises) sold out, out of stock; (stocks) exhausted, depleted

épuisement nm (de mar-chandises) selling out; (de stocks) exhaustion, depletion

équation nf equation

◊ **équation de la demande** demand equation

◊ **équation de réponse de marché** sales-response equation

◊ **équation de vente** sales equation

équipe nf team

◊ **équipe commerciale** marketing team

◊ **équipe de création** creative team

◊ **équipe promotionnelle** promotion team

◊ **équipe de vente** sales team

erreur nf error, mistake

◊ **erreur d'échantillonnage** sampling error

escompte nm (de commerce) discount; **accorder** ou **faire un escompte (à qn/sur qch)** to allow or give a discount (to sb/ on sth); **à escompte** at a discount; Can **50% d'escompte sur toute la marchandise** 50% discount on all goods

◊ **escompte sur les achats en gros** bulk discount, quantity discount

◊ **escompte de caisse** cash discount

◊ **escompte commercial** trade discount

◊ **escompte au comptant** cash discount

◊ **escompte professionnel** (au détaillant) trade discount

◊ **escompte d'usage** trade discount

espace *nm*

◇ *espace d'exposition* display area

◇ *espace de PLV* in-store advertising space

◇ *espace publicitaire* advertising space

◇ *espace de vente* sales area

> **"**
>
> Il y a un an, le Printemps de la Mode redéfinissait complètement son **espace de vente** en améliorant la fluidité de la circulation. Ce qui, in fine, a encouragé les vols.
>
> **"**

espèces *nfpl (argent)* cash; **payer en espèces** to pay in cash

espérance de vie *nf (d'un produit)* life expectancy, shelf life

essai *nm (de produit)* trial, test; **à l'essai** on a trial basis; **à titre d'essai** subject to approval; **acheter qch à l'essai** to buy sth on approval; **faire l'essai de qch** to test sth; **essais** *(procédure)* testing

◇ *essais comparatifs* comparative tests

◇ *essai gratuit* free trial

◇ *essai probatoire* feasibility test

◇ *essai de produit* product test

essayer *vt (produit)* to try (out), to test; **essayer une nouvelle marque** to try out a new brand

essor *nm (d'un secteur, de l'économie)* rapid growth; **en plein essor** *(secteur, économie,* booming

◇ *essor économique* economic boom

estimation des besoins *nf* needs assessment

étalage *nm (de marchandises)* display; *(dans une vitrine)* window display; **faire l'étalage** to put goods on display; *(dans une vitrine)* to dress the window(s); **mettre qch à l'étalage** to display sth in the window

◇ *étalage publicitaire* display advertising

étalager *vt* to display, to put on display

étaler *vt (marchandises)* to display

état *nm* **(a)** *(rapport)* form; *(des dépenses)* statement, list; *(des paiements, des marchandises)* list **(b)** *(condition)* state, condition; **en bon/mauvais état** *(marchandises)* in good/bad condition

◇ *état des ventes* statement of sales figures

étiquetage *nm (de marchandises)* labelling

étiqueter *vt (marchandises)* to label

étiquette *nf* label

◇ *étiquette de prix* price ticket, price tag, price label

◇ *étiquette promotionnelle* promotional label

◇ *étiquette de qualité* quality label

étranger, -ère *adj (devises, marché)* foreign

étude *nf* study; *(enquête)* survey; **études** *(activité)* research

◇ *étude ad hoc* ad hoc survey

◇ *étude AIO* AIO research

◇ *étude d'audience* audience study

◇ *étude des besoins* needs study, needs analysis

◇ *étude de cas* case study

◇ *étude client* customer survey

◇ *étude commerciale* marketing study

◇ *étude du comportement* behavioural study

◇ *étude du comportement du consommateur* consumer behaviour study

◇ *étude auprès des consommateurs* consumer survey

◇ *étude des créneaux* gap analysis

◇ *étude documentaire* desk research

◇ *étude de faisabilité* feasibility study

◇ *étude d'impact* impact study

◇ *étude longitudinale* longitudinal study

◇ *étude de marché* market study; **faire une étude de marché** to do market research

◇ *étude de marché standard* omnibus survey

◇ *étude marketing* marketing study

◇ *étude de mémorisation* recall study

◇ *étude de motivation* motivational study

◇ *étude de notoriété* awareness study

◇ *étude préliminaire* preliminary study

◇ *étude de produit* product analysis

◇ *étude prospective du marché* market study

◇ *étude qualitative* qualitative study

◇ *étude quantitative* quantitative study

◇ *étude de satisfaction de la clientèle* customer satisfaction survey

◇ *étude sur le terrain* field study

◇ *études sur les ventes* sales research

> **"**
>
> Soucieux de l'image que se font du centre commercial les consommateurs, il privilégie les **études clients** propres à chaque site. Les informations recueillies s'organisent autour de 4 axes: son environnement, son architecture extérieure et intérieure, sa communication et son offre. ... Ainsi, pas moins de trois vagues d'**études qualitatives** ont été réalisées depuis trois ans concernant le futur centre Val d'Europe qui ouvrira ses portes aux côtés de Disneyland Paris en septembre 2000.
>
> **"**

euro *nm (monnaie)* Euro

évaluation *nf* evaluation, assessment

◇ *évaluation des coûts* cost analysis

◇ *évaluation économique* economic appraisal

◇ *évaluation du marché* market appraisal

◇ *évaluation post-achat* post-purchase evaluation

◇ *évaluation des stocks* stock control

évaluer *vt* to evaluate, to assess; **évaluer les coûts de qch** to cost sth

éventail *nm* (*de produits*) range

◇ *éventail des prix* price range

éventuel, -elle *adj* (*client*) potential, prospective

exclusif, -ive *adj* (*droit, produit, distributeur*) exclusive

exclusivité *nf* (*droit*) sole or exclusive rights (**de** to); **avoir un contrat d'exclusivité** to have an exclusive contract; **nous avons l'exclusivité de la vente de ce produit** we have the (sole) rights for this product

◇ *exclusivité à la marque* brand exclusivity

exécuter *vt* (*commande*) to fill

exempt, -e *adj* **exempt de droits** duty-free

exhiber *vt* (*objet, marchandises*) to exhibit

exonérer *vt* (*marchandises*) to exempt from import duty

expansion *nf* (*du marché*) growth

expédier *vt* (*marchandises*) to dispatch, to ship; **expédier des marchandises par navire** to send goods by sea, to ship goods; **expédier des marchan-**dises par fret aérien to air freight goods

expéditeur, -trice 1 *ad* (*bureau, compagnie, gare*) shipping, dispatching

2 *nm,f* (*de marchandises*) shipper, consigner; (*par ba*teau) shipper

expédition *nf* (**a**) (*envoi*) (*d*marchandises) dispatch, shipment; **expéditions** (*service* dispatch department, shipping department (**b**) (*marchandises* consignment, shipment

◇ *expédition par avion* airfreighting

◇ *expédition par bateau* shipping

◇ *expédition par chemin de fer* sending by rail

◇ *expédition par mer* shipping, shipment

exploration des besoins et des désirs *nf* needs-and-wants exploration

export *nm* export, exportation

exportateur, -trice 1 *adj* (*pays*) exporting; (*secteur*) export; **être exportateur de qch** to export sth

2 *nm,f* exporter

exportation *nf* (*action*) export, exportation; (*produit*) export; **faire de l'exportation** to export; **le montant des exportations a augmenté de 10% cette année** exports have risen by 10% this year; **ce produit marche très fort à l'exportation** this product is doing very well on the export market; **réservé**

à l'exportation reserved for export, for export only

exporter 1 vt (marchandises) to export (**vers** to)

2 **s'exporter** vpr (marchandises) to be exported (**vers** to); **ce genre de produit s'exporte mal** this type of product is not good for exporting

exposant, -e nm,f (dans une foire) exhibitor

exposer vt (produits, marchandises) to display; **exposer des marchandises en vente** to display goods for sale

exposition nf (a) (foire) exhibition, show (b) (de marchandises) display

◇ **exposition commerciale** trade exhibition

◇ **exposition interprofessionnelle** trade exhibition

◇ **exposition sur le lieu de vente** point-of-sale display

◇ **exposition sur le marché** market exposure

◇ **exposition au public** audience exposure

exposition-vente nf display (where the items are for sale)

extension nf expansion, extension

◇ **extension de la gamme** range stretching

◇ **extension de la ligne** line extension, line stretching

◇ **extension de marché** market expansion

◇ **extension de la marque** brand extension

extrapolation nf extrapolation

extrapoler 1 vt to extrapolate 2 vi to extrapolate; **extrapoler à partir de qch** to extrapolate from sth

fabricant, -e *nm,f* manufacturer

fabrication *nf (construction)* manufacture, production; **de fabrication française** made in France, French-made

fabriquer *vt* to manufacture; **fabriqué en France** made in France

facilité *nf (possibilité)* facility
◇ *facilités de crédit* credit facilities
◇ *facilité d'écoulement* saleability
◇ *facilités de paiement* payment facilities, easy terms
◇ *facilité de vente* saleability

facing *nm* shelf facing

facteur *nm (élément)* factor
◇ *facteur clé de succès* key factor
◇ *facteur coût* cost factor
◇ *facteur de demande* demand factor
◇ *facteur économique* economic factor

facturation *nf* invoicing, billing

facture *nf* invoice, bill; **établir** *ou* **faire une facture** to make out an invoice; **régler une facture** to settle an invoice; **conformément à la facture** as per invoice
◇ *facture d'achat* purchase invoice
◇ *facture de consignation* consignment invoice
◇ *facture de vente* sales invoice

facturer *vt (personne)* to invoice, to bill; *(produit, service)* to charge for; **facturer qch à qn** to invoice sb for sth, to bill sb for sth; **ils ne m'ont pas facturé la livraison** they didn't charge me for delivery

faiblesse *nf (d'un concurrent, d'un produit)* weakness

faisabilité *nf (d'un projet)* feasibility

familial, -e *adj (paquet, emballage, format)* family-sized

famille *nf* (a) *(ménage)* household (b) *(de produits)* family, line

fermé, -e *adj (question)* closed-ended, yes/no

fermeture *nf (d'un magasin, d'une entreprise)* closure, closing-down, *Am* closing-out

fiche *nf (formulaire)* form; *(papier)* sheet, slip; **remplir une fiche** to fill in *or* fill out a form

◇ **fiche d'appréciation** customer satisfaction questionnaire

◇ **fiche client** customer record

◇ **fiche fournisseur** supplier file

◇ **fiche d'observations** comment card

◇ **fiche prospect** potential-customer file

◇ **fiche technique** product information sheet

fichier *nm* file

◇ **fichier d'adresses** mailing list

◇ **fichier client** client file

fidèle 1 *adj (client)* loyal; **rester fidèle à un produit** to stick with a product; **fidèle à la marque** brand-loyal

2 *nmf* loyal customer

◇ **fidèle absolu** hard-core loyal

fidélisation *nf* building of customer loyalty

fidéliser *vt* to win the loyalty of; **fidéliser la clientèle** to develop customer loyalty

> 66
>
> Aux petits soins pour un consommateur fuyant comme le savon, les hypers rivalisent dans les promotions, les offres qu'on ne peut pas refuser, les cadeaux qui **fidélisent** l'inconstant client.
>
> 99

fidélité *nf* loyalty

◇ **fidélité absolue** hard-core loyalty

◇ **fidélité du client** customer loyalty

◇ **fidélité du consommateur** consumer loyalty

◇ **fidélité à la marque** brand loyalty

film publicitaire *nm (à la télévision)* commercial; *(au cinéma)* cinema advertisement

fin de série *nf (d'articles)* discontinued line

fixation des prix *nf* pricing

fixer *vt (prix)* to set, to fix

focalisation *nf* targeting

◇ **focalisation stratégique** strategic targeting

focaliser *vt* to target

foire *nf* (trade) fair

foire-échantillon, foire-exposition *nf* trade fair

fonction de demande *nf* demand function

force *nf (d'un produit, d'un concurrent)* strength

◇ **forces, faiblesses, opportunités et menaces** strengths, weaknesses, opportunities and threats, SWOT

◇ *Écon* **forces du marché** market forces

◇ **force de vente** sales force

format *nm (d'une annonce publicitaire)* format

formule *nf (méthode)* option

◇ **formules de crédit** credit options

◇ **formules de paiement** methods of payment, payment options

◊ *formules de rembourse-ment* repayment options

forte remise *nf* deep discount

fourni, -e *adj (approvisionné)* **bien/mal fourni** well-/poorly-stocked

fournir 1 *vt (approvisionner)* to supply; **fournir qch à qn** to supply sb with sth; **ce magasin nous fournit tout le matériel de bureau** this shop supplies us with all our office equipment

2 **se fournir** *vpr* **il se fournit chez nous** he is a customer of ours, he's one of our customers

fournisseur, -euse *nm,f* supplier

◊ *fournisseur exclusif* sole supplier

◊ *fournisseur principal* main supplier

◊ *fournisseur secondaire* secondary supplier

foyer *nm (domicile)* household, household unit

frais *nmpl* expenses, costs; **à grands frais** at great expense

◊ *frais d'achat* purchase costs

◊ *frais d'agence* agency fee

◊ *frais de commercialisation* marketing costs

◊ *frais commerciaux* selling costs

◊ *frais de courtage* brokerage, commission

◊ *frais de distribution* distribution costs

◊ *frais d'envoi* carriage costs

◊ *frais d'expédition* shipping costs, forwarding costs

◊ *frais facturables* chargeable

expenses

◊ *frais de livraison* delivery charges

◊ *frais de port (de mar chandises)* carriage; *(de let tres, de colis)* postage

◊ *frais de portage* carriage

◊ *frais de port et d'emballage* postage and packing

◊ *frais de publicité* advertising costs

◊ *frais de transport* carriage

franc, franche *adj (gratuit)* free; **franc de douane** duty paid; **franc de tout droit** duty free, free of duty; **franc de port** carriage paid, carriage free

franchisage *nm* franchising

franchise *nf* (a) *(exonération)* exemption; **importer** *ou* **faire entrer qch en franchise** to import sth duty-free; **en franchise d'impôt** exempt from tax, tax free (b) *(de commerce)* franchise; **ouvrir un magasin en franchise** to open a franchise

> **"**
>
> Les frères McDonald exploitent leur concept par le système de la **franchise** depuis un certain temps: ils laissent à d'autres le soin de griller les steaks et empochent les royalties.
>
> **"**

franchisé, -e *nm,f* franchisee

franchiser *vt* to franchise

franchiseur, -euse *nm,* franchisor

franco *adv* **franco (de port**

free, carriage paid; **livré franco delivered** free; **livraison franco frontière française** delivered free as far as the French border; **franco (à) domicile** delivery free, carriage paid; **échantillons franco sur demande** free samples available on request; **franco de douane** free of customs duty; **franco d'emballage** free of packing charges; **franco de port et d'emballage** postage and packing paid; **franco de tous frais** free of all charges; **franco transporteur** free carrier

fréquence *nf* frequency

◇ *fréquence absolue* absolute frequency

◇ *fréquence d'achat* purchase frequency

◇ *fréquence d'utilisation* usage frequency

66 ⎯⎯⎯⎯⎯⎯⎯⎯⎯

Le marché des jeux vidéo est un jackpot incroyable: la durée de vie d'une console est de cinq ans, la **fréquence d'achat** de trois à quatre jeux par an.

⎯⎯⎯⎯⎯⎯⎯⎯ **99**

fret *nm* (**a**) *(cargaison, transport)* freight (**b**) *(coût du transport)* freight (charges)

◇ *fret aérien* airfreight

◇ *fret payé* freight paid

◇ *fret au poids* freight by weight

frontale *nf* shelf facing

gadget publicitaire *nm* advertising gimmick

gagner *vt (part de marché)* to capture; **nos concurrents gagnent du terrain** our competitors are gaining ground

galerie marchande *nf Br* shopping centre, *Am* shopping mall

gamme *nf (de produits)* range, series; *(de prix, de couleurs)* range; **étendre sa gamme de produits** to widen one's product range; **bas de gamme** *(de qualité inférieure)* bottom-of-the-range; *(peu prestigieux)* downmarket; **haut de gamme** *(de qualité supérieure)* top-of-the-range; *(prestigieux)* upmarket; **milieu de gamme** middle-of-the-range

> "
>
> "Quand nous avons gagné ce compte l'année dernière, nous avons cherché à donner à Morgan une image plus **haut de gamme**," explique-t-elle.
>
> "

garantie *nf (d'un produit)* guarantee, warranty; **sous garantie** under guarantee

◊ **garantie illimitée** unlimited warranty

◊ **garantie légale** legal guarantee

◊ **garantie limitée** limited warranty

◊ **garantie prolongée** extended warranty

◊ **garantie de remboursement** money-back guarantee

◊ **garantie totale** full warranty

garantir *vt (produit, service)* to guarantee; **cet appareil est garanti deux ans** this appliance is guaranteed for two years; **nous garantissons un délai de livraison d'une semaine** we guarantee delivery within seven days

géant, -e *adj (carton, paquet)* giant-sized

gel *nm (des prix)* freeze

geler *vt (prix)* to freeze

générique *adj (publicité, marché, produit)* generic

géodémographique *adj* geodemographic

géomarketing *nm* geomarketing

gérant, -e *nm,f (d'un magasin)* manager

gérer *vt (magasin)* to manage, to run

gestion *nf (d'une entreprise)* management

◇ **gestion de comptes-clés** key-account management

◇ **gestion des coûts** cost management

◇ **gestion de la distribution** distribution management

◇ **gestion de la distribution physique** physical distribution management

◇ **gestion du marketing** marketing management

◇ **gestion de marque** brand management

◇ **gestion de produits** product management

◇ **gestion qualité** quality control, quality management

◇ **gestion des stocks** stock control

gisement de clientèle *nm* pool of customers, potential customers

global, -e *adj (budget, demande)* total; **le budget global de publicité excède les coûts de production** the total publicity budget is higher than the production costs

globalisation *nf* globalization

globaliser *vt* to globalize

GM *nm (abrév* **grand magasin)** department store

GMS *nfpl (abrév* **grandes et moyennes surfaces)** large and medium commercial outlets

> **"**
>
> Lentement mais sûrement, hypermarchés et supermarchés accentuent leur poids sur la distribution de carburants. À ce titre, l'année qui vient de se terminer leur a permis de franchir un cap symbolique, les **GMS** vendant désormais plus d'un litre d'essence sur deux.
>
> **"**

gondole *nf (présentoir)* gondola

gouffre financier *nm (produit)* financial disaster, dog

grand, -e *adj*

◇ **grande distribution** mass distribution

◇ **grand magasin** department store

◇ **grandes et moyennes surfaces** large and medium commercial outlets

◇ **grande surface** superstore, hypermarket

◇ **grande surface spécialisée** specialist superstore

graphe *nm* graph, chart

◇ **graphe en ligne** line chart

graphique *nm (schéma)* graph, chart; **tracer un graphique** to plot a graph; **faire le graphique de qch** to chart sth

◇ **graphique d'acheminement** flow chart

◇ **graphique des activités** activity chart

◇ **graphique à** *ou* **en barres** bar

chart

◇ *graphique circulaire* pie chart

◇ *graphique en colonnes* bar chart

◇ *graphique d'évolution* flow chart

gratuit, -e *adj (échantillon, livraison)* free

gratuitement *adv* free of charge

griffe *nf (marque)* label

> Côté print, on retrouve les grands classiques, les belles annonces presse sur papier glacé pour des **griffes** de luxe qui plaisent toujours autant, ou encore les visuels qui invitent à la nostalgie des tendres années.

gros *nm (en commerce)* wholesale (trade); **acheter en gros** to buy wholesale; *(en grosse quantité)* to buy in bulk; **vendre en gros** to sell wholesale; **de gros** *(prix, commerce)* wholesale

grossiste *nmf* wholesaler

groupage *nm (de paquets)* bulking; *(de commandes, d'envois, de livraisons)* groupage, consolidation

groupe *nm* group

◇ *groupe cible* target group

◇ *groupe de consommateurs* consumer group

◇ *groupe de détaillants* retailer co-operative

◇ *groupe de prospects* prospect pool

◇ *groupe de référence* reference group

◇ *groupe suivi* control group

◇ *groupe test de consommateurs* consumer test group

groupé, -e *adj (commandes, envois, livraisons)* grouped, consolidated

groupe-cible *nm* target group

grouper *vt (paquets)* to bulk; *(commandes, envois, livraisons)* to group, to consolidate

groupe-témoin *nm* focus group, control group, consumer panel

GSS *nf (abrév* **grande surface spécialisée)** specialist superstore

> La quasi totalité des secteurs représentés dans les galeries commerciales ont profité du courant d'achat de décembre. Les ventes des grandes surfaces à dominante alimentaire ont progressé de 5,3% et celles de **GSS** de 6,2%.

guérilla *nf* guerilla attack

guerre des prix *nf* price war

habillage *nm (de marchandises)* packaging

◊ **habillage transparent** blister pack

habiller *vt (marchandises)* to package

habitude *nf* habit

◊ **habitudes d'achat** purchasing habits

hausse *nf* increase, rise (**de** in); **une hausse de 4%** a 4% rise; **une hausse des prix** a price increase; **être à la hausse** to go up; **les prix ont subi une forte hausse** prices have increased sharply, prices have shot up

hausser 1 *vt* to raise, to put up; **le prix a été haussé de 10%** the price has gone up by 10%

2 *vi* to rise; **faire hausser les prix** to force up prices

haut *nm (du marché)* high end, top end

hétérogène *adj (marché, produits)* heterogeneous

homogène *adj (marché, produits)* homogeneous

horizontal, -e *adj (concen-tration, intégration)* horizontal

hors *prép* **hors taxe** excluding tax; *(à la douane)* duty-free

hors-média 1 *adj (publicité, promotion, coûts)* below-the-line

2 *nm* below-the-line advertising

> **❝**
>
> En ce qui concerne la communication, c'est le **hors-média** qui tient le haut du pavé avec pas moins de 95% des investissements (montant non révélé). Cette activité comprend, outre le marketing direct, les mailings effectués tous les ans pour recruter la clientèle – la quantité d'adresses, le nombre et le coût des mailings restent bien entendu top secret.
>
> **❞**

hypermarché *nm* hypermarket, superstore

hypersegmentation *nf* hypersegmentation

identificateur de marque *nm* brand identifier

identification *nf*
- *identification des besoins* need identification
- *identification de la marque* brand recognition

identité *nf*
- *identité graphique* logo
- *identité de marque* brand identity

IGP *nf* (*abrév* **indication géographique protégée**) = designation of a product which guarantees its authentic origin and gives the name protected status

îlot *nm* (*pour étaler des marchandises*) island

ILV *nf* (*abrév* **information sur le lieu de vente**) point-of-sale information

image *nf* (*illustration*) picture; (*façon dont on est perçu*) image
- *images à compléter* picture completion
- *image de marque* (*d'un produit*) brand image; (*d'une société*) corporate image
- *image de produit* product image

imitation *nf* (*produit*) imitation

impact *nm* (*d'une publicité, d'une campagne*) impact

" —

…En plus, si la méchanceté a de l'**impact**, elle est également appréciée. Pour preuve, le film Piq et Croq pour Vache qui rit, qui arrive en troisième position du score d'agrément avec 88 %.

" —

implantation *nf* (*d'un magasin, d'un rayon*) location (*établissement*) setting up

implanter 1 *vt* (*magasin, rayon*) to locate; (*établir*) to set up; **implanter un produit sur le marché** to establish a product on the market
2 **s'implanter** *vpr* (*magasin, rayon*) to be located; (*être établi*) to be set up

implication *nf* (*du consommateur*) involvement

import *nm* importation

importateur, -trice 1 *adj* importing

2 *nm,f* importer; **c'est l'importateur exclusif de cette marque pour la France** they are the sole French importers of this brand

importation *nf (action)* importing; *(produit)* import
◇ *importation en franchise* duty-free import

importer *vt (marchandises)* to import; **importer des marchandises des États-Unis en France** to import goods from the United States into France

import-export *nm* import-export

imprimé publicitaire *nm* advertising leaflet, publicity handout

INC *nm (abrév* **Institut national de la consommation)** = French consumer research organization

incitation *nf* incentive
◇ *incitation à l'achat* buying incentive
◇ *incitation à la vente* sales incentive

indicateur *nm* indicator
◇ *indicateurs d'alerte* economic indicators, business indicators
◇ *indicateur (d'activité) économique* economic indicator

indice *nm (chiffre indicateur)* index
◇ *indice des prix* price index
◇ *indice des prix à la consommation* consumer price index
◇ *indice des prix de détail* retail price index

◇ *indice des prix de gros* wholesale price index
◇ *indice de richesse vive* consumer purchasing power index

indirect, -e *adj (coûts, vente)* indirect

industrie *nf* Écon industry
◇ *industrie de consommation* consumer goods industry
◇ *industrie des loisirs* leisure industry

industriel, -elle *adj (marché, marketing)* industrial

inférieur, -e *adj (marchandises, qualité)* inferior

inflation *nf* Écon inflation
◇ *inflation des prix* price inflation

inflationniste *adj* Écon inflationary

influenceur *nm* influencer

information *nf (renseignement)* (piece of) information; **informations** information; **nous vous adressons ce catalogue à titre d'information** we are sending you this catalogue for your information
◇ *information commerciale* market intelligence
◇ *information sur le lieu de vente* point-of-sale information
◇ *informations primaires* primary data
◇ *informations secondaires* secondary data

inhibiteur *nm* inhibitor

initiateur *nm* initiator

innovateur, -trice 1 *adj*

(produit, entreprise) innovative **2** *nm,f* innovator

◇ *innovateur continu* continuous innovator

◇ *innovateur tardif* laggard

innovation *nf* innovation

◇ *innovation continue* continuous innovation

◇ *innovation de produit* product innovation

inondation *nf (du marché)* flooding

inonder *vt (marché)* to flood; **le marché des produits de luxe est inondé de contrefaçons** the luxury goods market is flooded with imitation products

insérer *vt (publicité, annonce)* to place (**dans** in)

insertion *nf* advertisement

◇ *insertion publicitaire* advertisement

❝

Les campagnes de marketing direct lui permettent de passer sur TF1, France 2 et M6 à moindre coût, le matin ou l'après-midi. Plus de 60 passages sont programmés pour un budget de 300 000 F. Deux **insertions** sont aussi prévues dans *Télé Star* et *Télé Poche*.

❞

institut *nm (organisme)* institute

◇ *Institut national de la consommation* = French consumer research organization

◇ *institut de sondage* polling

company

instrument de vente *nm* sales tool

intégration *nf Écon* integration

◇ *intégration en amont* backward integration

◇ *intégration en aval* forward integration

◇ *intégration horizontale* horizontal integration

◇ *intégration verticale* vertical integration

intelligence marketing *nf* marketing intelligence

intention d'achat *nf* intention to buy

interdiction *nf* ban

◇ *interdiction d'exportation* export ban

◇ *interdiction d'importation* import ban

interdire *vt* interdire qch d'exportation/d'importation to impose an export/import ban on sth

intérêt *nm* (a) *(sur un prêt)* interest; **à 5% d'intérêt** with 5% interest; **emprunter/prêter à intérêt** to borrow/lend at interest (b) *(avantage)* interest

◇ *intérêt du consommateur* consumer welfare

intermédiaire *nmf (dans une transaction)* middleman; **sans intermédiaire** directly; **je préfère vendre sans intermédiaire** I prefer to sell directly to the customer

◇ *intermédiaire agréé* authorized dealer

Internet *nm Ordinat* Internet; **acheter/vendre qch par l'Internet** to buy/sell sth over the Internet

interroger *vt* to interview, to question; **60% des personnes intérrogées ont déclaré n'avoir jamais entendu parler de ce produit** 60% of those questioned said that they had never heard of this product

interrompre *vt (produit)* to discontinue

intervenant, -e *nm,f*

◇ *intervenant sur le marché* market participant

invendable *adj (marchandises)* unmarketable, unsaleable

inventaire *nm (de marchandises) (procédure)* stocktaking, inventory; *(liste)* stocklist, inventory; **faire** *ou* **dresser un inventaire** to stocktake, to take the inventory

◇ *inventaire d'entrée* ingoing inventory

◇ *inventaire de sortie* outgoing inventory

inventorier *vt (marchandises)* to make a stocklist *or* an inventory of

IRSM *nm (abrév* **impact sur la rentabilité de la stratégie marketing)** PIMS

ISO *nf (abrév* **International Standards Organization)** ISO

jargon *nm* jargon

◊ *jargon publicitaire* advertising jargon

JAT *adj* (*abrév* **juste à temps**) JIT

jetable *adj* (*emballage, produit*) disposable

jeter *vt* (*mettre au rebut*) to throw away; **jeter des marchandises sur le marché** to throw goods onto the market

jingle *nm* jingle

jury des consommateurs *nm* focus group

juste à temps *adj* (*achat, distribution, production*) just-in-time

label *nm (étiquette)* label

◇ *label d'exportation* export label

◇ *label de garantie* guarantee label

◇ *label d'origine* label of origin

◇ *label de qualité* quality label

laissé-pour-compte 1 *adj (article, marchandise)* rejected, returned

2 *nm (article, marchandise)* reject

lancement *nm (d'un produit, d'une marque, d'une entreprise)* launch

◇ *lancement sur le marché* market entry

◇ *lancement tardif* late entry

lancer 1 *vt (produit, modèle)* to launch; **lancer un nouveau produit sur le marché** to launch a new product on the market

2 se lancer *vpr* **se lancer sur le marché** to enter the market

leader *nm (produit, entreprise)* (market) leader; **cette entreprise est le leader mondial de la micro-informatique** this firm is the world leader in microcomputing

◇ *leader sur le marché* market leader

◇ *leader d'opinion* opinion former, opinion leader

> Patrick Mahé, directeur de la rédaction de l'hebdomadaire ne mâche pas ses mots. "En 12 ans, le titre a, en effet, perdu 14% de sa diffusion. Nous avons décidé que cette année serait celle de la fin de l'érosion. Il n'est pas possible de revenir aux 3,2 millions de 1987, mais nous devions nous conforter notre position de **leader**."

légende *nf (commentaire)* caption

lettre *nf (courrier)* letter

◇ *lettre de relance* follow-up letter

◇ *lettre type (pour mailing)* form letter

◇ *lettre de vente* sales letter

◇ *lettre de voiture* consignment note

libre *adj (non réglementé)* free

◇ *libre concurrence* free competition

◇ *libre service (technique de vente)* self-service; *(magasin)* self-service shop

❝

Les trois opérateurs ont tout intérêt à travailler dans le sens d'une simplification de leur produit. En commercialisant dans les hypermarchés une version packagée de son décodeur analogique, Canal+ a prouvé que, sur le marché de la télévision payante, le **libre service** fonctionnait aussi bien que sur d'autres marchés.

❞

licence *nf (permis)* licence
◇ *licence exclusive* exclusive licence
◇ *licence d'exportation* export licence
◇ *licence d'importation* import licence
◇ *licence de vente* selling licence

lieu *nm (endroit)* place
◇ *lieu de livraison* place of delivery, point of delivery
◇ *lieu de vente* point of sale

ligne *nf (de produits)* line, range
◇ *ligne de produits* line of products, product line

limite *nf (maximum ou minimum)* limit; **dans la limite des stocks disponibles** while stocks last
◇ *limite de crédit* credit limit

linéaire 1 *adj* linear
2 *nm* shelf space; *(étalage)* shelf display; **ce produit n'apparaît pas dans les linéaires des magasins non spécialisés** non-specialist shops do not stock this product

❝

Avec l'apparition des univers de consommation, on pourrait envisager un **linéaire** éclaté. Les biberons seraient vendus près des laits en poudre, la vaisselle à côté des petits pots et les peignes à la suite des shampoings. Pourtant Carrefour, qui a commencé à installer ses univers bébé, persiste à considérer la petite puériculture comme un rayon à part entière, à proximité des autres produits, mais rassemblés.

❞

liquidation *nf (de stocks)* selling off, clearance; *(d'un commerce)* closing-down, *Am* closing-out

liquider *(stocks)* to sell off, to clear; *(commerce)* to close down, *Am* to close out

liste *nf* list
◇ *liste d'adresses* mailing list, address list
◇ *liste d'attributs* attribute list
◇ *liste de clients* customer or client list
◇ *liste de colisage* packing list
◇ *liste de diffusion* mailing list
◇ *liste d'envoi* mailing list
◇ *liste des importations* import list

◇ *liste des prix* price list

◇ *liste de publipostage* mailing list

◇ *liste des tarifs* price list, tariff

livrable *adj (marchandises)* ready for delivery

livraison *nf (action, marchandises)* delivery; **faire** *ou* **effectuer une livraison** to make a delivery; **prendre livraison de qch** to take delivery of sth

◇ *livraison à domicile* door-to-door delivery

◇ *livraison franco* free delivery, delivered free

◇ *livraison franco à domicile* free home delivery

◇ *livraison franco par nos soins* carriage paid

◇ *livraison gratuite* free delivery, delivered free

◇ *livraison le jour même* same-day delivery

◇ *livraison lendemain* next-day delivery

◇ *livraison contre remboursement* *Br* cash on delivery, *Am* collect on delivery

livre *nm (registre)* book

◇ *livre d'échantillons* sample book

livrer *vt (marchandises, commande)* to deliver; **nous avons bien été livrés** we have received the delivery; **nous livrons à domicile** we deliver to your door; **vous serez livrés dès demain** you will receive delivery tomorrow; **livré franco domicile** delivered free

LJM *nf (abrév* **livraison le jour même)** same-day delivery

location-vente *nf* hire purchase, *Am* installment plan; **acheter qch en location-vente** to buy sth on hire purchase *or Am* on the installment plan

logistique commerciale *nf* marketing mix

logo *nm* logo

longitudinal, -e *adj (étude, recherche)* longitudinal, continuous

lot *nm (de marchandises)* batch

◇ *lot dépareillé* odd lot

◇ *lot d'envoi* consignment

luxe *nm* **de luxe** *(produit)* luxury

macroenvironnement *nm* macroenvironment

macromarketing *nm* macromarketing

macrosegment *nm* macrosegment

macrosegmentation *nf* macrosegmentation

magasin *nm* (**a**) *(commerce)* shop, store (**b**) *(entrepôt)* store, warehouse; **avoir qch en magasin** to have sth in stock

◇ *magasin de détail* retail shop or outlet

◇ *magasin détaxé* duty-free shop

◇ *magasin de discount* discount store

◇ Ordinat *magasin électronique* on-line shop

◇ *magasin d'exposition* showroom

◇ *magasin franchisé* franchise

◇ *magasin sous franchise exclusive* tied outlet

◇ Douanes *magasins généraux* bonded warehouse

◇ *magasin à grande surface* hypermarket

◇ *magasin hors taxe* duty-free shop

◇ *magasin laboratoire* = test shop used to monitor consumer behaviour

◇ *magasin de luxe* luxury goods shop

◇ *magasin de proximité* local shop

◇ *magasin à succursales (multiples)* chain store

◇ *magasin d'usine* factory shop, factory outlet

◇ *magasin de vente au détail* retail shop

magasinage *nm* *(de marchandises)* warehousing, storing; *(frais)* warehouse *or* storage charges

mailing *nm* (**a**) *(procédé)* mailing; **ce sont des clients que nous avons eus par mailing** we acquired these customers through a mailshot (**b**) *(envoi de prospectus)* mailshot; **faire un mailing** to do *or* send a mailshot

>
> Le premier **mailing** est parti en octobre. Envoyé à près de 200 000 foyers par mois sur le fichier des nouveaux abonnés de France Télécom … il

comprend un guide pratique de 20 pages conçu comme un véritable outil pour faciliter les démarches administratives.

"

maison *nf (entreprise)* firm, company, business

◊ *maison de courtage* brokerage house

◊ *maison de détail* retail company

◊ *maison d'exportation* export firm

◊ *maison de gros* wholesale firm

◊ *maison d'importation* import firm

◊ *maison de rabais* discount store

◊ *maison à succursales multiples* chain store

◊ *maison de vente par correspondance* mail-order company

majoration *nf (de prix)* increase, mark-up

majorer *vt (prix)* to increase, to raise (**de** by)

majorité *nf* majority

◊ *majorité conservatrice* late majority

◊ *majorité innovatrice* early majority

◊ *majorité précoce* early majority

◊ *majorité tardive* late majority

mandataire *nmf* authorized agent

manque à la livraison *nm* short delivery

manufacturer *vt* to manufacture

mapping *nm* mapping

marchand, -e 1 *adj (quartier, ville)* commercial

2 *nm,f (dans un magasin) Br* shopkeeper, *Am* storekeeper

◊ *marchand en gros* wholesaler, wholesale dealer

marchander 1 *vt (prix, article)* to bargain over, to haggle over

2 *vi* to bargain, to haggle

marchandisage *nm* marketing, merchandising

marchandise *nf* commodity; **marchandises** goods, merchandise

◊ *marchandises au détail* retail goods

◊ *marchandises en entrepôt* warehoused goods, goods in storage; *Douanes* bonded goods, goods in bond

◊ *marchandises à l'export* export goods

◊ *marchandises de gros* wholesale goods

◊ *marchandises à l'import* import goods

◊ *marchandises en magasin* stock in hand

◊ *marchandises d'origine* = goods of guaranteed origin

◊ *marchandises périssables* perishable goods, perishables

◊ *marchandises de qualité* quality goods

◊ *marchandises en vrac* bulk goods

marchandiser *vt* to merchandise

marchandiseur *nm* merchandiser

marché *nm* (a) *Écon* market; **mettre** *ou* **lancer un nouveau produit sur le marché** to launch a new product on the market; **ce produit n'a pas de marché** there is no market for this product; **arriver sur le marché** to come onto the market; **mettre qch sur le marché** to put sth on the market; **retirer qch du marché** to take sth off the market

(b) *(accord)* deal, bargain; *(plus officiel)* contract; **faire** *ou* **conclure un marché** to strike a deal *or* bargain, to clinch a deal

◇ **marché d'acheteurs** buyer's market

◇ **marché à la baisse** seller's market

◇ **marché des besoins** need market

◇ **marché captif** captive market

◇ **marché cible** target market

◇ **marché de concurrence** competitive marketplace

◇ **marché des consommateurs, marché de la consommation** consumer market

◇ **marché effectif** available market

◇ **marché à l'exportation** export market

◇ **marché extérieur** foreign market, overseas market

◇ **marché générique** generic market

◇ **marché global** global market

◇ **marché grand public** consumer market, mass market

◇ **marché gris** grey market

◇ **marché industriel** industrial market

◇ **marché intérieur** home market, domestic market

◇ **marché des intermédiaires** middleman's market

◇ **marché de masse** mass market

◇ **marché mondial** world market

◇ **marché monopolistique** monopoly market

◇ **marché national** national market, home market

◇ **marché noir** black market; **faire du marché noir** to buy and sell on the black market

◇ **marché d'outre-mer** overseas market

◇ **marché parallèle** parallel market, black market

◇ **marché porteur** growth market

◇ **marché primaire** primary market

◇ **marché principal** core market

◇ **marché de référence** core market

◇ **marché de renouvellement** repurchase market

◇ **marché de revente** second-hand market

◇ **marché secondaire** secondary market

◇ **marché témoin** control market, test market

◇ **marché test** test market

◇ **marché utile** addressable market

◇ **marché vendeur** seller's market

◇ *marché visé* target market

marchéage *nm* marketing mix, marketing spectrum

◇ *marchéage de distribution* retailing mix

marge *nf* margin; **avoir une faible/forte marge** to have a low/high (profit) margin; **nous faisons 30% de marge sur ce produit** we make a 30% margin on this product

◇ *marge arrière* refund *(given to distributors at end of financial year)*

◇ *marge bénéficiaire* profit margin

◇ *marge brute* gross margin

◇ *marge commerciale brute* gross profit margin

◇ *marge commerciale nette* net profit margin

◇ *marge du détaillant* retailer margin

◇ *marge du distributeur* distributor's margin

◇ *marge du grossiste* wholesaler margin

◇ *marge de l'importateur* importer's margin

◇ *marge nette* net margin

> **❝**
>
> Jean-Paul Gaultier n'a rien déboursé pour son site marchand, il ne traite pas la gestion des stocks, ni l'expédition ou la facturation, ni même la promotion du site. En échange, l'agence perçoit la même **marge** que les magasins (autour de 50% du prix de vente).
>
> **❞**

marketing *nm* marketing

◇ *marketing après-vente* after-sales marketing

◇ *marketing ciblé* niche marketing, target marketing

◇ *marketing commercial* trade marketing

◇ *marketing concentré* concentrated marketing

◇ *marketing de contact* direct marketing

◇ *marketing de différenciation, marketing différencié* differentiated marketing

◇ *marketing direct* direct marketing

◇ *marketing écologique* green marketing

◇ *Ordinat marketing électronique* on-line marketing

◇ *marketing global* global marketing

◇ *marketing de grande consommation* mass marketing

◇ *marketing indifférencié* undifferentiated marketing

◇ *marketing industriel* industrial marketing

◇ *marketing interactif* interactive marketing

◇ *marketing international* global marketing

◇ *marketing interne* internal marketing

◇ *marketing de masse* mass marketing

◇ *marketing sur mesure* customized marketing

◇ *marketing mix* marketing mix

◇ *marketing multinational* multinational marketing

◇ *marketing non-commercial*

non-business marketing

◇ *marketing de nouveaux produits* new product marketing

◇ *marketing one to one* one-to-one marketing

◇ *marketing opérationnel* operational marketing

◇ *marketing de relance* re-marketing

◇ *marketing relationnel* relationship marketing

◇ *marketing de réseau* multi-level marketing

◇ *marketing sélectif* selective marketing

◇ *marketing de stimulation* stimulation marketing, incentive marketing

◇ *marketing stratégique* strategic marketing

◇ *marketing téléphonique* telemarketing

◇ *marketing vert* green marketing

"

Le **marketing direct** permet de réduire d'environ 15 à 20% tant les coûts d'opérations commerciales et administratives que ceux des infrastructures (immobilier et technologie).

"

marquage *nm* branding, labelling

marque *nf (de produit)* (name) brand; *(sur l'article)* trademark; **grande marque** famous make, well-known brand; **de marque** *(produit)* branded

◇ *marque d'appel* loss leader

brand

◇ *marque clé* key brand

◇ *marque collective* label

◇ *marque de commerce* trademark, brand (name)

◇ *marque déposée* registered trademark

◇ *marque de distributeur* distributor's brand name, own brand

◇ *marque dominante* dominant brand

◇ *marque économique* economy brand

◇ *marque de fabricant* manufacturer's brand (name)

◇ *marque de fabrique* trademark, brand (name)

◇ *marque de garantie* certification mark

◇ *marque générale* family brand

◇ *marque générique* generic brand

◇ *marque globale* global brand

◇ *marque grand public* consumer brand

◇ *marque de magasin* store brand

◇ *marque multiple* multibrand

◇ *marque ombrelle* umbrella brand

◇ *marque d'origine* origin of goods label

◇ *marque de service* mark of quality, quality guarantee *(on range of services offered by company or manufacturer)*

◇ *marque de tête* brand leader

"

Dans l'optique de disposer de produits à marque propre ou à **marque de distributeur**

(MDD), les enseignes font appel à des industriels spécialisés, à qui elles demandent une prestation qui va de la fabrication de produits sur mesure conformément à un cahier des charges préétabli (contrat de sous-traitance), à la simple tâche de signer à **marque de distributeur** des produits préexistants (contrat de fourniture).

"

marquer vt (article, produit) to brand, to label

mass-médias nmpl mass media

matériel nm (équipement) material

◊ **matériel de PLV** point-of-sale material

◊ **matériel de présentation** display material

◊ **matériel de promotion** promotional material

◊ **matériel publicitaire** advertising material

matraquage publicitaire nm hype

matrice nf matrix

◊ **matrice BCG** Boston matrix

◊ **matrice croissance-part de marché** growth-share matrix

maturité nf (du marché) maturity

MDD nf (abrév **marque de distributeur**) distributor's brand name, own brand

mécanisme du marché nm market mechanism

mécénat nm patronage, sponsorship

◊ **mécénat d'entreprise** corporate sponsorship

média nm (support) medium; **les médias** the media; **une campagne publicitaire dans tous les médias** a media-wide advertising campaign

◊ **média de masse** mass media

◊ **média planner** media planner

◊ **média planning** media planning

◊ **média publicitaire** advertising media

médialogie nf media research

médiaplaneur nm media planner

médiatique adj media

médiatisation nf media coverage

médiatiser vt to give media coverage to

médium nm (support) medium

mémomarque nf brand name recall

mémorisation nf recall

◊ **mémorisation un jour après** day-after recall

◊ **mémorisation de la marque** brand name recall

menace nf (d'un produit, d'un concurrent) threat

ménage nm Écon household

mercaticien, -enne nm,f marketing expert, marketing consultant

mercatique nf marketing

merchandisage *nm* merchandising

merchandising *nm* merchandising

"

Le **merchandising** des devants de caisse laisse peu de place à l'improvisation car il repose sur un équilibre difficile à trouver. Sachant que chaque meuble dégage entre 80 et 100 000 francs de chiffre d'affaires annuel dans un hypermarché, les enseignes y regardent à deux fois avant de modifier la configuration de ces minirayons.

"

message *nm (dans la publicité)* message

◇ *message principal* core message

◇ *message publicitaire* advertisement

mesure *nf (action)* measurement, measuring; *(résultat)* measurement

◇ *mesure d'audience* audience measurement

◇ *mesure d'impact* impact measurement

◇ *mesure de satisfaction de la clientèle* customer satisfaction measurement

méthode *nf (façon de procéder)* method

◇ *méthode de la boule de neige* referral system

◇ *méthode d'échantillonnage* sampling method

◇ *méthode non probabilist* non-probability method

◇ *méthode probabiliste* probability method

◇ *méthode des quotas* quot sampling method

◇ *méthode de sélection* selection method

◇ *méthode de sondage* polling method

◇ *méthode de vente* sale technique, selling technique

méthodologie *nf* methodology

mètre linéaire *nm* linear metre

"

Le temps de parcours d'un client pour venir et revenir de son magasin est de vingt à vingt-cinq minutes. Il vient d'y passer cinquante minutes. Il a soif. Lorsqu'un hypermarché dispose d'une *vending machine*, il réalise 1 000 000 F de chiffre d'affaires au **mètre linéaire** et des marges de 30 à 40%.

"

mettre *vt* mettre qch en œuvre *(produit, campagne)* to implement sth

mévente *nf* slump (in sales), slack period; **c'est une période de mévente dans ce secteur** this sector is experiencing a slack period

micromarketing *nm* micromarketing

microsegment *nm* microsegment

microsegmentation *nf* microsegmentation

mise *nf*
◇ **mise en dépôt** warehousing
◇ **mis en œuvre** *(d'un produit, d'une campagne)* implementation
◇ **mise en page** *(d'une publicité)* layout
◇ **mise en place marketing** marketing implementation
◇ **mise au point** *(d'un produit)* development
◇ **mise en vente** *(d'un produit)* bringing onto the market, launching

mission *nf* brief
◇ **mission d'activité, mission d'entreprise** business mission

mix *nm (marchéage)* mix
◇ **mix média** media mix
◇ **mix de produits** product mix

mobile *nm*
◇ **mobile d'achat** buying inducement, purchasing motivator
◇ **mobile publicitaire** advertising mobile

modèle *nm* (a) *(exemplaire)* model; **le nouveau modèle de chez Renault** the new model from Renault; **ce modèle existe aussi en rouge** this model also comes in *or* is also available in red
(b) *(représentation schématique)* model
◇ **modèle du chemin critique** critical path model
◇ **modèle de comportement** d'achat purchasing behaviour model
◇ **modèle de décision, modèle décisionnel** decision model
◇ **modèle de décision en arborescence** decision tree
◇ **modèle de démonstration** demonstration model
◇ **modèle déposé** registered design
◇ **modèle déterministe** decision model
◇ **modèle familial** family model
◇ **modèle de prévision des ventes** sales forecast model
◇ **modèle de prise de décision(s)** decision-making model
◇ **modèle de relations réciproques** reciprocal relationships model

mondial, -e *adj (prix)* world, worldwide; *(commerce, consommation)* worldwide, global; **leur réseau de distribution mondial est leur atout principal** their worldwide distribution network is their main asset

mondialisation *nf* globalization

mondialiser *vt* to globalize

monopole *nm* monopoly; **avoir le monopole de qch** to have a monopoly on sth; **exercer un monopole sur un secteur** to monopolize a sector
◇ **monopole des prix** price monopoly
◇ **monopole de vente** sales monopoly

monopoliser *vt* to monopolize, to have a monopoly on

motif nm *(intention)* motive

◇ *motif d'achat* buying motive, purchasing motive

motivation nf motivation, incentive

◇ *motivation d'achat* buying motive, purchasing motive

◇ *motivation de consommateur* consumer motivation

mouvement de défense du consommateur nm consumer protection movement

moyen, -enne adj *(prix, coût, consommation)* average; d taille moyenne medium-sized

moyenne nf average

◇ *moyenne des ventes* sale average

multimarque nf multibrand

multinational, -e 1 adj multinational

2 nf **multinationale** multinational

multipostage nm volume mailing

myopie mercatique nf marketing myopia

négociant, -e *nm,f (dans le commerce)* wholesaler

net, nette *adj* net; **net de tout droit** exempt of duty

niche *nf* (market) niche

niveau *nm (degré)* level; **maintenir les prix à un niveau élevé** to maintain prices at a high level
◇ **niveau des besoins** need level
◇ **niveau de prix** price level

noir *nm* **acheter/vendre au noir** to buy/sell on the black market

nom *nm*
◇ **nom déposé** registered (trade) name
◇ **nom de famille global** blanket family name
◇ **nom générique** generic name
◇ **nom de marque** brand name

non-livraison *nf* non-delivery

non-réception *nf* non-delivery

norme *nf* standard
◇ **normes publicitaires** advertising standards

note de fret *nf* freight note

notoriété *nf* awareness

◇ **notoriété assistée** aided recall
◇ **notoriété de la marque** brand awareness
◇ **notoriété du produit** product awareness
◇ **notoriété publicitaire** advertising awareness
◇ **notoriété spontanée** spontaneous recall

> **“**
> "Nous avons 100 magasins et notre taille nous permet de communiquer en national," reprend Olivier Hamel. "Avec une **notoriété** faible, de 20% en spontané et de 17% en assisté, il devenait impératif de faire parler de nous."
> **”**

nouveau, -elle *adj* new
◇ **nouveau produit** new product
◇ **nouvel utilisateur** first-time user

nouveauté *nf* new product, innovation

novateur, -trice **1** *adj (produit, entreprise)* innovative **2** *nm,f* innovator

objectif *nm* objective, goal

◇ *objectif marketing* marketing goal

◇ *objectif publicitaire* advertising goal

◇ *objectif de vente* sales target

observation *nf* observation

◇ *observation en situation* personal observation

obsolescence *nf* obsolescence; **le taux d'obsolescence des ordinateurs est très élevé** the obsolescence rate of computers is very high, computers very quickly become obsolete

◇ *obsolescence calculée, obsolescence planifiée, obsolescence prévue* built-in obsolescence, planned obsolescence

occasion *nf* (a) *(bonne affaire)* bargain; **pour ce prix-là, c'est une occasion** it's a real bargain at that price

(b) *(article de seconde main)* second-hand item; **acheter qch d'occasion** to buy sth second-hand; **l'occasion** the second-hand trade; **l'occasion se vend bien** there's a brisk trade in second-hand goods

(c) *(circonstance favorable)* opportunity

◇ *occasion d'entendre* opportunity to hear

◇ *occasion de voir* opportunity to see

ODE *nf* (*abrév* **occasion d'entendre**) opportunity to hear

ODV *nf* (*abrév* **occasion de voir**) opportunity to see

office de publicité *nm* advertising agency

offre *nf* (a) *(proposition)* offer; *(action)* offering; **cette offre est valable jusqu'au 30 juin** this offer is valid until 30 June; **ils lui ont fait une offre avantageuse** they made him a worthwhile offer

(b) *Écon* supply; **l'offre et la demande** supply and demand; **lorsque l'offre excède la demande, les prix ont tendance à baisser** when supply exceeds demand, prices have a tendency to fall

◇ *offre de base* basic offer

◇ *offre de bon de réduction* coupon offer

◇ *offre d'échantillon gratuit* free sample offer

◇ *offre d'essai* trial offer

◇ *offre de lancement* introductory offer

◇ *offre à prix réduit* reduced-price offer

◇ *offre promotionnelle* promotional offer

◇ *offre de remboursement* money-back offer

◇ *offre spéciale* special offer, *Am* special

> **"**
>
> Le loup Soignon (Eurial) emblème de la marque, revient sur les écrans jusqu'au 28 février, avec un spot de quinze secondes annonçant une **offre promotionnelle** sur le fromage de chèvre Ste Maure Soignon. Il s'agit d'une **offre de remboursement** intégral sur le troisième Ste Maure acheté.
>
> **"**

oligopole *nm* oligopoly

opération *nf (campagne)* opération, campaign

◇ *opération marketing* marketing campaign

◇ *opération publicitaire* advertising campaign

opérationnel, -elle *adj (en activité)* operational

opportunités *nfpl* opportunities

optimal, -e, optimum *adj (prix)* optimal, optimum

optique *nf*

◇ *optique marketing* marketing orientation

◇ *optique produit* product orientation

◇ *optique publicitaire* advertising approach

◇ *optique vente* sales orientation

organe de publicité *nm* advertising medium

organigramme *nm* organization(al) chart, organigram

organisation *nf (groupement)* organization

◇ *Organisation internationale de normalisation* International Standards Organization

organisme *nm (organisation)* organization, body

◇ *organisme de crédit* credit organization

◇ *organisme de défense des consommateurs* consumer organization

orientation *nf*

◇ *orientation clientèle* customer orientation

◇ *orientation marché* market orientation

origine *nf (d'un produit)* origin

outil *nm (aide)* tool

◇ *outil de marketing* marketing tool

ouvert, -e *adj (question)* open-ended

ouverture *nf* opening, window of opportunity; **l'ouverture de nouveaux débouchés** the opening up of new markets

P *nm* **les quatre P** *(le marketing mix)* the four Ps

page de publicité *nf* commercial break

paiement *nm* payment; *(d'un compte)* payment, settlement; **effectuer** *ou* **faire un paiement** to make a payment; **recevoir un paiement** to receive a payment

◇ *paiement à la commande* cash with order

◇ *paiement (au) comptant* cash payment, payment in cash

◇ *paiement contre documents* payment against documents

◇ *Ordinat* *paiement électronique* electronic payment, payment by electronic transfer

◇ *paiement en espèces* payment in cash, cash payment

◇ *paiement en liquide* payment in cash, cash payment

◇ *paiement à la livraison* *Br* cash on delivery, *Am* collect on delivery

◇ *paiement partiel* part payment

◇ *paiement à tempérament* payment by *or* in instalments

◇ *paiement à terme* payment by *or* in instalments

pancarte *nf (dans un magasin)* showcard

panel *nm (échantillon)* panel

◇ *panel ad hoc* ad hoc panel

◇ *panel de consommateurs* consumer panel, shopping panel

◇ *panel de détaillants* retail panel

◇ *panel de distributeurs* distributor panel

◇ *panel d'essayeurs de produits* product testing panel

◇ *panel de téléspectateurs* television viewing panel

panéliste *nmf* panel member

panier *nm (présentoir)* dump bin

◇ *Écon* *panier de la ménagère* shopping basket

◇ *panier de présentation en vrac, panier présentoir* dump bin

◇ *panier à la sortie* check-out display

◇ *panier vrac* dump bin

panneau d'affichage, panneau publicitaire *nm* billboard, *Br* hoarding

paquet *nm (marchandise*

The four Ps
Les quatre P

name
features
performance
packaging

product
produit

nom
caractéristiques
performance
emballage

channels of distribution
retailing
wholesaling
transportation

place
lieu

circuits de distribution
vente en détail
vente en gros
transport

the marketing mix
le marketing mix

advertising
public relations
direct marketing
sales force

promotion
promotion

publicité
relations publiques
marketing direct
force de vente

discounts
costs
overheads
credit facilities

price
prix

remises
coûts
frais généraux
facilités de crédit

emballée) packet, pack

◇ *paquet échantillon* sample pack

◇ *paquet économique* economy pack

◇ *paquet familial* family-sized pack

◇ *paquet géant* giant-sized pack

◇ *paquet de présentation* presentation pack

parrain *nm (sponsor)* promoter, sponsor

parrainage *nm (sponsoring)* sponsorship

◇ *parrainage d'entreprises* corporate sponsorship

parrainer *vt (sponsoriser)* to sponsor

part *nf (fraction)* share

◇ *part de marché* market share

◇ *part de marché relative* relative market share

◇ *part de voix* share of voice

> 66
>
> "De 1991 à 1997, Total n'a cessé de prouver qu'elle se préoccupait des automobilistes et pas seulement de leur voiture," souligne Marie-Christine Dax. "La marque a très vite gagné un point de **part de marché** et a surtout préempté un territoire: le service."
>
> 99

partenaire *nm* (business) partner

partenariat *nm* partnership

passer 1 *vt (commande)* to place (**de qch** for sth; **à qn** with sb)

2 *vi (représentant)* **passer chez un client** to call on a client

patronage *nm* sponsorship, sponsoring; **sous le patronage de** sponsored by

patronner *vt* to sponsor

payable *adj* payable; **payable en 12 mensualités** payable in 12 monthly instalments; **payable à la commande** cash with order, payable with order; **payable comptant** payable in cash; **payable à la livraison** payable on delivery

payer *vt (facture, personne)* to pay; *(marchandises)* to pay for; **payer par chèque/par carte de crédit** to pay by cheque/credit card; **payer comptant, payer en liquide, payer en espèces** to pay (in) cash; **payer intégralement, payer en totalité** to pay in full; **payer à la livraison** to pay on delivery

pays *nm* country

◇ *pays exportateur* exporting country

◇ *pays d'origine* country of origin

◇ *pays de provenance* country of origin

PDV *nm (abrév* **point de vente**) POS

pénétration *nf (d'un marché)* penetration

> 66
>
> Entré dans une nouvelle phase de son développement, le journal veut à la

> fois accroître la notoriété de sa marque, affirmer sa spécificité, développer des produits différenciés et accroître sa **pénétration** auprès des cibles étudiants, jeunes cadres, cadres étrangers et dirigeants de PME.
>
> **"**

pénétrer *vt (marché)* to penetrate, to enter

PEPS (*abrév* **premier entré, premier sorti**) FIFO

percée *nf (sur un marché)* breakthrough; **leur société a fait une percée sur le marché de la micro-informatique** their company has broken into the microcomputer market

◊ *percée commerciale* market thrust

perception *nf (d'un consommateur, d'un client)* perception

◊ *perception de marque* brand perception

◊ *perception sélective* selective perception

percer *vi* **percer sur un marché** to break into a market

perdre *vt (clientèle, part de marché)* to lose

perdu, -e *adj (emballage)* one-way

performance *nf (d'une entreprise)* performance; **il faut améliorer les performances de notre entreprise** we must improve our company's performance

performant, -e *adj (entreprise)* successful

période *nf* period

◊ *période d'essai* trial period

◊ *période d'essai gratuit* free trial period

◊ *période d'essor* boom

◊ *période de réflexion* cooling-off period

permis *nm* permit

perspective *nf (avenir)* prospect, outlook

◊ *perspectives commerciales* market prospects

persuasion *nf* persuasion

perte *nf (de clientèle, de part de marché)* loss; **vendre qch à perte** to sell sth at a loss

◊ *pertes et profits* profit and loss

petit, -e *adj* small

◊ *petites annonces* classified advertisements, *Br* small ads, *Am* want ads

◊ *petit commerçant* small trader, shopkeeper

◊ *le petit commerce* the small retail trade

phase *nf (étape)* phase, stage

◊ *phase de commercialisation* marketing stage

◊ *phase de croissance* growth stage

◊ *phase de déclin* decline stage

◊ *phase de développement* development stage

◊ *phase de faisabilité* feasibility stage

◊ *phase d'introduction* introduction stage

phoning *nm* telesales

pige *nf* *(de la publicité concurrente)* monitoring

pilote *adj* *(échantillon, étude, prix)* pilot

piloter *vt* *(étude, campagne)* to pilot

pionnier *nm* *(société, produit)* pioneer; **entrer en pionnier sur le marché** to be the first on the market

> **❝**
>
> Le **pionnier** du supermarché on-line continue à perdre de l'argent et ses performances boursières s'en ressentent. Sur les neufs premiers mois de 1997, le spécialiste américain de la livraison à domicile a perdu 8,8 millions de dollars.
>
> **❞**

placard *nm* *(publicité)* poster
◊ *placard publicitaire* display advertisement

placement *nm* placement
◊ *placement de produit* product placement

placer **1** *vt* *(vendre)* to sell; **facile/difficile à placer** easy/difficult to sell
2 se placer *vpr* *(se vendre)* to sell; **ces marchandises se placent facilement** these goods sell easily

placier *nm* **(a)** *(représentant de commerce)* sales representative **(b)** *(qui fait du porte-à-porte)* door-to-door salesman

plafond de crédit *nm* credit ceiling, credit limit

plan *nm* *(projet)* plan, project
◊ *plan d'action* action plan
◊ *plan de campagne* campaign plan
◊ *plan de développement des produits* product planning
◊ *plan marketing* marketing plan
◊ *plan média* media plan
◊ *plan prévisionnel* forecast plan
◊ *plan prix* price plan

planification *nf* planning
◊ *planification budgétaire* budget planning
◊ *planification des opérations* operational planning
◊ *planification du produit* product planning
◊ *planification stratégique* strategic planning
◊ *planification des ventes* sales planning

planigramme *nm* flow chart

planning *nm* plan, schedule; **nous avons un planning très chargé cette semaine** we have a very busy schedule this week
◊ *planning de distribution* distribution schedule
◊ *planning de livraison* delivery schedule

plaquette publicitaire *nf* brochure

plus-produit *nm* competitive advantage

PLV *nf* *(abrév* **publicité sur le lieu de vente***)* point-of-sale promotion

> "
>
> La campagne est relayée dans les magasins par des **PLV** et des leaflets distribués en sortie de caisses, expliquant les engagements de l'enseigne.
>
> "

PME *nf (abrév* **petite et moyenne entreprise)** small business

poids mort *nm (produit)* dog, dodo

point *nm* (a) *(endroit)* point, place (b) *(stade)* point (c) *(sur une carte de fidélité)* point

◊ *point d'achat* point of purchase

◊ *points cadeau* points *(awarded when making a purchase and collected by the customer to receive a discount off subsequent purchases)*

◊ *point de distribution* distribution outlet

◊ *point d'interrogation (produit)* question mark

◊ *point mort* break-even point

◊ *point de part de marché* share point

◊ *point prix* price point

◊ *point de saturation* saturation point

◊ *point de vente* point of sale, POS; **disponible dans votre point de vente habituel** available at your local stockist

◊ *point de vente au détail* retail outlet

◊ *Ordinat point de vente électronique* electronic point of sale

◊ *point de vente multimarque* multibrand store

politique *nf (stratégie)* policy

◊ *politique d'assortiment diversifié* mixed merchandising

◊ *politique de commercialisation* marketing policy

◊ *politique de communication* promotional policy

◊ *politique de distribution* distribution policy

◊ *politique de marque* brand policy

◊ *politique de prix* pricing policy, price policy

◊ *politique de produit/prix* product/price policy

◊ *politique de promotion* promotional policy

◊ *politique de vente* sales policy

population *nf* population

◊ *la population active* the working population

◊ *population cible* target population

◊ *population mère* basic population

port *nm (de marchandises)* carriage

◊ *port avancé* carriage forward, freight collect

◊ *port compris* postage included

◊ *port dû* carriage forward

◊ *port et emballage* postage and packing

◊ *port franc, port payé* carriage paid

◊ *port payé, assurance comprise* carriage insurance paid

porte-à-porte *nm* door-to-door selling; **faire du porte-à-porte** to be a door-to-door salesman, *f* saleswoman

portée *nf (d'une publicité, d'une campagne)* reach

portefeuille *nm (ensemble)* portfolio

◇ *portefeuille d'activités* business portfolio, portfolio mix

◇ *portefeuille de marques* brand portfolio

◇ *portefeuille de produits* product portfolio

position *nf (d'une entreprise, d'un produit)* position

◇ *position clé* key position

◇ *position concurrentielle* competitive position

◇ *position stratégique* strategic position

positionnement *nm (sur un marché)* positioning

◇ *positionnement concurrentiel* competitive positioning

◇ *positionnement de la marque* brand positioning

◇ *positionnement de prix* price positioning

◇ *positionnement du produit* product positioning

◇ *positionnement par la qualité* quality positioning

◇ *positionnement stratégique* strategic positioning

"

Le magasin le plus sélectif de Paris a même choisi un pic de spécialité. Quatre grandes (et rares) marques de maquillage professionnel ont ainsi fait leur entrée. Ce **positionnement** haut de gamme correspond parfaitement à la cible du grand magasin. La moitié de la clientèle habite en effet dans les quartiers aisés de la capitale.

"

positionner 1 *vt (produit)* to position

2 **se positionner** *vpr* **se positionner à la hausse sur le marché** to move upmarket; **se positionner par rapport à la concurrence** to position oneself in relation to the competition

post-achat *adj* post-purchase

poste *nf (service)* mail, *Br* post; **envoyer qch par la poste** to send something by mail *or Br* post

post-test *nm* post-test

post-tester *vt* to post-test

potentiel, -elle 1 *adj (acheteur, marché)* potential 2 *nm* potential

◇ *potentiel du marché* market potential *(of market)*

◇ *potentiel sur le marché* market potential *(of product)*

◇ *potentiel publicitaire* advertising potential

◇ *potentiel de vente* sales potential

pourcentage *nm* percentage; **travailler au pourcentage** to work on a commission basis

pouvoir d'achat *nm* purchasing power, buying power

> *Représentant 33% de la population en 1998, 53% en 2020, les seniors sont aussi une réalité économique importante, avec un **pouvoir d'achat** estimé à 800 MsdF.*

pré-commercialisation *nf* pre-marketing

préconditionné, -e *adj* pre-packed, pre-packaged

préconditionner *vt* to pre-pack, to pre-package

préconisateur *nm* influencer, opinion leader

prédisposition à l'achat *nf* buyer-readiness

préemballé, -e *adj* pre-packed, pre-packaged

préemballer *vt* to pre-pack, to pre-package

pré-étude *nf* pilot study

préférence *nf* preference

◊ *préférence du consommateur* consumer preference

> *Créer la **préférence** en donnant l'image d'une marque dynamique, jeune et conviviale est indéniablement l'objectif d'un France Télécom croulant sous le poids de son statut institutionnel.*

pré-marketing *nm* pre-marketing

prescripteur, -trice *nm,f* opinion leader

présentation *nf (exposition)* display

◊ *présentation sur le lieu de vente* point-of-sale display

◊ *présentation en masse* mass display

◊ *présentation du produit* product display

◊ *présentation au sol* floor display

◊ *présentation à la sortie* check-out display

◊ *présentation en vrac* dump display

présenter *vt (marchandises)* to display

présentoir *nm* display stand, display unit; *(panier)* dump bin

◊ *présentoir de caisse* check-out display

◊ *présentoir au sol* floor display, floor stand

presse *nf* la presse the press

◊ *presse nationale* national press

◊ *presse professionnelle* trade press

prétendant, -e *nm,f* challenger

pré-test *nm* pre-test

◊ *pré-test publicitaire* copy test

pré-tester *vt* to pre-test

prévision *nf* forecast; *(activité)* forecasting; **nous avons constitué des stocks en prévision d'une hausse subite de la demande** we have built up stocks in anticipation of a sudden increase in demand

◇ **prévision de la base** grass-roots forecasting

◇ **prévisions budgétaires** budget estimates, budget forecasts

◇ **prévisions économiques** economic forecasts

◇ **prévision événementielle** hazard forecasting

◇ **prévision du marché** market forecast

◇ **prévisions qualitatives** qualitative forecasting

◇ **prévisions quantitatives** quantitative forecasting

◇ **prévision de ventes** sales forecast

◇ **prévision des ventes et profits** sales and profit forecast

prévisionnel, -elle adj (coût, budget) estimated

prévoir vt (augmentation, baisse, ventes) to forecast

prévu, -e adj (augmentation, baisse, ventes) forecast, projected

prime nf (a) (cadeau) free gift, giveaway; **recette donnée en prime avec ce produit** free recipe when you buy this product (b) (subvention) subsidy

◇ **prime auto-payante** self-liquidating premium

◇ **prime contenant** container premium

◇ **prime différée** on-pack offer

◇ **prime directe** with-pack premium

◇ **prime à l'échantillon** free sample

◇ **prime produit en plus** bonus pack

> Côté promotion, Bordas propose une **prime directe** sur sa collection de cahiers d'apprentissage maternelle (huit titres). Cette **prime** sera encartée dans un rabat pour éviter les risques de vol. Il s'agit d'un objet en plastique à monter, sur le thème de la locomotion: bateau, avion, camion de pompiers – en tout huit objets différents.

prime time nm (à la télévision) prime time

prise de décision(s) nf decision-making

prix nm (coût) price; **à moitié prix** half price; **acheter qch à bas prix** to buy sth at a low price or cheaply; **mettre un prix à qch** to price sth, to put a price on sth

◇ **prix d'acceptabilité** psychological price

◇ **prix d'achat** purchase price

◇ **prix affiché** sticker price, displayed price

◇ **prix d'appel** loss leader price

◇ **prix cassés** knockdown prices

◇ **prix catalogue** catalogue price, list price

◇ **prix (au) comptant** cash price

◇ **prix conseillé** recommended retail price

◇ **prix conseillé par le fa-**

bricant manufacturer's recommended price

◇ *prix coûtant* cost price; **acheter/vendre qch au prix coûtant** to buy/sell sth at cost (price)

◇ *prix demandé* asking price

◇ *prix de demi-gros* trade price

◇ *prix directeur* price leader

◇ *prix d'écrémage* skimming price

◇ *prix d'équilibre* target price

◇ *prix exceptionnel* bargain price

◇ *prix à l'exportation, prix (à l')export* export price

◇ *prix de fabrique* manufacturer's price

◇ *prix facturé, prix de facture* invoiced price

◇ *prix de faveur* preferential price

◇ *prix fixe* fixed price

◇ *prix forfaitaire, prix à forfait* fixed price, all-inclusive price

◇ *prix de gros* wholesale price

◇ *prix hors taxe* price net of tax, price before tax

◇ *prix à l'importation, prix (à l')import* import price

◇ *prix imposé* retail price maintenance

◇ *prix de lancement* introductory price

◇ *prix magique* odd numbers price

◇ *prix marchand* trade price

◇ *prix marqué* marked price

◇ *prix minimum rentable* break-even price

◇ *prix net* net price

◇ *prix offert* offer price, selling price

◇ *prix officiel* standard price

◇ *prix optimum* optimal price

◇ *prix de pénétration* penetration price

◇ *prix préférentiel* preferential price

◇ *prix de prestige* premium price, prestige price

◇ *prix promotionnel* promotional price

◇ *prix psychologique* psychological price

◇ *prix psychologique optimum* optimal psychological price

◇ *prix de rabais* reduced price, discount price

◇ *prix recommandé* recommended retail price

◇ *prix réduit* reduced price, discount price

◇ *prix de revient* cost price

◇ *prix de solde* bargain price

◇ *prix standard* standard price

◇ *prix taxé* standard price

◇ *prix taxe comprise* price inclusive of tax

◇ *prix tout compris, prix tous frais compris, prix toutes taxes comprises* all-inclusive price

◇ *prix de transport* freight price

◇ *prix unique* flat price

◇ *prix unitaire, prix à l'unité* unit price

◇ *prix d'usine* factory price

◇ *prix vendeur* offer price, selling price

◇ *prix à la vente* sticker price, displayed price

◇ *prix de vente* selling price

◇ *prix de vente imposé* resale price maintenance

prix-courant *nm* price list, catalogue

processus *nm* process

◇ *processus d'achat* purchasing process

◇ *processus de diffusion, processus de distribution* distribution process

producteur, -trice 1 *adj* productive

2 *nm,f* producer; **ce pays est le premier producteur de composants électroniques du monde** this country is the world's largest producer of electronic components

production *nf* production; **la production ne suit plus la consommation** production is failing to keep up with demand

◇ *production juste à temps* just-in-time production

produit *nm (article)* product

◇ *produits d'achat courant* convenience goods

◇ *produits alimentaires, produits d'alimentation* food products

◇ *produit d'appel* loss leader, traffic builder

◇ *produit augmenté* augmented product

◇ *produit ciblé* niche product

◇ *produits de consommation* consumables, consumable goods

◇ *produits de consommation courante* convenience goods

◇ *produit dérivé* by-product

◇ *produit drapeau* own-brand product

◇ *produit écologique* green product

◇ *produit d'élite* premium product

◇ *produits étrangers* foreign produce, foreign goods

◇ *produit final* end product

◇ *produit fini* finished product, end product

◇ *produit générique* generic product

◇ *produits de grande consommation* consumer products

◇ *produit d'imitation* imitative product

◇ *produit innovateur* innovative product

◇ *produits de luxe* luxury goods

◇ *produits manufacturés* manufactured goods

◇ *produit de marque* branded product, brand name product

◇ *produit sans marque* unbranded product

◇ *produit à marque du distributeur* own-brand product

◇ *produit sans nom* no-name product

◇ *produit novateur* innovative product

◇ *produits d'origine nationale* domestic products

◇ *produit ouvré* finished product, end product

◇ *produits du pays* home produce

◇ *produits périssables* perishable goods, non-durable goods

◇ *produit de prestige* premium product

◇ *produits de second choix* seconds, rejects

◇ *produits spécialisés* speciality goods

◊ *produit de substitution, produit substitut* substitute product

◊ *produit tactique* me-too product, follow-me product

◊ *produit vert* green product

> "
>
> Le développement en alimentaire est rendu difficile par de nombreuses lourdeurs. Parce qu'il faut produire en masse, vous pouvez difficilement réaliser de petites séries, en diffusant des **produits d'élite** qui deviendront, par la suite, des **produits de grande consommation**.
>
> "

profil *nm* profile

◊ *profil de la clientèle* customer profile

◊ *profil du consommateur* consumer profile

◊ *profil démographique* demographic profile

◊ *profil géodémographique* geodemographic profile

◊ *profil du marché* market profile

◊ *profil de produit* product profile

◊ *profil psychologique* psychological profile

◊ *profil socio-démographique* sociodemographic profile

profit *nm* profit; **faire** *ou* **réaliser des profits** to make a profit

◊ *profit brut* gross profit

◊ *profit net* net profit

◊ *pertes et profits* profit and loss

programme *nm (planning)* programme, schedule; **arrêter un programme** to draw up *or* arrange a programme

◊ *programme des annonces* advertising schedule

◊ *programme de fidélisation* loyalty programme

◊ *programme de stimulation* incentive scheme

◊ *programme des ventes* sales programme, sales schedule

prohibition *nf* ban

◊ *prohibition d'entrée, prohibition à l'importation* import ban

◊ *prohibition de sortie* export ban

projection *nf (prévision)* projection

◊ *projection des ventes* sales projection

promesse *nf* claim

◊ *promesse mensongère* false claim

◊ *promesse produit* claim *(made about a product)*

◊ *promesse unique de vente* unique selling point *or* proposition

◊ *promesse de vente* promise to sell

> "
>
> Les spots mettent en avant la **promesse produit** de manière simple et conceptuelle, tout en conservant les valeurs de plaisir et de gourmandise qui sont des bases de Yoplait.
>
> "

promo *nf Fam (promotion)* promo

promoteur, -trice *nm,f* promoter

◇ *promoteur des ventes* sales promoter

promotion *nf (offre spéciale)* promotion; **articles en promotion** items on promotion *or Am* on special; **notre promotion de la semaine** this week's special offer *or Am* special; **faire une promotion sur un produit** to promote a product; **faire la promotion de qch** to promote sth

◇ *promotion collective* tie-in promotion

◇ *promotion sur le lieu de vente* point-of-sale promotion, in-store promotion

◇ *promotion on-pack* on-pack promotion

◇ *promotion de prestige* prestige promotion

◇ *promotion spéciale* special promotion

◇ *promotion des ventes* sales promotion

promotionnel, -elle *adj (brochure)* promotional; *(tarif)* special; *(budget)* promotional, publicity

promouvoir *vt (article)* to promote, to publicize

pronostic *nm* forecast

◇ *pronostic du marché* market forecast

proposition *nf (suggestion)* suggestion, proposal; *(offre)* offer; **faire** *ou* **formuler une proposition** to make a proposal

◇ *proposition de prix* price proposal

◇ *proposition unique* unique proposition

◇ *proposition unique de vente* unique selling point *or* proposition, USP

prospect *nm* prospective customer, prospect

◇ *prospects à forte potentialité* hot prospect pool

> Aujourd'hui, 70% des abonnés à CanalSatellite sont des abonnés à Canal+, le reste sont des **prospects** purs.

prospecté, -e *nm,f* prospective customer, prospect

prospecter **1** *vt (client)* to canvass; *(marché)* to explore; **prospecter la clientèle** to prospect for new cusomers
2 *vi* to prospect

prospecteur, -trice *nm,f* canvasser

prospection *nf* canvassing, prospecting; **faire de la prospection** to explore the market

◇ *prospection du marché* market exploration

◇ *prospection téléphonique* telephone canvassing

◇ *prospection sur le terrain* field research

prospectus *nm (de publicité)* leaflet; *(de plusieurs pages)* brochure

protection du consommateur *nf* consumer protection

provision *nf* *(réserve)* stock, supply; **faire provision de qch** to build up a stock of sth

psychologie *nf* psychology

◊ *psychologie commerciale* marketing psychology

◊ *psychologie des consommateurs* consumer psychology

◊ *psychologie de la publicité* advertising psychology

PU *nm* *(abrév* **prix unitaire**) unit price

pub *nf Fam (abrév* **publicité**) **(a)** *(secteur)* advertising; **elle travaille dans la pub** she works in advertising; **faire de la pub pour qch** to advertise sth **(b)** *(message)* ad

public *nm (d'un produit, d'une publicité)* audience

publicitaire 1 *adj (dépenses, campagne)* advertising

2 *nmf (personne)* advertising executive; **c'est une publicitaire** she works in advertising

publicité *nf (secteur)* advertising; *(message)* advert, advertisement; *(couverture)* advertising, publicity; **être/travailler dans la publicité** to be/work in advertising; **faire de la publicité pour qch** to advertise *or* publicize sth; **passer une publicité à la télévision** to advertise on TV

◊ *publicité par affichage* poster advertising

◊ *publicité agressive* hard sell

◊ *publicité d'amorçage* advance publicity

◊ *publicité de bouche à oreille* word-of-mouth advertising

◊ *publicité collective* group advertising

◊ *publicité comparative* comparative advertising

◊ *publicité concurrentielle* competitive advertising

◊ *publicité continue* drip advertising

◊ *publicité directe* direct advertising, direct mail advertising

◊ *publicité d'entreprise* corporate advertising

◊ *publicité extérieure* outdoor advertising

◊ *publicité générique* generic advertising

◊ *publicité goutte-à-goutte* drip advertising

◊ *publicité informative* informative advertising

◊ *publicité institutionnelle* institutional advertising, corporate advertising

◊ *publicité intensive* saturation advertising

◊ *publicité isolée* solus advertisement

◊ *publicité sur le lieu de vente* *(activité)* point-of-sale advertising; *(promotion)* point-of-sale promotion

◊ *publicité de marque* brand advertising

◊ *publicité média* media advertising, above-the-line advertising

◊ *publicité mensongère* misleading advertising; *(message)* misleading advertisement

◊ *publicité sur panneau* billboard advertising

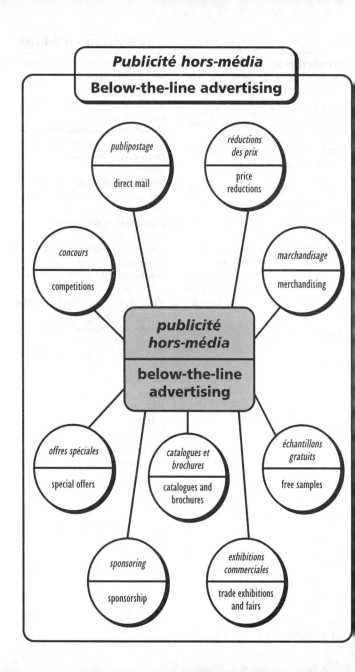

◇ *publicité périphérique* perimeter advertising

◇ *publicité au point de vente* point-of-sale advertising

◇ *publicité de prestige* prestige advertising

◇ *publicité de produit* product advertising

◇ *publicité par publipostage* direct mail advertising

◇ *publicité rédactionnelle* advertorial

◇ *publicité à réponse directe* direct response advertising

◇ *publicité subliminale* subliminal advertising

◇ *publicité télévisée* television advertising; *(message)* television advertisement

◇ *publicité par voie d'affiches* poster advertising

> **"**
>
> Incontournable relais des marques dans les rayons, les **publicités sur le lieu de vente** sont un peu comme les vitrines de Noël des boutiques d'antan: elle sont censées attirer l'œil, susciter l'envie et provoquer l'achat.
>
> **"**

publicité-médias *nf* media advertising, above-the-line advertising

publicité-produit *nf* product advertising

publipostage *nm* mailshot, mailing; **faire un publipostage** to send a mailshot *or* mailing

◇ *publipostage groupé* volume mailing

publireportage *nm* advertorial

> **"**
>
> Depuis 8 ans, l'agence Qualpige post-teste les **publireportages** qu'elle réalise pour ses clients. Bilan: des scores élevés, des campagnes efficaces. … Les performances des **publireportages** sont très variables selon la qualité de la réalisation. Ceux de Qualpige obtiennent d'ailleurs des scores largement supérieurs à la moyenne. "Nos articles sont faciles à lire, les informations sont intéressantes et nous faisons un vrai travail de réflexion sur le fond et la forme des messages."
>
> **"**

puissance *nf (pouvoir)* power

◇ *puissance d'achat* buying power, purchasing power

◇ *puissance de vente* selling power

QCM *nm* (*abrév* **questionnaire à choix multiple**) multiple-choice questionnaire

qualitatif, -ive *adj* qualitative

qualité *nf* (*d'un produit*) quality; **de qualité supérieure, de première qualité** good-quality, high-quality; **de mauvaise qualité, de qualité inférieure** poor-quality

◇ *qualité marchande* merchantable quality

◇ *qualité perçue* perceived quality

quantitatif, -ive *adj* quantitative

quantité *nf* quantity; **acheter qch en grande quantité** to buy sth in bulk

question *nf* question

◇ *question à choix multiple* multiple-choice question

◇ *question de contrôle* check question, control question

◇ *question dichotomique* dichotomous question

◇ *question fermée* closed-ended question, yes/no question

◇ *question filtre* check question

◇ *question ouverte* open-ended question

questionnaire *nm* questionnaire

◇ *questionnaire à choix multiple* multiple-choice questionnaire

◇ *questionnaire pilote* pilot questionnaire

quota *nm* quota

◇ *quota d'échantillonnage* sampling quota

◇ *quota de ventes* sales quota

◇ *quotas volontaires à l'export* voluntary export restraint

rabais *nm* reduction, discount; **un rabais de 500 francs** a 500-franc reduction *or* discount; **acheter/vendre qch au rabais** to buy/sell sth at a discount *or* at a reduced price; **faire** *ou* **accorder un rabais sur qch** to give a discount on sth; **il nous a fait un rabais de 20%** he gave us a 20% discount

rabattre *vt (déduire)* to take off, to deduct; **il a rabattu 5% sur le prix affiché** he took 5% off the marked price

rang *nm (dans une hiérarchie)* rank; **cette entreprise occupe le premier rang mondial du marché des composants électroniques** this company is number one in the world in the electronic component market; **l'entreprise a été reléguée au cinquième rang pour la production d'appareils électroménagers** the company has slipped to fifth place in the white goods market

rappel *nm* (**a**) *(de marchandises défectueuses)* recall (**b**) *(en publicité)* follow-up

rappeler *vt (marchandises défectueuses)* to recall

rapport *nm* (**a**) *(compte-rendu)* report; **faire** *ou* **rédiger un rapport (sur)** to make *or* to draw up a report (on) (**b**) *(proportion)* ratio, proportion

◇ *rapport commercial* market report

◇ *rapport d'étude de marché* market study report

◇ *rapport de faisabilité* feasibility report

◇ *rapport qualité-prix* quality-price ratio, value for money; **être d'un bon rapport qualité-prix** to be good value for money

◇ *rapport de vente* sales report

rayon *nm* (**a**) *(dans un magasin)* department; **le rayon des surgelés** the frozen food department; **nous n'avons plus en rayon** we're out of stock (**b**) *(d'une étagère)* shelf

◇ *rayon d'action (d'une campagne publicitaire)* range

◇ *rayon des soldes* bargain counter

rayonnage *nm* shelving, shelves

R-D *nf (abrév* **recherche et développement)** R & D, R and D

réachat nm rebuy, repurchase

◊ **réachat modifié** modified rebuy

réacheter vt to rebuy, to repurchase

réaction nf reaction; (des consommateurs) feedback

◊ **réaction émotionnelle** emotional response

réassortiment nm (d'un magasin) restocking; (stock) new stock

réassortir 1 vt (magasin) to restock

2 **se réassortir** vpr to replenish one's stock; **se réassortir en qch** to renew one's stock of sth

rebut nm (article) reject

recensement nm (de marchandises) inventory

recenser vt (marchandises) to inventory, to take stock of

récépissé nm receipt

◊ **récépissé de douane** customs receipt

◊ **récépissé d'entrepôt** warehouse receipt

réceptif précoce nm early adopter

réception nf (d'une commande, de biens) receipt; **à payer à la réception** Br cash or Am collect on delivery

réceptionnaire nmf (de marchandises) consignee

réceptionner vt (marchandises) to take delivery of

réceptivité des consommateurs nf consumer acceptance

recette nf takings, earnings, revenue; **faire recette** to be profitable or a success; **on a fait une bonne/mauvaise recette** the takings were good/poor; **la recette était meilleure la semaine dernière** the takings were up last week

◊ **recette annuelle** annual earnings

◊ **recette journalière** daily takings

recevoir vt (courrier, marchandises, commande) to get, to receive

recherche nf research; **faire des recherches (sur qch)** to do research (into sth)

◊ **recherche ad hoc** ad hoc research

◊ **recherches sur les besoins des consommateurs** consumer research

◊ **recherche commerciale** marketing research

◊ **recherche et développement** research and development

◊ **recherche documentaire** desk research

◊ **recherche longitudinale** longitudinal research, continuous research

◊ **recherche marketing** market research

◊ **recherche de motivation** motivation research, motivational research

◊ **recherche opérationnelle** operational research

◊ **recherches par panel** panel research

◊ **recherche sur les prix** pricing

research

◇ *recherche de produits* product research

◇ *recherche par sondage* survey research

◇ *recherches sur le terrain* field research

réclame *nf* (a) *(secteur)* advertising; *(annonce)* advertisement; **faire de la réclame pour qch** to advertise sth (b) *(promotion)* **en réclame** on offer

recommercialiser *vt* to remarket

reconditionner *vt (marchandises)* to repackage

reconnaissance *nf (identification)* recognition

◇ *reconnaissance des besoins* need recognition

recueil des données *nm* data collection

recul *nm* decline, drop; **les ventes ont subi un recul** sales have dropped

rédacteur, -trice *nm,f*

◇ *rédacteur publicitaire* copywriter

redorer *vt (société, image)* to repackage

réduction *nf (rabais)* reduction; **faire une réduction de 15% (à qn)** to give (sb) a 15% reduction

◇ *réduction des prix* price reduction

réduit, -e *adj (prix, marchandises)* reduced

référence *nf (produit)* listed product

> "Nous avons mis en place plus de 550 **références** contre environ 450 dans l'ancienne configuration," confie Jean Métro, directeur du magasin. "Compte tenu de l'importance de la production locale, nous avons également apporté un soin particulier à notre sélection de bourgognes rouges et blancs, qui représentent 10% de l'offre totale."

référencement *nm (d'un produit)* listing

référencer *vt (produit)* to list

refrain publicitaire *nm* (advertising) jingle

refus de vente *nm* refusal to sell

refuser *vt (marchandises)* to reject

régie publicitaire *nf* advertising sales agency

région test *nf* test area

réglementation *nf* regulation

◇ *réglementation des prix* price regulation

règlement *nm (d'un compte)* settlement; *(d'une facture)* payment, settlement; **en règlement de votre compte** in settlement of your account; **faire un règlement par chèque** to pay by cheque

◇ *règlement à la commande* cash with order

◊ *règlement en espèces* cash payment, cash settlement

régler *vt (compte)* to settle; *(facture)* to pay, to settle; *(achat)* to pay for; **régler qch en espèces** to pay cash for sth; **régler qch par chèque** to pay for sth by cheque

relance *nf* (a) *(d'un produit, d'une marque, d'une entreprise)* relaunch (b) *(d'un client)* follow-up

◊ *relance téléphonique* telephone follow-up

> Malgré une promesse de vente à NRJ de quelque 15 MF, il tente, cette année-là, une **relance** de la dernière chance en se positionnant sur une niche qui fait alors fureur au nord de la France: la dance.

relancement *nm (d'un produit)* relaunch

relancer *vt* (a) *(ventes)* to boost (b) *(produit)* to relaunch (c) *(client)* to follow up

relatif, -ive *adj (part de marché)* relative

relations *nfpl* relations

◊ *relations clientèle* customer relations

◊ *relations publiques* public relations

relevé *nm* statement

◊ *relevé d'achat journalier* purchase diary

◊ *relevé de vente* sales report

remboursable *adj (argent, achat)* refundable; *(prêt)* repayable

remboursement *nm (d'un achat)* refund; *(d'un prêt)* repayment

rembourser *vt (argent, achat, personne)* to refund; *(prêt)* to repay

remise *nf (rabais)* discount, reduction; **une remise de 10%** a discount of 10%, 10% off; **faire une remise sur qch** to allow a discount on sth; **faire une remise à qn** to give sb a discount

◊ *remise de caisse* cash discount

◊ *remise de fidélité* customer loyalty discount

◊ *remise de marchandisage* merchandising allowance

◊ *remise sur marchandises* trade discount

◊ *remise promotionnelle* promotional discount

◊ *remise quantitative, remise pour quantité, remise sur la quantité* bulk discount, quantity discount

◊ *remise saisonnière* seasonal discount

◊ *remise d'usage* trade discount

remue-méninges *nm* brainstorming; **un remue-méninges** a brainstorming session

rendu *nm* returned article, return; **faire un rendu** to return *or* exchange an article

renouveler *vt (commande, achat)* to repeat

rentabilité *nf* profitability, cost-effectiveness (**de** of); *(des ventes)* return (**de** on)

◊ *rentabilité directe du produit* direct product profitability

rentable *adj* profitable, cost-effective; **la campagne n'a pas été très rentable** the campaign has not been very profitable *or* cost-effective

renvoi *nm (de marchandises)* return, sending back

renvoyer *vt (marchandises)* to return, to send back

repli stratégique *nm (du marché)* strategic withdrawal

répondant, -e *nm,f (d'un questionnaire)* respondent

répondre **répondre à** *vt ind (question)* to reply to, to answer

réponse *nf (à une question)* answer, reply, response

◊ *réponse payée* reply paid

◊ *réponse stimulée* stimulus response

repositionnement *nm (d'un produit)* repositioning

◊ *repositionnement réel* real repositioning

repositionner **1** *vt (produit)* to reposition

2 se repositionner *vpr* **se repositionner à la baisse** to move downmarket; **se repositionner à la hausse** to move upmarket

reprendre **1** *vt (marchandises invendues, articles en solde)* to take back

2 *vi (affaires, économie)* to recover, to pick up

représentant, -e *nm,f* representative, agent; **je suis représentant en électroménager** I'm a representative for an electrical appliances company

◊ *représentant de commerce, représentant commercial* sales representative

◊ *représentant dûment accrédité* duly authorized agent

◊ *représentant exclusif* sole agent

◊ *représentant multi-carte* freelance representative *(working for several companies)*

représentatif, -ive *adj (échantillon)* representative

représentation *nf* representation; *(agence)* agency; **faire de la représentation, être dans la représentation** to be a (sales) representative

◊ *représentation exclusive* sole agency; **avoir la représentation exclusive de** to be sole agents for

représenter *vt* **(a)** *(agir au nom de)* to represent, to be a representative for **(b)** *(corres-*

pondre à) to account for, to represent; **ceci représente 10% du budget des ventes** this accounts for *or* represents 10% of the sales budget

reprise *nf* (a) *(des affaires)* recovery (b) *(de marchandises invendues, d'articles en solde)* taking back, return; **nous ne faisons pas de reprise** goods cannot be returned

◊ *reprise économique* economic recovery

réseau *nm* network

◊ *réseau d'affichage* outdoor network

◊ *réseau commercial* sales network

◊ *réseau de distribution* distribution network

◊ *réseau de vente* sales network

> **"**
>
> Enfin, dès le premier semestre 1998, une opération de stimulation du **réseau de vente** a touché 200 points de vente sur les 1000 qui distribuent les produits.
>
> **"**

résistance des consommateurs *nf* consumer resistance

responsabilité *nf (morale)* responsibility (**de** for); *(légale)* liability (**de** for); **avoir la responsabilité de qch** *(en avoir la charge)* to be in charge of sth; **elle a la responsabilité du service après-vente** she's in charge of the after-sales department

◊ *responsabilité du fabricant* manufacturer's liability

◊ *responsabilité du produit* product liability

responsable 1 *adj* responsible (**de** for); **être responsable de qch** *(en avoir la charge)* to be in charge of sth; **elle est responsable du service après-vente** she's in charge of the after-sales department

2 *nmf (personne qui a la charge)* person in charge (**de** of)

◊ *responsable de budget* account executive

◊ *responsable commercial* business manager

◊ *responsable des comptes-clients* account handler

◊ *responsable du marketing* marketing manager

◊ *responsable des relations publiques* public relations officer

résultats *nmpl* performance

rétention *nf (d'un message publicitaire)* retention

◊ *rétention sélective* selective retention

retour *nm (de marchandises)* return; **marchandises de retour, retours** returns; **vendu avec possibilité de retour** sold on a sale or return basis

réunion *nf (assemblée)* meeting

◊ *réunion de groupe (pour étude de marché)* group meeting

◊ *réunion de remue-méninges* brainstorming session

revendable *adj* resaleable

revendeur, -euse *nm,f* retailer; *(d'articles d'occasion)* second-hand dealer

revendre 1 *vt* to resell
2 **se revendre** *vpr* **ce genre de produit ne se revend pas facilement** this sort of product isn't easy to resell

revente *nf* resale

revenu disponible *nm* disposable income

riche *adj (fortuné)* wealthy, affluent

richesse *nf* wealth, affluence
◊ *la richesse vive* consumer purchasing power

risque perçu *nm* perceived risk

ristourne *nf (rabais)* discount; **une ristourne de 15%** a 15% discount; **faire une ristourne à qn** to give sb a discount
◊ *ristourne de fidélité* customer loyalty discount

ristourner *vt (réduire)* to give a discount of; **il nous a ristourné 15% du prix** he gave us a 15% discount

rival, -e *nm,f & adj* rival

rivaliser *vi* **rivaliser avec qn** to compete with sb; **ils rivalisent avec nous pour la conquête du marché** they're competing with us to dominate the market

rotation *nf (des stocks)* turnover; **le délai de rotation des stocks est de quatre mois** stocks are turned round every four months

rupture *nf* **être en rupture de stock** *(magasin, fournisseur)* to be out of stock

> Ce magazine … est une façon positive de les remercier de leur fidélité et de leur attachement à l'enseigne. Et lorsque nous sommes **en rupture de stock**, les jeunes nous le réclament: le magazine fait désormais partie des services que nous leur devons.

sacrifié, -e *adj (prix)* rock-bottom; *(article)* at a rock-bottom price

sacrifier *vt (marchandises)* to sell at rock-bottom prices

salle *nf* room

◇ **salle de démonstration** showroom

◇ **salle d'exposition** showroom; *(pour une foire)* exhibition hall

salon *nm (exposition)* exhibition, trade fair

satisfaction *nf* satisfaction

◇ **satisfaction de la clientèle** customer satisfaction

◇ **satisfaction du consommateur** consumer satisfaction

saturation *nf (du marché)* saturation; **arriver à saturation** to reach saturation point

saturé, -e *adj (marché)* saturated

SAV *nm (abrév* **service après-vente)** after-sales service

scénario d'achat *nm* buying situation

score *nm* score

◇ **score d'agrément** approval rating, approval score

◇ **score d'attribution** attribution score

◇ **score de mémorisation** recall score

◇ **score de reconnaissance** recognition score

> Le ballet aquatique réalisé par Jean-Pierre Roux et accompagné d'une musique extraite du film *Les Hommes préfèrent les blondes* de Howard Hawks obtient un **score de reconnaissance** de 91%. Autant dire que presque tous les téléspectateurs qui l'ont vu s'en souviennent.

séance de créativité *nf* brainstorming session

secteur *nm* (a) *Écon (d'une activité)* sector (b) *(d'un représentant)* area, patch

◇ **secteur en expansion** growth sector

◇ **secteur de la grande distribution** mass distribution sector

- ◇ *secteur primaire* primary sector
- ◇ *secteur secondaire* secondary sector
- ◇ *secteur tertiaire* tertiary sector
- ◇ *secteur de vente* sales area, sales territory

séduction *nf (d'un produit)* appeal

- ◇ *séduction du client* customer appeal

segment *nm (du marché)* segment

- ◇ *segment démographique* demographic segment
- ◇ *segment géodémographique* geodemographic segment
- ◇ *segment géographique* geographic segment
- ◇ *segment socio-démographique* sociodemographic segment

> **"**
>
> Deux ans à peine après leur lancement, les sauces exotiques Goûtez le monde signées Amora s'octroient 20% des ventes du **segment** des sauces à cuisiner.
>
> **"**

segmentation *nf* segmentation

- ◇ *segmentation par avantages recherchés* benefit segmentation
- ◇ *segmentation comportementale* behaviour segmentation
- ◇ *segmentation démographique* demographic segmentation
- ◇ *segmentation fondée sur les besoins* needs-based segmentation
- ◇ *segmentation géodémographique* geodemographic segmentation
- ◇ *segmentation géographique* geographic segmentation
- ◇ *segmentation du marché* market segmentation
- ◇ *segmentation psychographique* psychographic segmentation
- ◇ *segmentation socio-démographique* sociodemographic segmentation
- ◇ *segmentation stratégique* strategic segmentation
- ◇ *segmentation par styles de vie* lifestyle segmentation

segmenter *vt (marché)* to segment

sélection *nf (échantillon)* selection

- ◇ *sélection au hasard* random selection

sélectionner *vt (choisir)* to select

sensibilité *nf* sensitivity

- ◇ *sensibilité compétitive* competitive awareness
- ◇ *sensibilité aux marques* brand sensitivity
- ◇ *sensibilité aux prix* price sensitivity

sensible *adj* sensitive; **sensible aux marques** brand-sensitive; **sensible aux prix** price-sensitive

service nm (a) *(département)* department (b) *(prestation)* service (c) *Écon* **services** *(secteur)* services; **les biens et les services** goods and services

◇ *service des achats* purchasing department

◇ *service d'action commerciale* marketing department

◇ *service après-vente (département)* after-sales department; *(prestation)* after-sales service

◇ *service clientèle, service clients (département)* customer service department; *(prestation)* customer service

◇ *service des commandes* order department

◇ *service commercial* sales department

◇ *service commercial export* export department

◇ *service consommateurs (département)* customer service department; *(prestation)* customer service

◇ *service contrôle qualité, service de contrôle de qualité* quality control department

◇ *service d'études* research department

◇ *service d'étude marketing* market research department

◇ *service des expéditions* dispatch department

◇ *service export, service des exportations* export department

◇ *service du marketing* marketing department

◇ *service perçu* perceived service

◇ *service premier* premium service

◇ *service de presse* press office

◇ *service de publicité* advertising department, publicity department

◇ *service de relation clientèle (département)* customer service department; *(prestation)* customer service

◇ *service des ventes* sales department

◇ *service vente-marketing* sales and marketing department

SET nf *Ordinat* *(abrév* **secure electronic transaction)** SET®

seuil de rentabilité nm break-even (point); **atteindre le seuil de rentabilité** to break even, to reach break-even point

signature musicale publicitaire nf *(advertising)* jingle

SIM nm *(abrév* **système d'information marketing)** MIS

site nm (a) *(emplacement)* site (b) *Ordinat (sur le Web)* site

◇ *Ordinat* **site marchand** e-commerce site

◇ *site témoin* test site

◇ *Ordinat* **site Web** Web site

> **❝**
>
> La première étude s'appuie sur 55 **sites marchands** qui représenteraient, selon Benchmark Group, 80% du volume échangé sur le Web en France.
>
> **❞**

situation *nf (circonstances)* situation

◇ *situation d'achat* buying situation

◇ *situation de nouvel achat* new-buy situation

slogan *nm* slogan

◇ *slogan publicitaire* advertising slogan

société *nf* (a) *(entreprise)* company (b) *(communauté)* society

◇ *la société d'abondance* the affluent society

◇ *société de consommation* consumer society

◇ *société d'études* research company

◇ *société d'études de marché* market research company

◇ *société d'exportation* export company

◇ *société de marketing* marketing company

◇ *société de vente par correspondance* mail-order company

socio-démographique *adj* sociodemographic

sociologique *adj (enquête)* sociological

socio-style *nm* lifestyle group

solde *nm (promotion)* sale; *(marchandise)* sale item; **en solde** *(marchandise) Br* in the sale, *Am* on sale; **acheter** *ou* **avoir qch en solde** to buy *or* get sth *Br* in the sale *or Am* on sale; **mettre** *ou* **vendre qch en solde** to sell sth off

◇ *solde de fermeture* closing-down sale

◇ *solde de fin de saison* end-of-season sale

◇ *solde après inventaire* stocktaking sale

solder *vt (stock)* to sell off, to discount

soldeur, -euse *nm,f* discount trader

sonal *nm (advertising)* jingle

sondage *nm (enquête)* poll, survey; *(activité)* sampling; **faire un sondage (sur qch)** to carry out a poll *or* survey (on sth)

◇ *sondage aléatoire* random sampling

◇ *sondage d'opinion* opinion poll

◇ *sondage par quotas* quota sampling

sondé, -e *nm,f* respondent

sonder *vt (dans une enquête)* to poll; **sonder l'opinion** to carry out *or* to conduct an opinion poll; **10% de la population sondée** 10% of those polled

sortir **1** *vi* **sortir sur le marché** *(produit)* to come onto the market

2 *vt (nouveau produit)* to bring out, to launch

sous-produit *nm* by-product

soutien commercial *nm* sales support

spécialiste *nmf* specialist; **c'est un spécialiste du marketing** he's an expert in marketing

◇ *spécialiste produit* product specialist

sponsor *nm* sponsor

sponsoring *nm* sponsorship

"
"Nous sommes par ailleurs engagés dans des actions de **sponsoring**. Notre principal engagement en la matière est réalisé en Formule 1 aux côtés de l'écurie McLaren depuis plus de 4 ans. C'est pour nous une formidable occasion de faire des relations publiques auprès de nos plus grands comptes."
"

sponsoriser *vt* to sponsor

spot *nm* advert, commercial
◇ **spot publicitaire** advert, commercial
◇ **spot télé, spot TV** TV advert, TV commercial

stabiliser se stabiliser *vpr* (prix, demande, ventes) to level off, to level out

stabilité *nf* (des prix, de la demande, des ventes) stability

stable *adj* (prix, demande, ventes) stable

stand *nm* (d'exposition) stand
◇ **stand d'exposition** exhibition stand

standard *adj* (modèle, prix, taille) standard

star *nf* (produit) star

"
Une soixantaine de nouveaux jeux Nintendo 64 vont être mis sur le marché pour cette fin d'année 1998. Parmi eux, Zelda: cent heures de suspense et de jeu qui vont faire un carton. Ce concept existe déjà sur nos consoles 8 et 16 bits: Zelda est devenue une **star**, vendue à près de 6 millions d'ex. dans le monde.
"

statistique *nf* (donnée) statisti
◇ **statistiques démographiques** demographics

stimulant *nm* (pour relancer, stimulus; (pour encourager) incentive
◇ **stimulants de vente** sales incentives

stimulation *nf* incentive

stock *nm* (des marchandises) stock; **en stock** in stock; **nous n'avons plus ce modèle en stock** we no longer have this model in stock, this model is out of stock; **dans la limite des stocks disponibles** while stocks last, subject to availability; **constituer des stocks** to build up stocks; **épuiser les stocks** to deplete or exhaust stocks

stocker *vt* (marchandises) to stock; (en grande quantité) to stockpile

stratégie *nf* strategy
◇ **stratégie de croissance** growth strategy
◇ **stratégie de différenciation** differentiation strategy
◇ **stratégie de distribution** distribution strategy
◇ **stratégie de distribution intensive** intensive distribution strategy

◇ *stratégie de diversification* diversification strategy

◇ *stratégie de globalisation* globalization strategy

◇ *stratégie d'imitation* imitation strategy, me-too strategy

◇ *stratégie marketing* game plan, marketing strategy

◇ *stratégie de la marque* brand strategy

◇ *stratégie de pénétration* market penetration strategy

◇ *stratégie de positionnement* positioning strategy

◇ *stratégie promotionnelle* promotional strategy

◇ *stratégie publicitaire* advertising strategy

◇ *stratégie pull* pull strategy

◇ *stratégie push* push strategy

> **❝**
>
> Bricolag, enseigne de bricolage implantée en Martinique, confie son budget de communication à LM Y&R. L'agence nantaise a dû repenser la **stratégie publicitaire** du magasin martiniquais afin de lui construire une image différente de celle établie en métropole.
>
> **❞**

structure *nf (du marché, d'une enquête)* structure

structuré, -e *adj (enquête)* structured

style de vie *nm (du consommateur, du client)* lifestyle

substitut *nm (produit)* substitute

◇ *substitut rapproché* close substitute

succursale *nf* branch

suite *nf* follow-up; **donner suite à qch** *(demande, lettre)* to follow sth up; *(commande)* to deal with sth

suivant, -e *nm,f* follower; *(sur le marché)* market follower

◇ *suivant immédiat* early follower

suiveur *nm* follower; *(sur le marché)* market follower

suivi *nm (relance)* follow-up; **assurer le suivi de qch** *(commande)* to deal with sth; *(produit)* to continue to stock sth

supérieur, -e *adj (produit, marchandises)* of superior quality; *(qualité)* superior

supermarché *nm* supermarket

support *nm (médium)* medium

◇ *support de publicité, support publicitaire* publicity medium, advertising medium

surabondance *nf (de marchandises)* surfeit, glut

surcharger *vt (marché)* to glut, to overload

surface *nf*

◇ *surface d'exposition, surface de présentation* display space

◇ *surface au sol* floor space

◇ *surface de vente* sales area

> **"**
>
> Deux questions majeures se posent au hard discount à l'aube de l'an 2000: la **surface de vente** et l'assortiment. Faut-il réduire la première ou élargir le second, quitte à prendre quelques libertés avec le hard pur et dur?
>
> **"**

surplus nm (revenu) disposable income

surpositionnement nm over-positioning

surpositionner vt to over-position

surveillance nf (des prix) monitoring

surveiller vt (prix) to monitor

survendre vt to overcharge for

survente nf overcharging

système nm (structure) system

◇ **système de contrôle de stocks** stock control system

◇ **système de distribution** distribution system

◇ **système d'information marketing** marketing information system

◇ **système d'intelligence marketing** marketing intelligence system

tactique *nf* tactics
◇ *tactique commerciale* marketing tactics

taille *nf (du marché, de part de marché, d'un segment)* size

tarif *nm (prix)* rates; *(tableau des prix)* price list
◇ *tarif d'entrée* import list
◇ *tarif des insertions* advertising rates
◇ *tarif de la publicité* advertising rates

tarification *nf* pricing
◇ *tarification géographique* geographic pricing
◇ *tarification de pénétration du marché* market penetration pricing

tassement *nm (du marché, des ventes, de la demande)* drop, downturn; **l'augmentation de la TVA a provoqué un léger tassement de nos ventes** the rise in VAT has caused a slight drop in our sales

tasser se tasser *vpr (marché, ventes, demande)* to drop, to fall

TAT *nm (abrév* **thematic apperception test** *ou* **test d'apperception thématique)** TAT

taux *nm (montant, pourcentage)* rate
◇ *taux d'attribution* attribution rate
◇ *taux de change* exchange rate
◇ *taux de couverture* coverage rate
◇ *taux d'escompte* discount rate
◇ *taux d'exclusivité à la marque* brand exclusivity rate
◇ *taux d'inflation* rate of inflation
◇ *taux de mémorisation* recall rate
◇ *taux de notoriété (d'un produit)* awareness rating
◇ *taux de pénétration (d'un marché)* rate of penetration
◇ *taux de réachat* rebuy rate, repurchase rate
◇ *taux de refus* refusal rate
◇ *taux de renouvellement* rate of renewal
◇ *taux de répétition* frequency rate
◇ *taux de réponse* response rate
◇ *taux de rotation (des stocks)* turnover rate

taxe *nf* (a) *(prélèvement)* tax; **hors taxe** exclusive of tax; **toutes taxes comprises** inclusive of tax (b) *(prix fixé)* con-trolled price; **vendre qch à la taxe** to sell sth at the controlled price

◇ **taxe à l'exportation** export tax

◇ **taxe à l'importation** import tax

◇ **taxe de luxe** tax on luxury goods, luxury tax

technico-commercial, -e
1 *adj (service)* technical sales
2 *nm,f* sales technician, sales engineer

technique *nf* technique

◇ **techniques commerciales** marketing techniques

◇ **techniques marchandes** merchandising techniques

◇ **techniques promotionnelles** promotional techniques

◇ **technique de sondage d'opinion** opinion measurement technique

◇ **techniques de vente** sales techniques

téléachat *nm* teleshopping

télédémarchage *nm* telephone canvassing

télémarketing *nm* telemarketing

téléspectateur, -trice *nm,f* television viewer

télévendeur, -euse *nm,f* telesales person

télévente *nf* telephone selling; **téléventes** telesales

témoignage *nm (publicité)* testimonial advertising

tempérament *nm* **à tempérament** on hire purchase, *Am* on the installment plan; **acheter qch à tempérament** to buy sth on hire purchase *or Am* on the installment plan

tendance *nf* tendency, trend

◇ **tendances conjoncturelles** economic trends

◇ **tendances de la consommation** consumer trends

◇ **tendance du marché** market trend

termes *nmpl (d'une vente, d'un accord, de paiement)* terms

terminal *nm (pour payer)* terminal

◇ *Ordinat* **terminal électronique de paiement** electronic payment terminal

◇ *Ordinat* **terminal de paiement en ligne** on-line terminal

◇ **terminal point de vente** point-of-sale terminal

terrain *nm (lieux d'étude)* field; **sur le terrain** in the field

territoire *nm (d'un représentant)* territory

◇ **territoire exclusif** exclusive territory

◇ **territoire de vente** sales territory

test 1 *adj (zone, département)* test

2 *nm* test; **tests** *(procédure)* testing

◇ **test d'acceptabilité** acceptance test

◇ **test d'aperception thématique** thematic apperception test

◇ **test aveugle** blind test

◇ **test de concept** concept test

◇ **test comparatif** comparison test

◇ **test auprès des consommateurs** consumer test

◇ **test du lendemain** day-after recall test

◇ **test de marché** market test

◇ **test de mémorisation** memory test, recall test

◇ **test monadique** monadic test

◇ **test de performance** performance test

◇ **test sur place** field test

◇ **test de préférence** preference test

◇ **test de produit** product test

◇ **test de rappel** recall test

◇ **test de reconnaissance** recognition test

◇ **test de vente** market test

tester *vt* to test; **tester qch sur le marché** to test-market sth

tête *nf* **par tête** *(par personne)* per capita, per head

◇ **tête de gondole** aisle end display, gondola end

texte publicitaire *nm* advertising copy

TG *nf (abrév* **tête de gondole**) aisle end display, gondola end

> 66
>
> Bressor Alliance organise deux opérations concernant ses fromages à pâte persillée, Grièges Affineur et Bleu des Burgons (rayon LS). À partir du mois de février, et tout au long de l'année, Grièges Affineur sera présent lors de 360 **TG** multimarques dans les hypermarchés. Les consommateurs pourront goûter Grièges Affineur et un dépliant leur sera remis.
>
> 99

théorie *nf* theory

◇ **théorie de la décision** decision theory

◇ **théorie des jeux** game theory

ticket nm

◇ **ticket de caisse** till receipt, Am sales slip

◇ **ticket d'entrée** = cost of entering the market

tierce partie de confiance nf Ordinat trusted third party

Toile nf Ordinat **la Toile** the Web

total, -e 1 adj (demande, dépenses, ventes) total

2 nm total; **le total s'élève à 10 000 francs** the total comes to 10,000 francs

tournée de présentation nf road show

tourniquet nm (présentoir) stand, spinner

TPC nf Ordinat (abrév **tierce partie de confiance**) TTP

TPV nm (abrév **terminal point de vente**) point-of-sale terminal

trade marketing nm trade marketing

traitement de données nm data processing

traiter vt (données) to process

tranche d'âge nf (dans une étude de marché) age group

transfert nm (d'argent) transfer

◇ Ordinat **transfert de fonds électronique** electronic funds transfer

◇ Ordinat **transfert de fonds électronique sur point de vente** electronic funds transfer at point of sale

transitaire nm forwarding agent

transport nm (de marchandises) transport, shipping

◇ **transport aérien, transport par avion** air transport, airfreight

◇ **transports routiers** road transport, road haulage

transporter vt (marchandises) to transport; **transporter qch par avion** to airfreight sth, to transport sth by air; **transporter qch par mer** to transport sth by sea; **transporter qch par route** to transport sth by road

transporteur nm carrier

travail nm work

◇ **travail complémentaire** follow-up work

◇ **travail sur le terrain** field work

TVA nf (abrév **taxe à la valeur ajoutée**) Br VAT, Am sales tax; **soumis à la TVA** subject to Br VAT or Am sales tax

UAS *nf (abrév* **unité d'activité stratégique**) SBU

ultracompétitif *adj (société, prix)* very highly competitive

union *nf (association)* union
◇ *Union des annonceurs* = organization which defends the interests of advertisers
◇ *union douanière* customs union

unité *nf (article)* unit; **les ventes ont dépassé les 3 000 unités** sales have passed the 3,000 mark; **acheter/vendre qch à l'unité** to buy/sell sth individually *or* singly
◇ *unité d'activité stratégique* strategic business unit

univers *nm (nombre de personnes dans un groupe, dans un segment)* universe

> **"**
> Certes, le consommateur achète rarement des draps et des serviettes le même jour, mais les fournisseurs – communs aux deux **univers** – conçoivent leurs collections de lit et de salle de bains autour des mêmes thèmes.
> **"**

utile *adj (marché, audience)* addressable

usine *nf* factory

utilisateur, -trice *nm,f* user
◇ *utilisateur final* end-user
◇ *utilisateur pilote* lead user
◇ *utilisateur tardif* late adopter

utiliser *vt (produit)* to use

vache à lait *nf (produit)* cash cow

vague *nf (de publicités)* run, series

valeur *nf* value; **prendre/perdre de la valeur** to go up/down in value; **avoir de la valeur** to be of value; **être sans valeur** to be of no value

◇ **valeur ajoutée** added value
◇ **valeur distinctive** distinctive value
◇ **valeur perçue** perceived value
◇ **valeur à la revente** resale value

vedette *nf (produit)* star

veille *nf* monitoring

◇ **veille marketing** marketing intelligence

vendable *adj* saleable, sellable

vendeur, -euse *nm,f (dans un magasin) Br* sales assistant, *Am* (sales) clerk; *(dans une entreprise)* sales representative

◇ **vendeur à domicile** door-to-door salesman
◇ **vendeur export** exporter
◇ **vendeur par téléphone** telesales person

vendre 1 *vt (produit, article, service)* to sell; *(commercialiser)* to market; **vendre qch à qn** to sell sb sth, to sell sth to sb; **vendre moins cher que qn** to undercut sb; **vendre comptant** to sell for cash; **vendre à crédit** to sell on credit; **vendre au détail** to sell retail, to retail; **vendre en gros** to sell wholesale; **vendre à perte** to sell at a loss

2 se vendre *vpr (produit, article)* to be sold; **le nouveau modèle ne se vend pas bien** the new model isn't selling well

vente *nf (transaction)* sale; *(activité)* selling; **réaliser une vente** to make a sale; **la vente** *(secteur)* sales; **elle est dans la vente** she's in sales; **ventes**

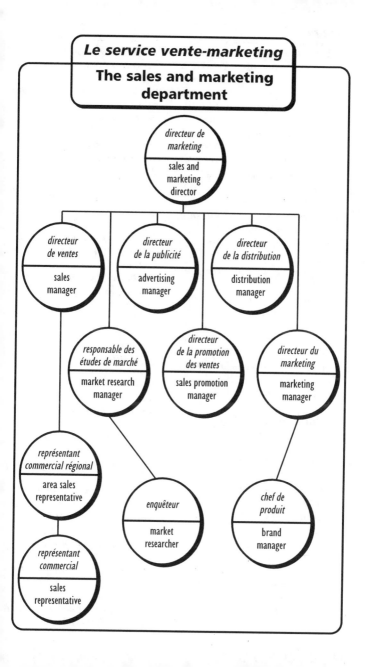

(dans la comptabilité) sales, turnover; **en vente** for sale, on sale; **en vente libre** freely available; **mettre qch en vente** to put sth up for sale, to offer sth for sale; **en vente dans tous les grands magasins** on sale at all leading stores; **vente et marketing** sales and marketing

◇ *Suisse* **vente action** bargain offer

◇ **ventes de base** baseline sales

◇ **vente à (la) commission** commission sale

◇ **vente (au) comptant** cash sale

◇ **ventes aux comptes-clés** key-account sales

◇ **vente par correspondance** mail-order (selling)

◇ **vente à crédit** credit sale; *(à tempérament)* hire purchase, *Am* installment plan

◇ **vente sur description** sale by description

◇ **vente au détail** retailing, retail selling

◇ **vente directe** *(méthode)* direct selling; *(transaction)* direct sale

◇ **vente à distance** distance selling

◇ **vente à domicile** door-to-door selling

◇ **vente domiciliaire** home (party) selling, party-plan selling

◇ **vente sur échantillon** sale by sample

◇ *Ordinat* **vente électronique** on-line selling

◇ **vente à l'essai** sale on approval

◇ **vente en l'état** sale as seen

◇ **ventes export, ventes à l'exportation** export sales

◇ **vente avec faculté de retour** sale or return

◇ **vente forcée** inertia selling

◇ **vente à froid** cold selling

◇ **vente en gros** wholesaling

◇ **vente indirecte** *(méthode)* indirect selling; *(occurrence)* indirect sale

◇ **vente sans intermédiaire** direct selling

◇ **vente jumelée** tie-in sale

◇ *Ordinat* **vente en ligne** on-line sales; *(transaction)* on-line selling

◇ **vente de liquidation** closing-down sale

◇ **vente par lot** banded pack selling

◇ *Ordinat* **vente et marketing assistés par ordinateur** computer-aided sales and marketing

◇ **vente parallèle** parallel selling

◇ **vente personnelle** personal selling

◇ **vente de porte-à-porte** door-to-door selling

◇ **vente avec prime** premium selling

◇ **vente promotionnelle** promotional sale

◇ **ventes de prospection** missionary selling

◇ **vente pyramidale** pyramid selling

◇ **vente de référence** reference sale

◇ **vente répétée** repeat sale

◇ **vente par réseau coopté** multi-level marketing

◇ *vente en semi-gros* small wholesaling

◇ *vente par téléphone* (*méthode*) telephone selling

◇ *ventes par téléphone* (*transactions*) telephone sales, telesales

◇ *vente à tempérament* hire purchase, *Am* installment plan

> **"**
>
> Les **ventes en ligne** sur le Web devraient représenter de 3 à 5% du chiffre d'affaires de la **vente à distance** fin 2001, soit entre 2,5 et 4 milliards de francs.
>
> **"**

vente-marketing *nf* sales and marketing

vépéciste *nm* mail-order organization

vérificateur, -trice de comptes *nm,f* auditor

vérification *nf* (*des comptes*) auditing

vérifier *vt* (*comptes*) to audit

versement *nm* (*paiement*) payment; (*paiement partiel*) instalment; **en plusieurs versements** by *or* in instalments; **premier versement** down payment

◇ *versement à la commande* down payment

◇ *versement comptant* cash payment

◇ *versement d'espèces* cash payment

◇ *versement en numéraire* payment in cash

◇ *versement partiel* instalment

verser *vt* (*argent*) to pay

vidéo promotionnelle *nf* promotional video

vie économique *nf* (*d'un produit*) economic life

ville test *nf* test city

viser *vt* (*clientèle, public*) to target

visite *nf* (*d'un représentant*) call

◇ *visite d'affaires* business call

◇ *visite à froid* cold call

◇ *visite de relance* follow-up visit

visiter *vt* (*client*) to call on

vitrine *nf Br* shop window, *Am* store window; **mettre des marchandises en vitrine** to display goods in the window

volume *nm* (*quantité*) volume

◇ *volume d'achats* purchase volume, volume of purchases

◇ *volume des exportations* volume of exports

◇ *volume des importations* volume of imports

◇ *volume des ventes* sales volume, volume of sales

voyageur, -euse *nm,f*

◇ *voyageur de commerce, voyageur représentant placier* sales representative

VPC *nf* (*abrév* **vente par correspondance**) mail-order (selling)

> **"**
>
> "Aujourd'hui, un foyer sur deux commande en **VPC**, alors que tous les foyers

achètent en boutique. Nous développons donc nos enseignes. Nous réalisons 60% de notre chiffre d'affaires en magasins et 40% en **VPC**."

"

vrac nm en vrac (marchandises) loose; (cargaison) bulk; **faire le vrac, transporter le vrac** to transport goods in bulk

vraquier nm bulk carrier

VRC nf (abrév **vente par réseau coopté**) MLM

VRP nm (abrév **voyageur représentant placier**) sales rep

◊ **VRP multi-carte** freelance rep (working for several companies)

Web nm Ordinat **le Web** the Web

World Wide Web nm Ordinat **le World Wide Web** the World Wide Web

WWW nm Ordinat (abrév **World Wide Web**) WWW

zéro défaut nm zero defects

zone nf area, zone

◊ **zone de chalandise** catchment area (of shop)

◊ **zone commerciale** retail park

◊ **zone test** test area

MODELES DE CORRESPONDANCE MARKETING

i. Présentation générale et style – Passer une commande

GAMESMASTER

14 Pitt Street
TUNBRIDGE WELLS
Kent
TN1 6BG

adresse de l'expéditeur au centre ou coin

Our Ref: Watts/646
Your Ref: n/462

(NB: États- July 1999)

20 July, 1999

Ms Karen Fraser
Administrator
Harris Computer Supplies
77 Park Avenue
LONDON
E17 6BG

adresse complète du destinataire, fonctions en toutes lettres, dans le coin gauche

graphe verture

Dear Ms Fraser,

formules d'appel: Dear Mr/Mrs/Ms... ou Dear Sir/Madam (si l'on ne connaît pas le nom du destinataire) ou Dear John/ etc.

Thank you for sending a copy of your most recent catalogue. I would now like to place an order for some of the products advertised.

paragraphe d'exposition

I enclose a completed order form herewith. I assume the amount payable will be subject to the usual trade discount; please advise if this is not the case.

nande de firmation

I look forward to receiving your confirmation of my order, and would be obliged if you could advise me in advance of the planned delivery date so that I can reorganize my stock accordingly.

formule de transition

Yours sincerely,

nature

Sarah Parker

Sarah Parker
Manager

nom

fonctions

formule de politesse renvoyant aux formules d'appel Mr/Mrs/Ms, ou Yours faithfully (pour la formule d'appel Dear Sir, Madam) ou With best wishes, Regards correspondant à une formule d'appel personnalisée (comme le prénom)

Remarque: "business@harrap.fr" est une adresse électronique factice dont le rôle est d'indiquer à l'utilisateur qu'il s'agit du supplément destiné aux francophones.

business@harrap.fr

ii. Facture de livraison

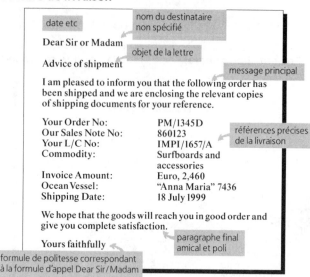

date etc

nom du destinataire
non spécifié

Dear Sir or Madam

objet de la lettre

Advice of shipment

message principal

I am pleased to inform you that the following order has been shipped and we are enclosing the relevant copies of shipping documents for your reference.

Your Order No:	PM/1345D
Our Sales Note No:	860123
Your L/C No:	IMPI/1657/A
Commodity:	Surfboards and accessories
Invoice Amount:	Euro, 2,460
Ocean Vessel:	"Anna Maria" 7436
Shipping Date:	18 July 1999

références précises de la livraison

We hope that the goods will reach you in good order and give you complete satisfaction.

paragraphe final amical et poli

Yours faithfully

formule de politesse correspondant à la formule d'appel Dear Sir/Madam

iii. Réponse à une facture

date etc

Dear Mr McGregor

Payment of [Invoice no BD767] (or goods shipped)

accusé de réceptic de livraison

Thank you for the prompt delivery of our order no. C00145.

Please find enclosed a cheque for US\$ 3,600 in payment of your invoice no. BD767 of 15 January 1999.

message principal avec mention des références de la facture et de la date

Yours sincerely

L. van der Linde

L. van der Linde

business@harrap.fr

Remarque: "business@harrap.fr" est une adresse électronique factice dont le rôle est d'indiquer à l'utilisateur qu'il s'agit du supplément destiné aux francophones.

iv. Publipostage

$B R A C O M S A$

25 rue Consolat 13100 Aix-en-Provence France Tel. Fax.

Simon Software Inc
291 Howard Street
Santa Fe   code postal ("zip code"
New Mexico 87051   aux États-Unis)
USA

7 February 2000

Dear Sir/Madam

Publishing Opportunities in Europe   Para 1, 1. présentation de la
                                                      société
                                              2. objet de la lettre

We are an established publisher of European trade and business journals
with high visibility throughout the Economic Community, central and
eastern Europe. Currently we are offering special advertising rates and
benefits to new customers.
                                              pourquoi faire appel aux
                                              services de la société

This is an excellent opportunity for your company to increase its share of
the IT market in the dynamic European market place.

Please find enclosed two copies of our journals, with our compliments. If
you wish to pursue our offer (attached) or require any further information,
please contact our enquiry line on Freefone 0800 3765.   comment prendre
                                                              contact avec la société

I look forward to hearing from you and to our possible future partnership.

Yours sincerely   conclusion
                       positive,
                       ouverture
J. C. Moreau   sur l'avenir

J. C. Moreau
Sales Director

Remarque: "business@harrap.fr" est une adresse électronique factice dont le rôle est d'indiquer
à l'utilisateur qu'il s'agit du supplément destiné aux francophones.

v. Réponse à une demande de renseignements

RANDONNEE MATOS

33 Rue Diderot
75012 Paris
France
Tel . . . (E-mail . . .)

(Ms) Laura Little
Rocksport Climbing Ltd
18 New Street
Birmingham
United Kingdom

Ms est une formule
d'appel de plus en plus
utilisée dans la
correspondance
commerciale pour
s'adresser aux femmes

date à droite

2 March, 1999

Dear Ms Little

On ajoute parfois Re: avar
l'objet de la lettre mais cet
emploi est déconseillé

Re: Mountaineering wholesale products

Thank you for your enquiry of 28 February about our products.
I enclose our current catalogue and price list with details of
discounts and delivery dates.

If you require any further information, please contact me. I look
forward to hearing from you soon.

Yours sincerely

Angelica Rosetti

Angelica Rosetti

vi. Fax, notes de service

- Ne faire figurer que les informations essentielles, comme les jours et heures, les lieux et les personnes.

- Les phrases peuvent être rédigées dans un style télégraphique: seuls les noms, adjectifs et expressions les plus importants seront ainsi employés.

- Les abréviations et les acronymes sont souvent utilisés pour remplacer des mots voire des expressions entières.

- Classer par ordre de priorité les différents points du message au moyen de tirets.

- Les voyelles peuvent parfois être omises. Ainsi, on écrira "yr lttr dtd . . ." pour "your letter dated".

- Veiller au ton général du message — les messages courts et factuels peuvent sembler froids. Il est donc conseillé d'ajouter des formules de politesse informelles, comme, par exemple, "Best Wishes, Clive".

Attn[1]: Gordon Richardson

Date: Monday 18 September

Re: New date for sales conference

Conference now starts Thurs[2] 21 Sept[3] at 10 a.m., Caledonian Hotel, Edinburgh. There will be a drinks party for all delegates Fri[4] 8 p.m. Pls[5] change yr[6] flight accordingly.

Call Sally a.s.a.p.[7] to confirm your attendance.

Regards,
John

Code
1. Attention
2. Thursday
3. September
4. Friday
5. please
6. your
7. as soon as possible

vii. Courrier électronique

- Une adresse électronique comprend deux parties. La première est constituée du nom du destinataire et la seconde du nom de domaine. Les deux parties sont séparées par une arrobase @ (que l'on prononce "at" en anglais).

- Le courrier électronique étant un moyen de communication rapide, les messages sont souvent rédigés en style télégraphique en utilisant de nombreux acronymes et abréviations. La concision du style et l'utilisation de formes abrégées peuvent parfois créer des problèmes. Il convient de n'utiliser que les abréviations et les acronymes dont vous savez qu'ils seront compris par votre correspondant.

- Pour indiquer que l'on hausse le ton au cours d'un message, on passe des lettres minuscules aux lettres majuscules. Il est donc recommandé d'éviter d'écrire un message en n'utilisant que des lettres majuscules dans la mesure où votre correspondant interprèterait cela comme un signe de mauvaise humeur de votre part.

- La convivialité du courrier électronique encourage une certaine familiarité, que l'on peut parfois regretter après-coup. Cette caractéristique a répandu le sentiment que les messages électroniques sont peu fiables, non durables, voire même inexacts, et ne valent donc pas la peine d'être cités.

- Il faut savoir que le courrier électronique est une forme de publication qui est donc soumise en tant que telle à la législation relative aux droits d'auteur et à la diffamation. Un message électronique doit par conséquent être considéré de la même façon que toute autre forme de communication écrite.

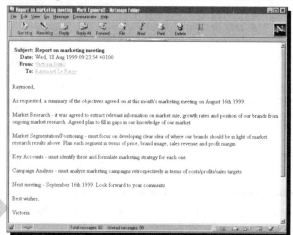

Remarque: "business@harrap.fr" est une adresse électronique factice dont le rôle est d'indiquer à l'utilisateur qu'il s'agit du supplément destiné aux francophones.

Sources of English Quotes

Sources de Citations Anglaises

ABC1 *Marketing* 1999

ABOVE-THE-LINE *Management: theory and practice* Cole, G A. London: D P Publications Ltd, Date unknown

ADSPEND *Marketing* 1998

ADVERTORIAL *Marketing* 1999

ASPIRATIONAL *Marketing* 1999

AVAILABLE Management training course (Business). Recorded on 26 March 1993

BABY BOOMER *The Economist* 1998

BANNER *Marketing* 1998

BELOW-THE-LINE *Marketing* 1998

BEST-PERCEIVED *Marketing* 1998

BLITZ *The Drum* 1998

BRAND *Marketing* 1998

BRAND-LED *Marketing Week* 1999

BROADCAST *Marketing* 1999

BUNDLE *The Guardian* 1989

CATEGORY *Marketing* 1999

CHALLENGER *Marketing* 1999

CLUSTER *Methods of social investigation* Mann, Peter H. Oxford: Basil Blackwell Ltd, 1985

COMPETITIVE *R&D Management: managing projects and new products* Date and publisher unknown

CONSUMER *Credit Management* Stamford, Lincs: Institute of Credit Management, 1992

COOLING-OFF PERIOD *Accountancy* London: Institute of Chartered Accountants, 1993

CORE *Mediaweek* 1998

COST *Advertising: What it is and how to do it* White, R. Maidenhead: McGraw-Hill Book Company, 1993

CREATIVE *Marketing* 1999

CUSTOMER *Marketing* 1998

CUSTOMER-FOCUSED *Marketing* 1999

DEMOGRAPHIC *Management: theory and practice* Cole, G A. London: D P Publications Ltd, Date unknown

DEPTH *The sociology of housework* Oakley, A. Oxford: Blackwell, 1990

DIRECT *Debrief* 1996

DOG *Marketing Week* 1999

DOOR DROP *Marketing* 1999

DUAL-BRANDED *Marketing* 1999

EMOTIONAL *Marketing* 1999

EXPAND *Marketing* 1999

FLAGSHIP *Marketing* 1999

FLOOR *Marketing* 1999

FOOTFALL *Marketing* 1999

GATEKEEPER *Elements of Marketing* Morden A R. London: D P Publications Ltd, 1987

GLOBAL *Marketing* 1998

GROW *Unigram X* APT Data Services Ltd, 1993

HALO EFFECT *Marketing* 1999

LAYOUT *Marketing* 1999

LICENSE *Marketing* 1999

LIFESTYLE *Marketing* 1999

LINEAR *Marketing* 1999

LOYALTY *Debrief* 1998

MAILING *Retailing: a manual for students* Leach, Helen. Oxford: Basil Blackwell Ltd, 1989

MARKET *Marketing* 1999

MARKETING *Marketing* 1998

MASTERBRAND *Marketing* 1998

MEDIA *Marketing Week* 1992

MULTIBRAND *Marketing* 1999

NEW *Marketing* 1998

ON-LINE *Marketing* 1999

OPPORTUNITY *Marketing* 1999

P *Elements of Marketing* Morden, A.R. London: D P Publications Ltd, 1987

PERCEPTION *Marketing* 1999

PERIMETER *Marketing* 1998

PITCH *Marketing* 1998

PLAYER *Marketing Week* 1999

POSTER *Marketing Week* 1992

POWER BRAND *Marketing* 1999

PREMIUM *Marketing* 1999

PRINT *Marketing* 1999

PROBLEM CHILD *Computergram International* Date and publisher unknown

PROFITABILITY *Marketing* 1999

PROSPECT *Marketing* 1999

PURCHASE *Marketing* 1999

PURCHASING *Marketing* 1998

REBRANDING *Marketing* 1999

RECALL *Advertising: What it is and how to do it* White, R. Mai-denhead: McGraw-Hill Bo Company, 1993

RELATIONSHIP   MARKE **ING** *Debrief* 1998

REPOSITION Dawson Interr. tional annual report 1993

RETAIL *Marketing* 1999

ROADSHOW *Marketing* 1999

SALE *Sales technique and manag ment* Lancaster, G & Jobber, London: Pitman Publishing, 199

SATURATION *The Face* 1992

SEGMENT *Debrief* 1998

SELLING *Guinness Globe* Da and publisher unknown

SHELF *Brand Packaging* 1998

SHOPPING *The Alton Hera* 1992

SIGHT *Accountancy* London: I stitute of Chartered Accou tants, 1992

SOFT SELL *In good faith* Lamor Stewart. Edinburgh: St Andrev Press, 1989

SPEND *Marketing* 1998

SPOILER CAMPAIGN *Marke ing* 1999

STRAPLINE *Marketing* 1999

TARGET *Marketing* 1999

TEASER *Marketing* 1998

TV *Marketing* 1998

UNDERCUT *The Economist* 199

USP *Advertising: What it is and ho to do it* White, R. Maidenhea McGraw-Hill Book Compar 1993

VOLUME *Marketing* 1999

YOUTH *Marketing* 1999

Sources de Citations Françaises

Sources of French Quotes

ACCORD *CB News* 1998
ACHAT *LSA* 1998
ACTEUR *Stratégies* 1999
AFFICHAGE *CB News* 1998
AGRÉMENT *Stratégies* 1999
ANNONCEUR *Stratégies* 1999
ASSORTIMENT *LSA* 1998
AUDIENCE *Stratégies* 1999
BON *CB News* 1998
BUDGET *Stratégies* 1999
CA *CB News* 1998
CAMPAGNE *L'Expansion* 1994
CATALOGUE *LSA* 1998
CIBLER *CB News* 1998
CŒUR DE CIBLE *Stratégies* 1999
COMMERCIALISER *CB News* 1998
COMMUNICATION *Mozaïk* 1999
COMPORTEMENT *LSA* 1998
COUVERTURE *Stratégies* 1999
DÉBOUCHÉ *LSA* 1998
DEVANT DE CAISSE *LSA* 1998
DIFFUSION *LSA* 1998
DIVERSIFICATION *Stratégies* 1999
ÉCRAN *CB News* 1998
EFFONDREMENT *L'Expansion* 1994
EMPLACEMENT *CB News* 1998
ENSEIGNE *LSA* 1998
ESPACE *CB News* 1998
ÉTUDE *LSA* 1998
FIDÉLISER *L'Expansion* 1994

FRANCHISE *Libération* 1998
FRÉQUENCE *CB News* 1998
GAMME *Stratégies* 1999
GMS *LSA* 1998
GRIFFE *Stratégies* 1999
GSS *LSA* 1998
HORS-MÉDIA *CB News* 1998
IMPACT *Stratégies* 1999
INSERTION *Stratégies* 1999
LEADER *Stratégies* 1999
LIBRE *LSA* 1998
LINÉAIRE *LSA* 1998
MAILING *CB News* 1998
MARGE *CB News* 1998
MARKETING *L'Expansion* 1994
MARQUE *LSA* 1998
MERCHANDISING *LSA* 1998
MÈTRE LINÉAIRE *LSA* 1998
NOTORIÉTÉ *Stratégies* 1999
OFFRE *LSA* 1998
PART *Stratégies* 1999
PÉNÉTRATION *CB News* 1998
PIONNIER *Stratégies* 1998
PLV *LSA* 1998
POSITIONNEMENT *LSA* 1998
POUVOIR D'ACHAT *CB News* 1998
PRÉFÉRENCE *CB News* 1998
PRIME *LSA* 1998
PRODUIT *Stratégies* 1999
PROMESSE *Stratégies* 1999
PROSPECT *Stratégies* 1999
PUBLICITÉ *LSA* 1998
PUBLIREPORTAGE *CB News* 1998